MW00666827

for Jessica

CONTENTS

The celebration of Advent is possible only to those who are troubled in soul, who know themselves to be poor and imperfect, and who look forward to something greater to come. He is, and always will be now, with us in our sin, in our suffering, and at our death. We are no longer alone. God is with us and we are no longer homeless.

—DIETRICH BONHOEFFER,
Advent Sunday, December 2, 1928

Every image is a revelation and representation of something hidden.

—JOHN OF DAMASCUS

Art inflames even a frozen, darkened soul to a high spiritual experience. Through art we are sometimes visited—dimly, briefly—by revelations such as cannot be produced by rational thinking.

—ALEXANDR SOLZHENITSYN

FOREWORD

When I find myself with a free day in a major city, I often look for an art museum. I wander the galleries, lingering mainly among the Impressionists and European Masters. Many museums offer listening devices that give background details on the important paintings, but I have little patience with the headsets or with the clumps of visitors that block the view of the paintings themselves. So, I move from painting to painting, reading the one-paragraph placard by each one, and leave the museum feeling nourished in some subliminal way—yet hardly enlightened.

I suspect that I am not alone in my naive approach to the visual arts. One of G. K. Chesterton's witticisms sums up an all-too-common bias: "In the Middle Ages we have art for God's sake, in the Renaissance we have art for man's sake, in the nineteenth century we have art for art's sake, and in the twentieth century we have no art for God's sake." A trained artist himself, Chesterton was stereotyping for effect, but in truth Christians have shown an ambivalence toward art of all kinds.

Unrivaled as a patron, and responsible for many of the finest creations, the church has at times undergone spasms of counter-reaction: whitewashing images during the iconoclasm controversy, banning and burning books, and destroying church organs. Though we moderns tend to demonstrate more tolerance, artists themselves often feel unappreciated and even estranged from the church.

Daily, art nourishes my own faith. As I write, classical music plays in the background, and I feast on books in my library. And as I've mentioned, I feel a strange gravitational tug toward art museums. What draws me? Beauty, of course—yet I sense something more. The journalist Malcolm Muggeridge put it this way: "Only mystics, clowns and artists, in my experience, speak the truth, which, as Blake was always insisting, is perceptible to the imagination rather than the mind." Artists communicate with a different, and often more penetrating, style than preachers and theologians.

The Bible itself demonstrates this principle, for God's *acts* get the bulk of attention, given far more weight than the dogma that later emerged. The apostle Paul's left-brain exegetical passages are the exception, not the rule, easily overwhelmed by passages devoted to narrative, poetry, wisdom literature, parables, prophetic visions, and, yes, the Pentateuch's meticulous descriptions of the visual arts.

If I hope to enrich my faith through the visual arts, I need a guide. When I enter museum galleries devoted to religious art, the paintings testify to a different era, with different principles of aesthetics at work. In this book, David Bannon's explorations show by example what makes art worth our effort and what it can do for the person of faith.

First, art offers an unexpected vantage point. For example, one does not expect a book of Advent meditations to bear the title *Wounded in Spirit*. As the season approaches, upbeat Christmas carols blare from speakers in the shopping malls, and the store clerks may offer a "Merry Christmas!" greeting. From where comes this melancholy counterpoint about wounded spirits?

From the Gospel of Luke, to be precise. The old man Simeon, assured he would live to see the Messiah, and having grown gray and frail waiting for the consolation of Israel, seasons his congratulations to Mary with these words: "And a sword will pierce your own soul too." Somehow, in the midst of joyous celebration, he foresees the shadow looming over the Incarnation: the slaughter of the innocents, the flight to Egypt, the tragic ending on an executioner's cross. Decades later, Paul would interpret these events for the Philippians through a theological lens: a member of the Godhead stripping away the prerogatives of divinity to become a human being, and not only that but one who came in the form of a slave, even one subject to death, yes, even that most ignoble death on a cross. Christmas Day was only the first of many humiliations that Jesus would undergo.

Depression and suicides spike at Christmas, as loneliness and the memories of lost loved ones invade the background cheer. My own father died in mid-December, before his twenty-fourth birthday, an untimely death that forever cast a pall over our family's Christmases. We know, all of us, the dissonance of which Simeon spoke to Mary: of love splattered with blood, of consolation that proves diffused and fleeting. Art brings that dissonance to the foreground, with a poignancy that wounds the spirit like a sword.

Second, art renders something unique to the artist's own experience of that dissonance. I know the author of this book: his own griefs, mistakes for which he has paid dearly, his inconsolable loss. It surprises me not at all that David Bannon would write an Advent book with such a title. I did not, however, know before reading these pages the personal trials of Tissot or Murillo or many of the artists discussed here.

Wounded in Spirit has become my guide, revealing what no one-paragraph summary in a museum could possibly make plain: the creator's internality that gets projected on a canvas for the rest of us to contemplate. For the artist, bringing hidden wounds into the light may become a move toward healing—although, paradoxically, complete healing might also dry up the font of creativity.

A depressed Rainer Maria Rilke once wrote, "Art is superfluous. . . . Can art heal wounds, can it take the bitterness away from death? It does not quiet despair, it does not feed the hungry, it does not clothe the freezing." Yes, art has its limits, but I would answer his rhetorical questions more positively. Art does at least contribute to the healing of wounds, by awakening a sense of companionship in those who receive it: *I am not alone*. More, art may present the needs of others in such a way as to arouse the very compassionate response that Rilke doubts: think of van Gogh's portrayals of peasants and coal miners, or the AIDS quilt that toured the nation, or photographs of refugees fleeing famine and war.

Great art operates on us at a deeper level than the rational. It *conveys* truth rather than arguing for it, and presents reality implicitly rather than explicitly. After seeing Hans Holbein's realistic painting of Christ's tortured body, Dostoevsky was haunted by it, and included the scene in his novel *The Idiot*. Thomas Merton, a self-indulgent dandy, became captivated by Byzantine mosaics on a visit to Rome; from them, he later said, he first learned the mystery of a God of infinite power, wisdom and love who had yet become man. Reciting the poem "Love" by George

Herbert led to Simone Weil's conversion: having committed it to memory, she repeated it almost as a mantra during violent headaches until somehow, without her willing it, the poem became a prayer. "It was during one of these recitations," she writes, "that Christ himself came down and took possession of me."

Finally, art forms a bridge between the artist's soul and our own. Every artist, regardless of the medium, wants someone to see or hear or read or otherwise receive the result that emerges from creative labor. The literary critic Cleanth Brooks observes, "In making us see our world for what it is, the artist also makes us see ourselves for what we are." In the process, art invites a form of meditation.

David Bannon widens the bridge of connection for me. His references to literature–Tolstoy, Byron, Shelley, Longfellow, Tennyson, Emerson, Shakespeare–enrich what I learn from the visual art he discusses. And in these pages I also meet familiar mentors of thought and theology: Buechner, Merton, Tillich, Heschel, Kierkegaard, Baillie, Rilke, Nouwen, Lewis, and of course the authors of the Bible.

Among all these mentors, some familiar and many new to me, I encounter art in a more restful, meditative way than if I were standing amid a buzzing museum crowd with a headset clutched to my ear. Within these pages I find much to contemplate, applying something of what took place in the artist to my own life. I am no longer staring at strange art in a museum in a new city. Now, the images come to me, held in my hands, along with the resources I need to understand and interpret them.

According to James Baldwin, "Every artist is involved with one single effort, really, which is somehow to dig down to where reality is." For the artist of faith, such as the representatives in this collection, reality includes the realm of eternity. Our modern, materialistic culture considers eternal matters as peripheral, not nearly so urgent as, say, making money and achieving success. The noise of surrounding culture tends to drown out a God who prefers to whisper, and we need prophetic prods in order to reorder our world.

Art freezes the moment, quickening the senses. "I am attempting to express what I saw in a flower which apparently others failed to see," explained Georgia O'Keefe.

In doing so, art nurtures that most human act, our ability to transcend the immediacy of time and space. The ordinary can become extraordinary, the instantaneous can become permanent—a form of *lectio divina* that requires no words.

Even as I write these words, my CD changer has made mechanical noises announcing a new disc under the laser. Instantly the room fills with the throaty sounds of a Russian male choir chanting prayers in a language I cannot understand. I stop typing, shove aside the papers on my desk, and close my eyes. Memories of a trip to St. Petersburg, Russia, come flooding back, including a visit to an onion-domed cathedral when I heard such sounds in person as they reverberated off the magnificent icon-covered dome above.

The following day I visited the Hermitage Museum. I walked into a room containing one of the world's largest collections of Rembrandt paintings. His massive rendition of *The Return of the Prodigal Son* was the first to catch my eye, a painting so evocative that Henri Nouwen spent two days sitting before it in a folding chair, meditating—and later wrote a book with that title about his encounter. The German siege of Leningrad imperiled all these paintings, which were saved only by a heroic rescue effort. Rembrandt's biblically themed portrayals survived not only that war, but also the atheistic frenzy of Bolsheviks who demolished churches and murdered forty two thousand priests.

Art endures. Later, a Christian convert from the darkest days of Stalin's reign wrote, "The task of a writer is to select more universal and eternal questions, the secrets of the human heart and conscience, the confrontation of life with death, the triumph over spiritual sorrow, the laws of the history of mankind that were born in the depths of time immemorial and that will cease to exist only when the sun ceases to shine." Aleksandr Solzhenitsyn devoted his life to honoring, by making permanent, the sacrifices of those who clung to such beliefs in a world gone mad.

Great religious art strives wordlessly for something similar. The paintings reproduced and discussed in these pages have become devotional for me in the best sense of the word: they inspire and inform my sense of devotion to the One who is eternally worthy.

—PHILIP YANCEY

INTRODUCTION

CHRISTIAN ART began in grief. The first known paintings were on tombs, funerary art deep in the catacombs of Rome. They portrayed Jesus primarily as the Good Shepherd or as the One who raised Lazarus and healed the paralytic. There were images from the Old Testament, as well, usually focusing on scenes of deliverance. Stories of renewal were easily understood and had symbolic significance to the often-illiterate followers of Jesus. While *texts* during the same period emphasized the Birth, the Passion, the Crucifixion, and the Resurrection, early Christian art did not. The healing Jesus seems to have had a special appeal.

This changed over time, as visual art began to depict a wider range of spiritual and liturgical experiences. Nativity scenes, for example, became as different as the artists who painted them. Some are works of sublime joy, others of deep and troubling grief. To understand the art, we must search out the hopes and wounds of the artists.

Wounded in Spirit is a book unlike most others that one might read during the season of Advent. There is joy in it, but there is also sorrow. For those who know loss, holidays can be a time of memory, tears, and prayer. There are joy-filled moments, to be sure, but they do not always come easily. *Wounded in Spirit* returns us to where Christian art began. In our wounds, we may once again encounter "God with us."

The reader may notice certain painters are absent: Michelangelo and da Vinci, say, or Rembrandt, Raphael, Rubens, Titian, Tintoretto, and van Dyck. Those artists are well known; their stories are often told. For this volume, I sought entries that are lesser known in one way or another: the famous whose religious pieces are easily overlooked (Gauguin and van Gogh) or buried under misapprehensions (Dürer, Thayer); the masters whose work is recognizable if their names are not (Caravaggio, Watteau); and the many fine artists who are all but forgotten in the hurly-burly of our modern world.

Many of us lack the ability or training to express our spiritual longings, our disappointments and hurts, our hopes despite all reason. Art speaks to us in ways words may not. It can be a source of solace and communion. Some of us make mistakes, bad ones sometimes, and we pay for them. In 2006 I was convicted of criminal impersonation. I was a fool, my intentions and actions were unjust, and I answered for it. The healing Jesus is as real to me today as he was to the grieving believers who drew him on catacomb walls. In 2015 my daughter, an artist, died of a fentanyl-laced heroin overdose. She was twenty-six. For many bereaved parents, the loss does not *define* us: it is *part* of us, just as our children were and always will be. Our souls have taken harm. I will be healed the moment I hold my daughter in my arms again. I wait for the advent of that day.

"*We each have to find our own personal pathway as we deal with loss*," wrote grief researcher Kenneth Doka. "Grief is as individual as fingerprints or snowflakes." This book is about artists who walked through their own dark valleys and the light they found there. Their wounds speak to us across the centuries: *We are not alone.*

USING THIS BOOK

EACH MEDITATION tells its own story. These meditations may be read in any order, apart from Advent or throughout the season. This book begins on December 1 and ends on Christmas Day.

Please pause at the paintings. We are so accustomed to rushing through life. The artists in this book offer us a moment to read, to consider, and, perhaps, to commune.

For those experiencing loss or grief, please do not skip the notes at the back of the book.

Advent Art and Meditations

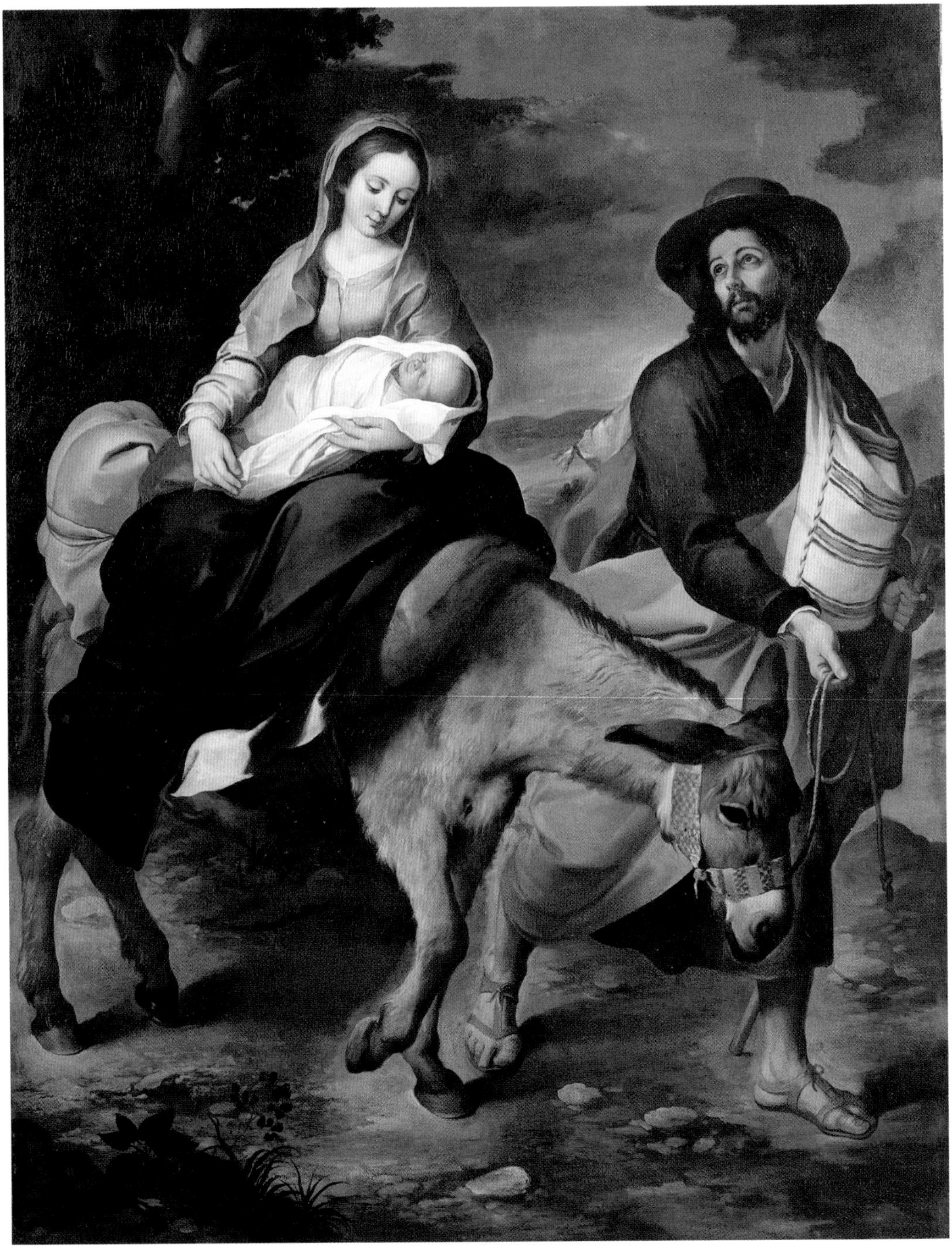

Murillo, *Flight into Egypt,* c. 1645, Musei di Strada Nuova, Genoa

An orphan finds a family

BARTOLOMÉ ESTEBAN MURILLO

(1617–1682), a Spanish painter

> *Even the sparrow has found a home, and the swallow a nest for herself, where she may have her young—a place near your altar,* LORD *Almighty, my King and my God.*
> —PSALM 84:3

BARTOLOMÉ MURILLO lost both his parents by the age of ten. This could have lent a certain darkness to his work, yet Bartolomé's paintings evoke quiet tenderness and the joys of everyday life.

After his parents died in 1627 and 1628, the young orphan moved in with his sister and her husband. Bartolomé became his brother-in-law's ward, a common procedure at the time, and took on his maternal grandmother's surname rather than that of his father.

By the age of ten most children understand the nature of death, though they mourn in ways that are quite different from those of adults. Studies show that bereaved children often feel abandoned and vulnerable; they may suffer from depression and be incapable of maintaining relationships throughout their lives. Repressed grief and hindered mourning can lead to anger, aggression, and antisocial behavior, but the devastating emotional and physical effects of the trauma need not be crippling. One telling difference, researchers have found, is a child's support at the time of the loss. Whatever Bartolomé's family life at his sister's home, it seems to have been nurturing and helpful. By age twenty-seven Bartolomé got married. He and his wife were to have eleven children together.

The year of his wedding, 1645, Bartolomé finished *The Young Beggar*, the first of many street children paintings. The artist seems to have had an affinity for the helpless. His portraits are known for their pathos and nostalgia for a Seville that never truly existed—a sentimentalizing, perhaps, of his own lost childhood. Yet he did not patronize his subjects. They retain an air of isolation and despair. Bartolomé's keen and compassionate eye quickly garnered favorable attention. He was commissioned by the Seville Cathedral. His career in Christian interpretations had begun.

Flight into Egypt may seem an ordinary painting at first glance, particularly the stiff Joseph in contemporary Spanish garb. But pause a moment. Bartolomé painted this scene shortly after his wedding; this plodding Joseph may have been intentional. The eye is led instead to the kindly animal and a loving Mary holding a quite realistic infant. These themes of domesticity and gentleness would dominate much of the artist's religious work.

Bartolomé continued this contemporary theme in one of his most famous works, *The Holy Family with a Bird*, painted five years after his marriage, around 1650. By now Bartolomé the orphan had a family of his own; this domestic scene is one of contentment and peace. Joseph is no longer an uncomfortable outsider. He supports the young Jesus, who expresses human delight in rescuing a bird from his puppy. The parents are every bit as present as the child. In painting the Savior of the world, Bartolomé may have been describing his own salvation.

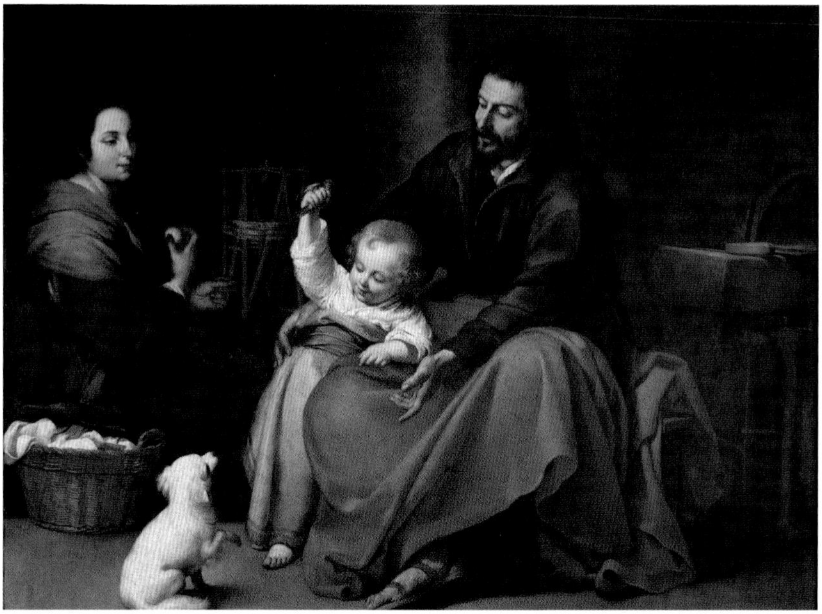

Murillo, *Holy Family with a Bird,* c. 1650, Prado Museum, Madrid

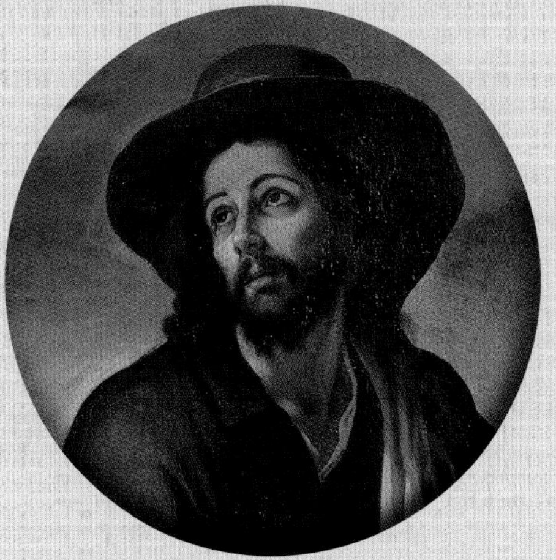

Art is a human activity, consisting in this, that one man hands on to others feelings he has lived through.
—LEO TOLSTOY

Life isn't much of a feast for children born to people who don't want them or can't afford them or are one way or another incapable of taking care of them and will one way or another probably end up abusing or abandoning them. And yet, and yet. Who knows what treasure life may hold for even such children as those, or what treasures even such children as those may grow up to become?
—FREDERICK BUECHNER

You need something to love,
if only a single face,
and more faces remain
than death has taken.

Think, what part of love
was taken with that face?
From each, from what remains,
death has taken nothing.
—FRIEDRICH RÜCKERT

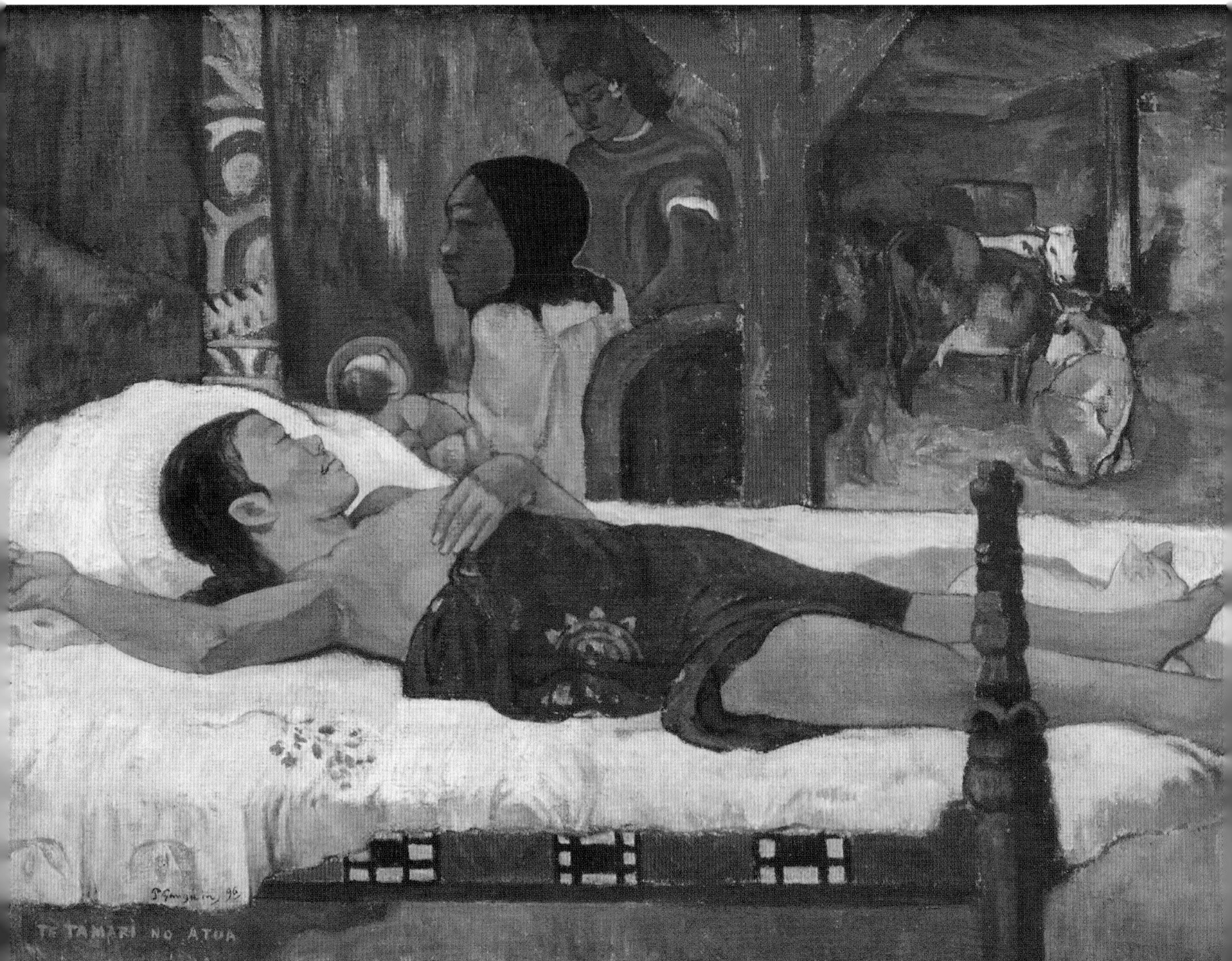

Gauguin, *Te tamari no atua, The Son of God*, 1896, Neue Pinakothek, Munich

There are no easy answers

EUGÈNE HENRI PAUL GAUGUIN

(1848–1903), a French painter

> *I will have mercy on whom I will have mercy, and I will have compassion on whom I will have compassion.*
> —EXODUS 33:19B

THERE IS MORE OF ULTIMATE REALITY IN AN APPLE BY CÉZANNE than in a Jesus by Hoffman," Paul Tillich said. Thomas Merton had a similar thought: "Expressionism is the style best suited to genuine religious art." Still, whether speaking of expressionism, post-impressionism, synthetism, or any other-*ism*, we might first take into account the artist.

Paul Gauguin was notoriously lascivious and unreliable in nearly every aspect of his life. He often left his family for sensual adventures in exotic locales. His experiments in art were at times bold and reflected genius; at other times, they bordered on the repulsive. Yet they were honest, often cruelly so, and in them Gauguin asked questions that demand answers to this day.

Gauguin and his wife, Mette, had five children. Their marriage dissolved over time until Paul finally left his family in 1894. Two years later he had a sixth child, a daughter, with his Tahitian mistress. The mother, Pau'ura, was fourteen; Paul was forty-eight. The infant died within a few days of her birth on Christmas Day, 1896. Gauguin memorialized the scene in art. Commonly known in English as *Nativity* or *The Birth*, Paul's Polynesian title, *Te tamari no atua*, is more poignant: *The Son of God*.

It is one of the most shocking nativities ever painted. There are no shepherds or wise men. Joseph is absent, though Gauguin may have seen himself in that role. The divine child is barely noticeable in the background. Our attention is drawn instead to Mary, exhausted from her labor. Paul had grown up with a religious education. *The Son of God* represents his uniquely radical interpretation of traditional Christian imagery.

The painting has a sense of grief and tenderness rarely seen in Gauguin's other work. The religious pieces from five years earlier are far more overt. Observe the yellow and green haloes of mother and child and the hint of light around the animals. They are subtle but not the source of the painting's moving pathos. A warm glow surrounds them, in sharp contrast to the gathering dark; this is the true halo. *The Son of God* was Gauguin at his best: more suggestive than descriptive, at once exhausted and serene.

The next year, 1897, Gauguin lost another daughter, this time to pneumonia. Aline was ten years old, and by all accounts she held a special place in the artist's heart. "I have lost my daughter. I no longer love God," Paul wrote in his final letter to Mette, which she never answered. "Like my mother she was called Aline; everyone loves after his own fashion, for some love is most intense at the grave, for others–I do not know. Her tomb is far away, the flowers, all that is an illusion. Her tomb is here near me; my tears are the living flowers." Paul accused God of "injustice and malice," and like Job and the prophets, felt free to express his despair: "It really looks as if somewhere up there in the higher regions I have an enemy who never for a moment will leave me in peace."

The same month Gauguin was served an eviction notice. Bereaved parents are often warned not to make any major changes the first year after losing a child, and then to take small steps on the inevitable and healthy paths that life may offer them later. Paul took out a loan he could ill afford to build a new home. By December, he faced foreclosure. He found himself nearly bankrupt, and his health failed him. He had broken an ankle in a brawl; the pain and morphine addiction to treat it were a constant misery. He suffered a series of strokes; his eyesight was failing; his body was beset with syphilitic lesions, and he often succumbed to bouts of fever. The crushing weight of grief drove Paul to despair.

Gauguin's first reaction to Aline's death was shock. "The news did not move me, trained as I am to suffering," he wrote in April 1897; "then each day, as memories came back, the wound opened more deeply, and at this moment I am completely discouraged." Entire books have been written about Paul's many failings, yet few pause to consider the direct link between Aline's death and his

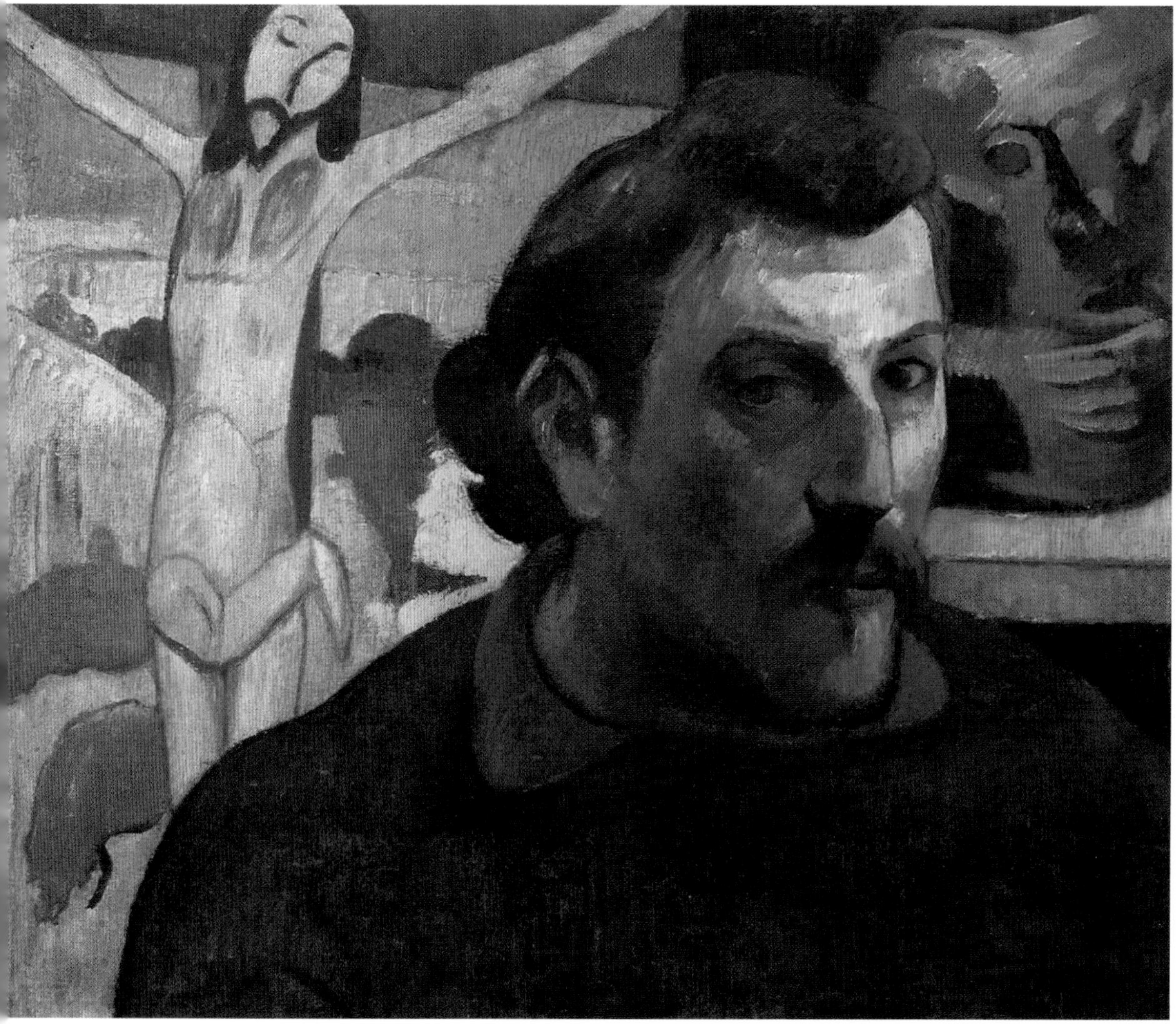

Gauguin, *Portrait of the Artist with Yellow Christ*, 1889, Musée d'Orsay, Paris

masterpiece. After finishing it, he tried to kill himself with arsenic but found, to his surprise, he could not.

Where Do We Come From? What Are We? Where Are We Going? is Gauguin's spiritual testament, a painting of hope and reconciliation that offers no easy answers. The questions themselves were deeply rooted in his five years at seminary as a child under Bishop of Orléans Félix-Antoine-Philibert Dupanloup. *Where?*

dominated much of Paul's religious art. "Where does the execution of a painting begin?" he wrote. "Who knows when, in the depths of the artist's soul the work was begun–unconsciously, perhaps?" In *Where Do We Come From? What Are We? Where Are We Going?* Gauguin found the will to go on. He probably named the piece after he recovered from his suicide attempt. "Not a title," he wrote, "but a signature."

Bereavement often opens religious paths to transformation and growth, a new appreciation for life as well as recognition of its transience and frailty, closer relationships, appreciation of others, personal strength, humility, compassion, and marked spirituality. It can lead to a quest for meaning and new discoveries of what that entails. This may have been true for Gauguin. He did not change, but his art reflects a better, more meditative Paul. Themes of belief and suffering had haunted him, and then, in 1889, he began painting a flurry of paintings that culminated in two great religious masterpieces, *The Son of God* and *Where Do We Come From? What Are We? Where Are We Going?*

There are also two self-portraits from this period that are suggestive of Paul's internal struggles. *Self-Portrait with Halo* has a somewhat whimsical tone–using bright colors against jarring themes. Paul holds a snake beneath the tempting fruit of the Garden of Eden; above his head is the halo of Christ. Which is he? Or is he both? The artist had no ready reply. *Portrait of the Artist with Yellow Christ* asks the same questions in a more profound way. Over one shoulder stands the crucified Jesus; over the other stands a prosaic tobacco jar. Between them is Gauguin: inscrutable, expressionless save for his penetrating eyes, wounded and searching. Observe the tones of his sweater, repeated in the background and in the shadows of the jar. As in *Halo*, the mysteries of good and evil remain unanswered.

This was not the dogmatic religion of Gauguin's youth. Through art and suffering and despite himself, he sought transcendence. His son, Clovis, died in 1900 of an infection following a hip operation. Clovis was the third child Paul had lost. Gauguin himself died three years later.

The creators of modern art have been able to see the meaningless of our existence; they participated in its despair. At the same time they have had the courage to face it and to express it in their pictures and sculptures. They had the courage to be themselves.

—PAUL TILLICH

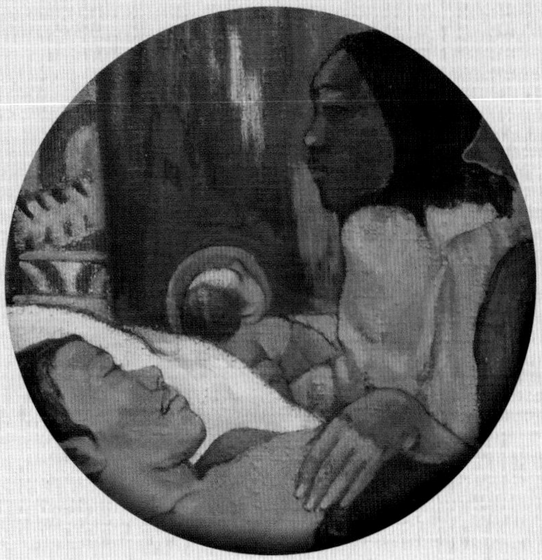

Suffering experienced through bereavement can be an impetus for transformative spiritual experience. Indeed, grief is a vital part of our very human life, an experience that can open compassion, and an important phase of maturation giving depth and humility to life; it can be regarded as a gift. Grief can ruin or mature us.

—CRYSTAL PARK and ROSHI JOAN HALIFAX

Holly-tree

So I am myself, and so my poem,
like the holly, is prickly and rough below,
where the cattle would graze and gnaw;
but from above the leaves have no sting,
to sway in heaven's breeze, in spring light,
or to birdsong.

—FRIEDRICH RÜCKERT

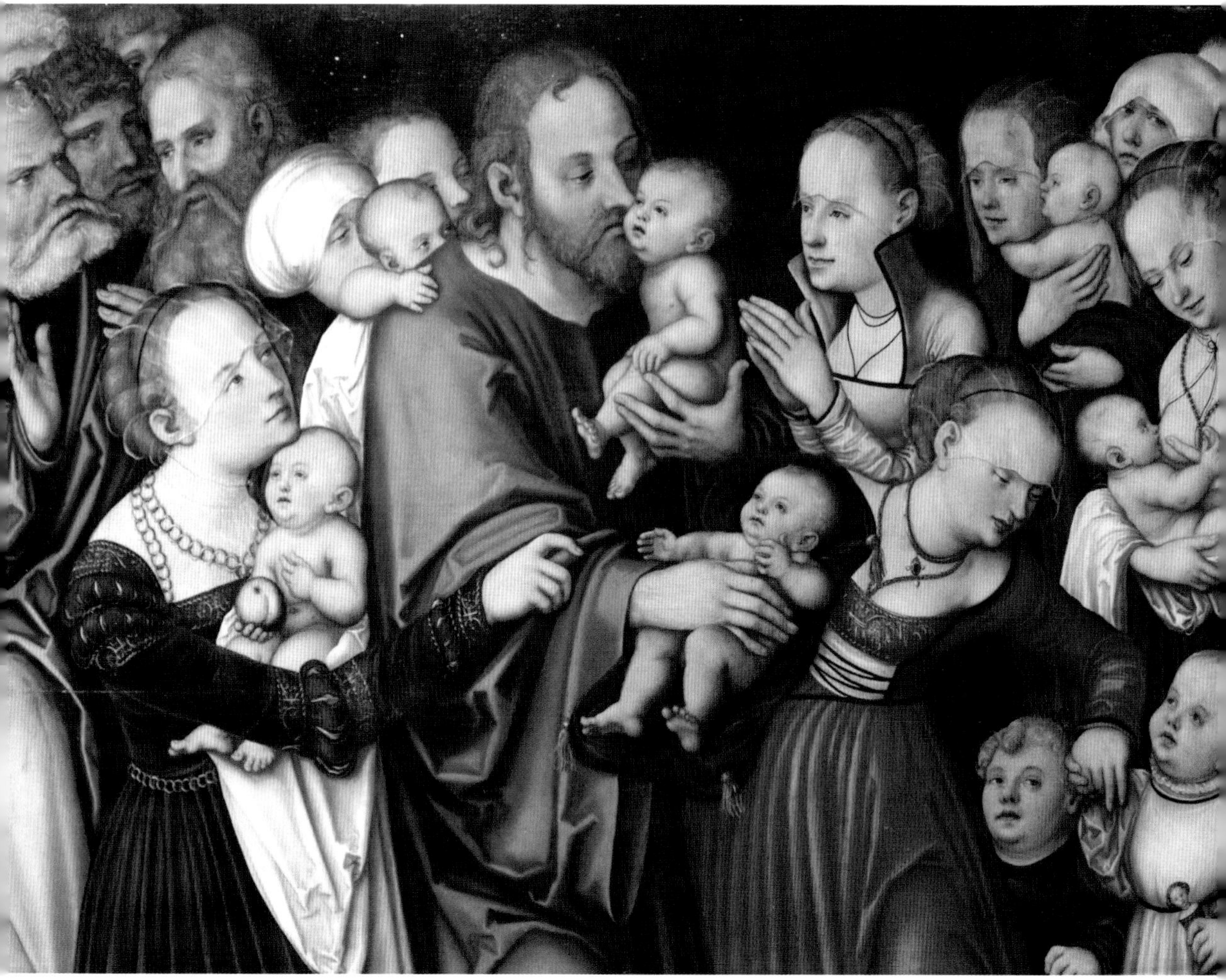

Cranach, *Christ Blessing the Children*, c. 1538, Städel Museum, Frankfurt

Two friends have no place to hide

LUCAS CRANACH THE ELDER

(1472–1553), a German painter

In him was life, and the life was the light of all people.
–JOHN 1:4 (NRSV)

LUCAS CRANACH was a son of the Reformation. He and Martin Luther were lifelong friends. Lucas was present when Martin renounced his vows; he served as a witness at Martin's wedding. Lucas named his first son Johann "Hans" Lucas Cranach. Thirteen years later he would be godfather to Martin's first child, Johannes "Hans" Luther. The two men were tied together by belief and temperament. Both were prone to moments of wisdom, devotion, and excess–Lucas with art, Martin with words.

After his first son was born, Lucas added to his religious works some rather mean-spirited anti-Catholic leaflets. Martin's early letters famously condemned mourning as a lack of faith. Yet neither stance was as absolute as it might seem.

Lucas would come to embrace the iconography and representative art that he and other reformers had once condemned. Martin's thoughts on sorrow changed, as well. He had once been fond of quoting Job to the bereaved, "The Lord gave and the Lord has taken away; may the name of the Lord be praised," instructing them to "cheerfully give God what is his." But Martin's views shifted when his daughter died. Firsthand experience changes us. As Luther wrote to a friend in August 1528:

> My small daughter, my little Elisabeth has died. How strangely wretched it has left my spirit . . . so that I am moved by the pity of it, for I would never before have believed that fathers' spirits could grow so tender towards their children.

Lucas may have understood Martin's shock. The artist's eldest son, Hans, died in 1537. The next year Lucas completed *Christ Blessing the Children*. The

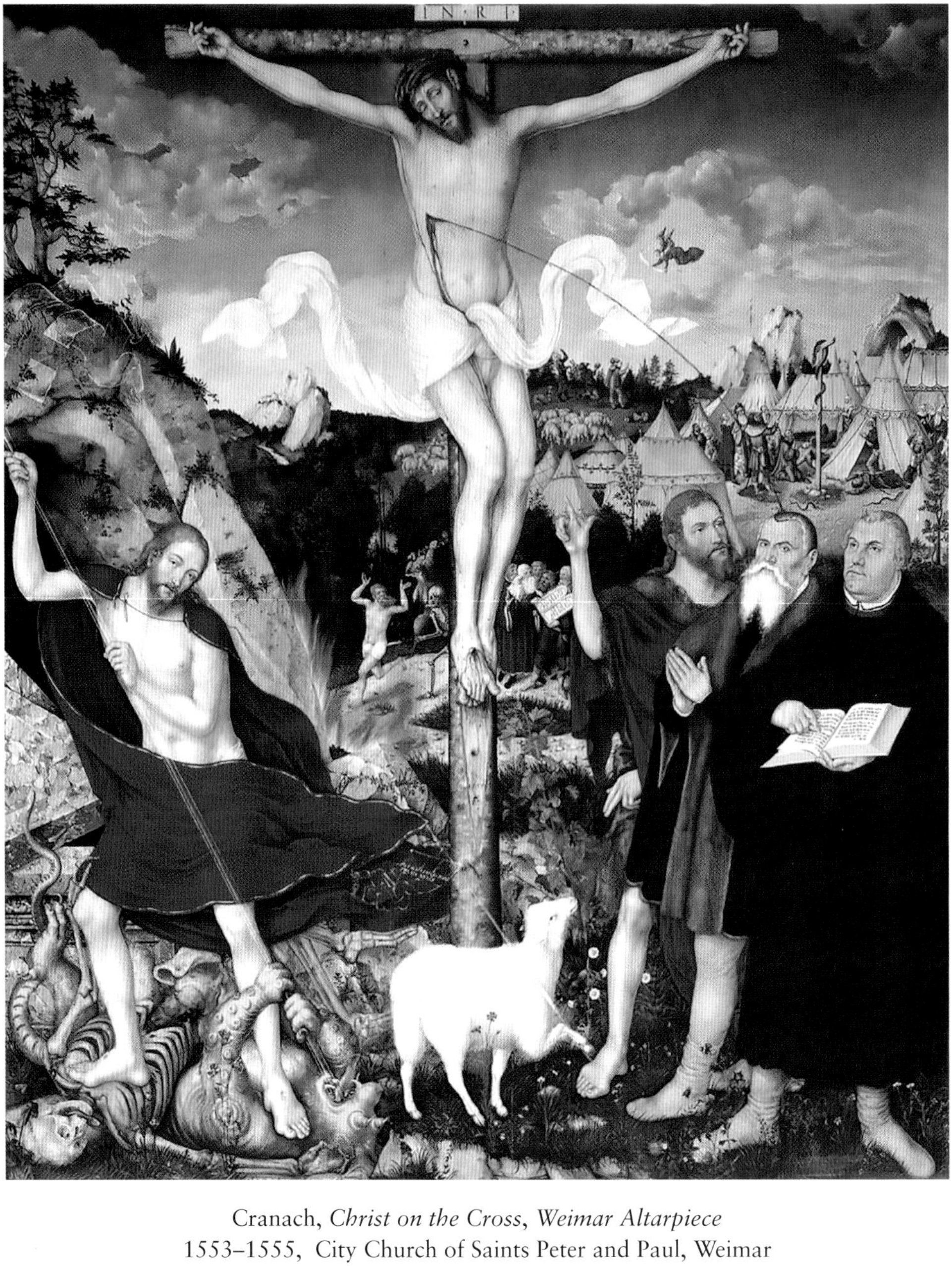

Cranach, *Christ on the Cross*, *Weimar Altarpiece*
1553–1555, City Church of Saints Peter and Paul, Weimar

apostles are fussy, and the mothers are devout or distracted, but two faces surprise us. In the upper right, a woman looks to us with overwhelming sorrow—a grief that is reflected, of all places, in the face of Jesus.

Martin's second daughter, Magdalena, died in his arms in September 1542. "I would gladly have kept my daughter," he would say later, "for I love her very much, if God had wanted to leave her with me." In a letter to a friend dated October 9 of that year, Martin displayed characteristics common to many grieving parents: gratitude for the assurance that his daughter was with God mingled with anger at her absence.

> My dearest daughter Magdalena has departed this life for the heavenly Father, falling asleep full of faith in Christ. I have mastered my paternal feelings, but only through a certain defiant raging against death; in this anger I have soothed my tears. I loved her very much.

At his daughter's funeral, Martin mourned over her narrow coffin. "The bed is too small for her because she has now died. . . . The separation vexes one way beyond all measure. It is a marvelous thing to know that she is certainly in peace and that all is well with her and yet to be so sad!" Shortly afterward he "broke down in tears and, with sobs wracking his body, quickly left his daughter." Luther himself died four years later.

His friend's "defiant raging against death" was not lost on Lucas. Cranach's final work, an altarpiece finished by another son, Lucas the Younger, gives a distinct impression of two worlds combined. Lucas began painting *Christ on the Cross* the year he died, 1553. Jesus hangs crucified, the splatter from his wound grotesque; yet to the left he stands clothed in a blood-red robe, triumphant over Satan and death. The victorious Christ and Lucas are looking directly at us. From the cross, Jesus seems to be glancing at the bereaved fathers. Martin points to a single passage, "The blood of Jesus purifies us from all sin," blood that lands directly on Lucas.

Those pure disciples themselves and those watercolor women—who so disconcertingly turned into The Christians overnight—were complex and selfish humans also, who lived in the material world, and whose errors and evils were not pretty but ugly, and had real consequences. If they were just like us then Christ's words to them are addressed to us, in full and merciful knowledge—and we are lost. There is no place to hide.

—ANNIE DILLARD

I thought to teach my little girl weaving;
she learned soon enough to spin me!
I bought a spinning wheel;
and all the silk for spinning!
Oh my hope, poor little thread!
Never to see that first thread spun.
Now she weaves, she is weaving
over her grave, in the light.

—FRIEDRICH RÜCKERT

If I am not in His grace, may God so place me;
if I am, may God so preserve me.
—ST. JOAN OF ARC

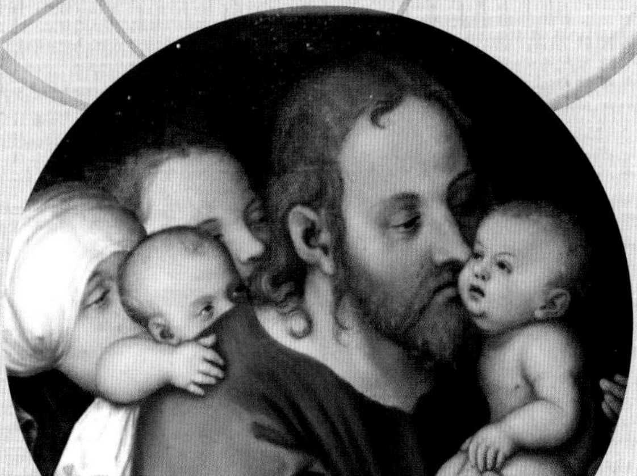

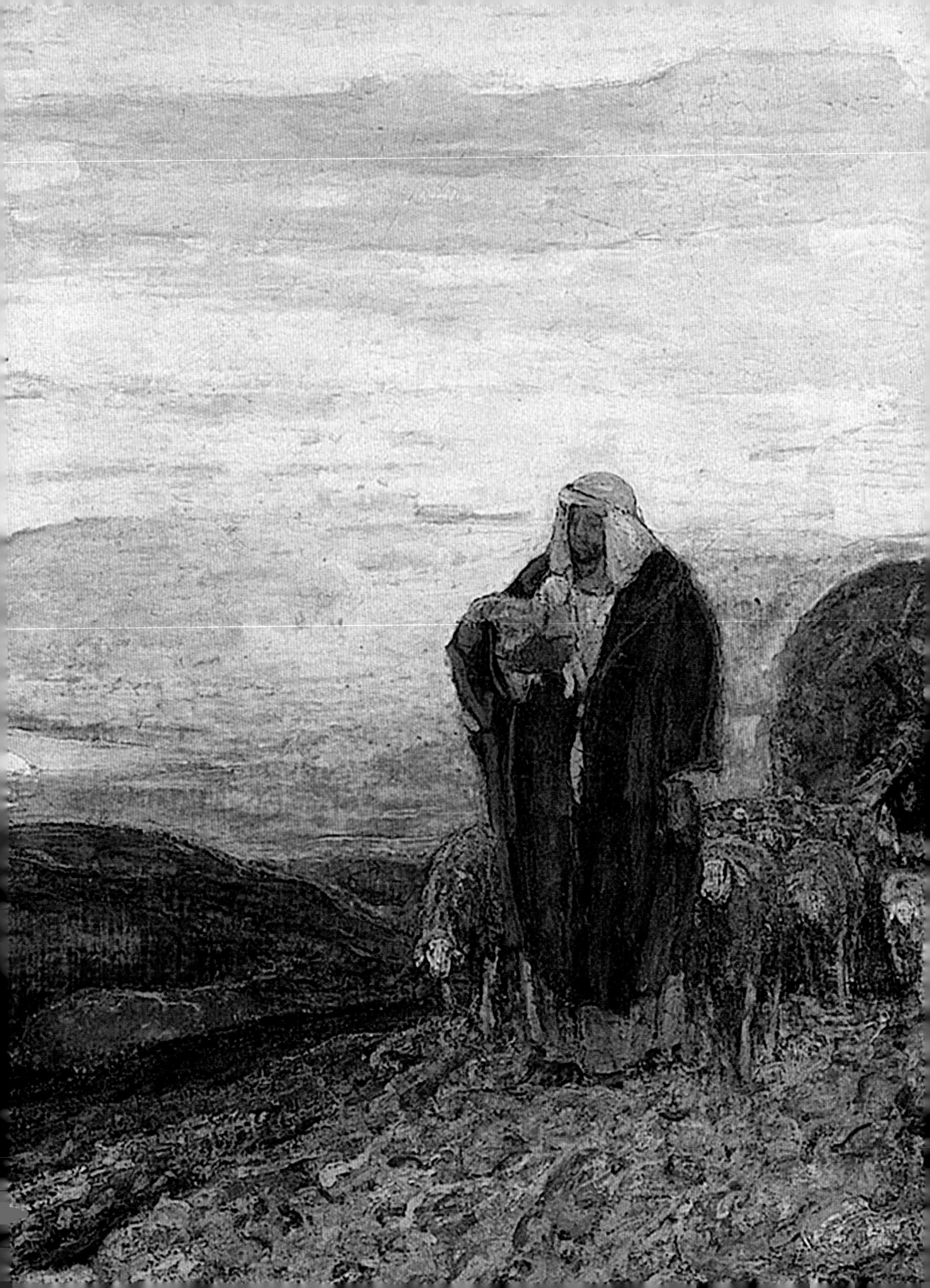

An artist sees through the haze

HENRY OSSAWA TANNER

(1859–1937), an American painter

We do not know what to do, but our eyes are on you.
—2 CHRONICLES 20:12B

HENRY TANNER did not let circumstances define him. He defied all labels. He refused to be identified solely as "the son of a slave" or "black" or even "Christian." He was all of those, but not *only* those.

Henry seems to have enjoyed being an artist. His mother had been enslaved in Virginia; she escaped via the Underground Railroad. When he painted her portrait, he used a simple title: *Portrait of the Artist's Mother.* His wife, Jessie, was a Swedish-American opera singer. Rather than focus on her accomplishments or the racial tensions of a mixed marriage, even in France, Henry again preferred clarity over extravagance: *Portrait of the Artist's Wife.* He called his autobiographical sketch *The Story of an Artist's Life.* These may seem to have undertones of false modesty or narcissism, but the titles were, in fact, common in his vocation. He chose them over self-aggrandizing descriptors.

Henry saw his task as a calling, in a way, whether depicting people, street scenes, or spiritual themes. "The want of high ideals in religious art will, as in other things, be fatal," he wrote. There is evidence in his work of what he envisioned those high ideals to be. In *Christ and His Mother Studying the Scriptures*, Henry used his wife and their son, Jesse, as models. This painting reveals an overwhelming sense of tenderness and love between mother and child and, clearly, between artist and subjects. *The Return of the Holy Women* is another example of these themes, to which he added a profound expression of both—grief. Henry explained:

> The moon has risen, a shepherd returns with his flock, all unconscious of the terrible tragedy of the morning, or the sorrowing figures, one of them, Mary, supported by John, in front of him. All is tranquility and loveliness, only within the souls of that sorrowing mother and those loving disciples is there turmoil and sorrow.

◀ Tanner, *The Good Shepherd*, 1930, private collection

Henry would use similar tones again and again in his depictions of Jesus. "'The Good Shepherd' was a favorite subject of his," Henry's son, Jesse, wrote of his father. Henry's mother had escaped slavery; his father was an Episcopal bishop. Whatever the church's influence may have been, the independent artist saw more than a Sunday School reading in this pastoral image. It was, to him, a living reality that he spent decades attempting to capture on canvas. As Jesse observed:

> Christ watches over his flock . . . "Let God Guide us" was his principal reason for prayer. This guidance was achieved, he believed, through a receptive state of mind that allows us to know God's will. It is this sort of mystical fourth dimension that my father attempted to give his religious paintings, and which is sensed by so many of his admirers.

This "mystical" element is palpable in Henry's *The Good Shepherd* paintings from 1903 to 1920. We can almost feel the artist's struggle to communicate his inner vision of Jesus. Unlike the soft lines of his portraits of Mary, his Shepherd is hazy, bold, lost in shadow and somewhat harsh surroundings. But this apparent distance is deceptive. The overall mood is one of comfort. A decade later, Henry would create his masterpiece on the subject after traveling with sorrows of his own.

His wife, Jessie, died in 1925. Henry mourned her deeply, and he was inactive for years. The few paintings we have from this period provide a hint of his despair. Henry's *Sodom and Gomorrah* from 1920 shows Lot and his daughters in the foreground; there is energy in the terrifying colors. *The Destruction of Sodom and Gomorrah*, painted four years after Jessie's death, is also a work of desolation: a land hopeless, helpless, bereft, bereaved. Only later did Henry come to a sense of peace. "It has often seemed to me that, when bowed by some sorrow," he wrote, "nature seemed more radiant than ever before."

Henry's *The Good Shepherd* from 1930 combines many elements from his earlier attempts: vibrant colors, bold lines muted by soft tones. But there are differences. Nature seems more inviting than merciless. Now it is the sheep that are hazy and blurred. The Shepherd, tender and loving, is clearly visible at last.

The artist should preach nothing—not even his own autonomy. His art should speak its own truth, and in so doing it will be in harmony with every other kind of truth—moral, metaphysical, and mystical.
—THOMAS MERTON

My role, I think, is done,
paid in full, this pound of flesh,
excluded, expelled, expunged,
extolled, endured, lamented.
For in grief all joy must cease;
lead me, I am sated, away from the feast!
My reason for living is gone!
Or my grief would be too much.
For my heart, I feel, since it took
this harm, breathes through sighs alone.
—FRIEDRICH RÜCKERT

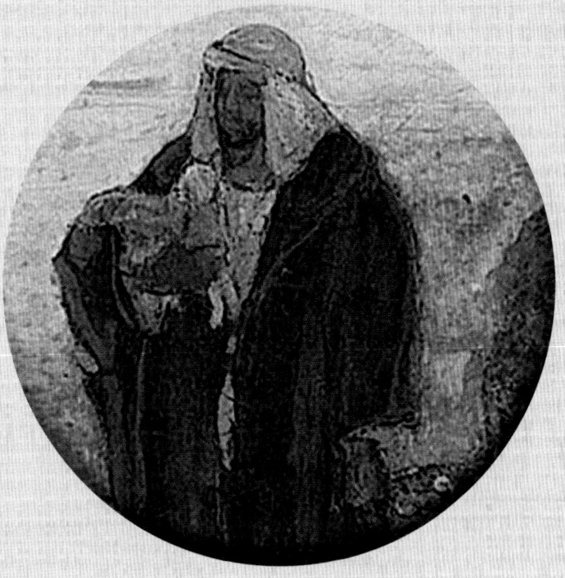

God is both transcendent
and immanent, both *more*
than the universe and
present in the universe.
Mystical experiences
involve a sense of
reconnection to what is.
—MARCUS BORG

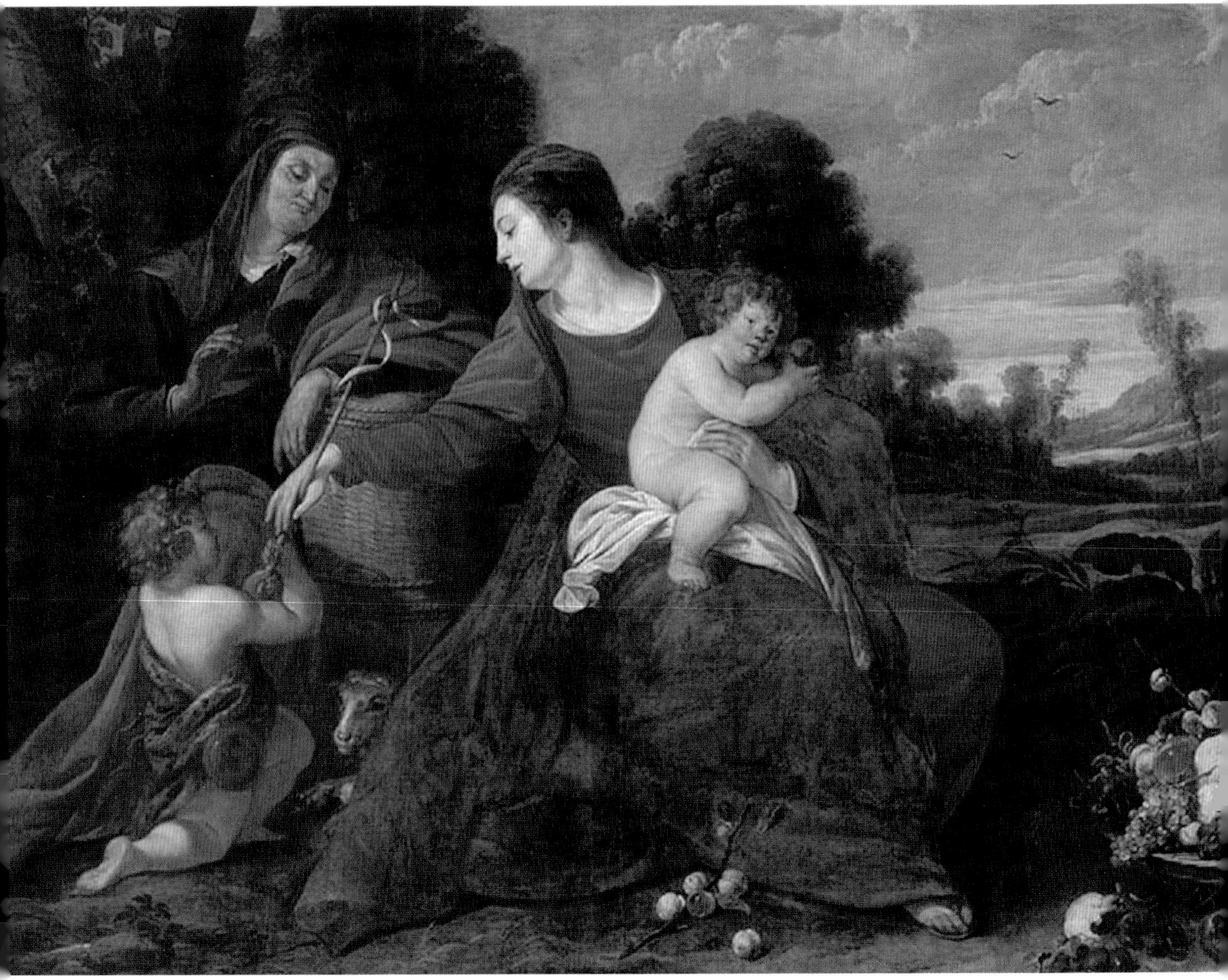

Wildens, *The Holy Family*, 1637, Royal Museum of Fine Arts, Antwerp

Through shadow to light

JAN WILDENS

(1586–1653), a Flemish painter

> *Peace I leave with you; my peace I give you. I do not give to you as the world gives. Do not let your hearts be troubled and do not be afraid.*
> —JOHN 14:27

JAN WILDENS was a master of detailed landscapes. Many of the great artists of the day used him to provide backgrounds to their work, particularly his close friend, Peter Paul Rubens. But for all the quiet joy of Jan's nature scenes, they do not compare to the hushed serenity of his later work. Jan's wife died in 1624. They had two sons, born a year apart. Both were painters like their father. The eldest, Jan Baptist, died in 1637. He was only seventeen.

Popular entertainment often portrays the grief-stricken as brooding or haunted. Jan was the opposite. Like so many who experience loss, he seems to have been solely interested in moments of peace. One researcher found that of more than three hundred bereaved mothers and fathers interviewed, "over 90 percent indicated that they had lost their fears of death" as a result of losing their children. Now they know true loss and pain; it is their constant companion. They seek only comfort and quiet. This is evident in Jan's *Infant Christ and St. John*. The landscape is a delight to the eye, and the children, though stylized, seem happy.

The year his son died, 1637, Jan collaborated with Theodoor Rombouts on *The Holy Family*. It was customary to paint Joseph and Mary with Jesus, but as with *Infant Christ and St. John*, Jan seems to have been drawn to the traditional scenes when *two* children were present. It is not difficult to imagine the artist recalling a similar scene with his two boys when they were young. This is not as odd or tragic as it may seem. Philosopher Thomas Attig observes that in remembering such small joys, the bereaved experience a connection to someone that will, after all, forever be a part of their lives. Attig insists there is a "life-affirming potential of loving in

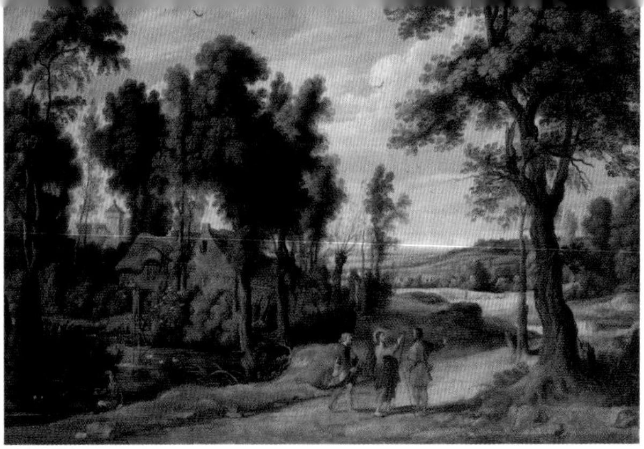

Wildens, *Christ and His Disciples on the Road to Emmaus*, 1640s, Hermitage Museum, Saint Petersburg

separation" that validates the fervent desire to remain linked to those who have died. Doing so is not only healthy and inevitable; to deny it may be crippling. It is a source of poignant, nearly spiritual solace. We can sense a measure of Jan's longing.

By the 1640s, Jan was making full use of vibrant, lush colors. His atmospheric light seems to increase an overall sense of serenity. *Landscape with Peasants*, for example, combines a tinge of nostalgia and foreboding with genuine playfulness. Jan seems to have taken particular care with light and dark in *Joseph Sold by His Brothers*. Again returning to siblings and loss, he uses dark, oppressive colors for the foreground and the brothers. The background and Joseph are bathed in calm, penetrating light, a hint of a future day when they would be reunited after many trials. Jan achieved a similar effect in *Christ and His Disciples on the Road to Emmaus*. Here the wanderers' road is not unpleasant but most assuredly shadowed—the opposite of the serenity that lies ahead.

In 1653 Jan's second son died. Jeremias was thirty-two. Jan did not write down his feelings, but consider the words of a woman who contracted cancer after her daughter died: *I used to think cancer was the worst thing that could happen to anyone. I had no idea.* Sixteenth-century Spanish historian Solomon ibn Verga related the story of a Jew who was exiled in 1492 and put ashore on an uninhabited island. The man watched as his wife and two sons died. This was his response:

> Lord of the universe: You are doing much to make me desert my faith. But I assure You that neither the sufferings that You have brought upon me, nor that which You shall yet bring upon me, will be of any avail.

Jan died that same year.

I think your heart needs to be broken, and broken open, at least once to have a heart at all or to have a heart for others.

—RICHARD ROHR

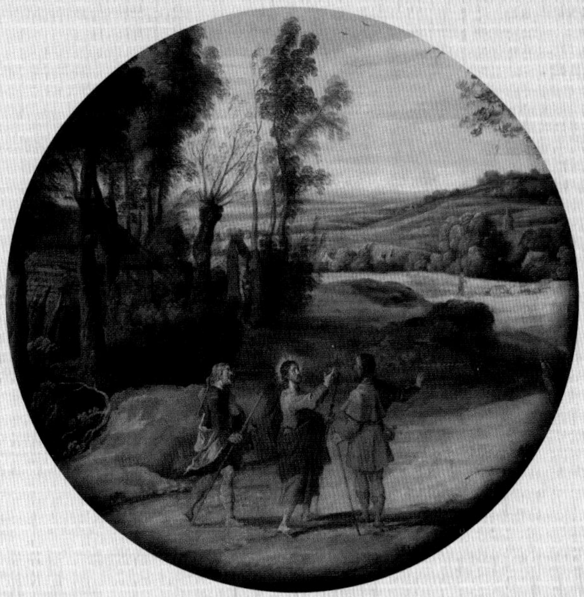

Yet a little while

Heaven is not far, tho' far the sky
  Overarching earth and main.
It takes not long to live and die,
  Die, revive, and rise again.
Not long: how long? Oh, long re-echoing song!
O Lord, how long?

—CHRISTINA ROSSETTI

God enters into the suffering of all creatures and experiences their life. God sees the suffering from the inside; God does not look at it from the outside, as through a window. God is internally related to the suffering of the people. God enters fully into the hurtful situation and makes it his own. In spite of the suffering God undergoes, God's salvific will does not waver; God's steadfast love endures forever. In this respect, God offers the supreme example of what to do with suffering.

—TERENCE FRETHEIM

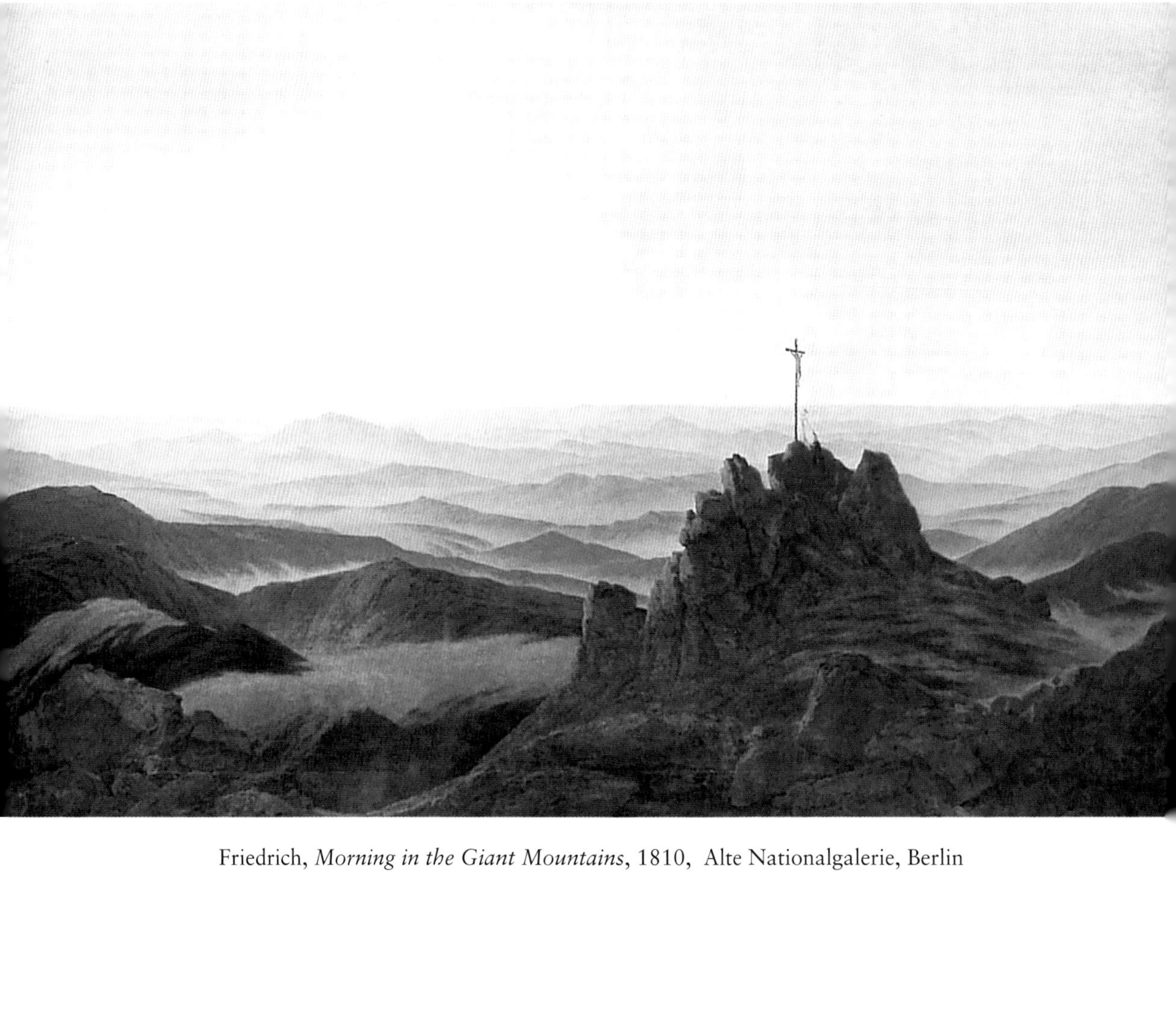

Friedrich, *Morning in the Giant Mountains*, 1810, Alte Nationalgalerie, Berlin

Nature offers solace

CASPAR DAVID FRIEDRICH

(1774–1840), a German painter

To you, God, . . . silence is praise.
—PSALM 65:1 (CJB)

CASPAR FRIEDRICH was skating under the Greifswald city wall. He had cajoled his younger brother, Christoffer, into daring the frozen moat. It was December 8, 1787. The ice gave way. The smaller boy pulled his brother to safety, losing his own life in the process. Caspar was thirteen; Christoffer was twelve.

Caspar knew about death. His mother passed when he was seven, his sister when he was eight. He would lose another sister in 1791. Christoffer's sacrifice was something else entirely. Studies show that losing a younger sibling is similar in some ways to losing a child. Despite this, the death of a sibling gets very little social acknowledgment. Others may have consoled Casper with the usual well-meant platitudes: his final act placed him with the angels, he's happier now, and so on.

In his young mind, Caspar may have felt responsible: *he* had failed to keep Christoffer safe; *he* had convinced him to go out on the ice. When their lives were in danger, *he* should have rescued his little brother, not the other way around; Christoffer gave his life for *him*; Christoffer's death was *his* fault. The sense of guilt can seem inescapable. Of those who lose a loved one in an accident, 78 percent feel persistent guilt; for suicides it is 92 percent. This was the one loss that Caspar never quite learned to live with.

Caspar was a true Romantic-era artist. His work captures the seen and unseen in nature. *The Cross in the Mountains*, painted as an altarpiece in 1808, was a revelation to the art world. It freed Christian faith from the confines of man-made churches and the conventions of landscape paintings. It depicts a *gipfelkreuz*, or summit cross, known to have been erected in Catholic regions of the Alps since the thirteenth century. "The firs stand around the cross," Caspar wrote of the piece,

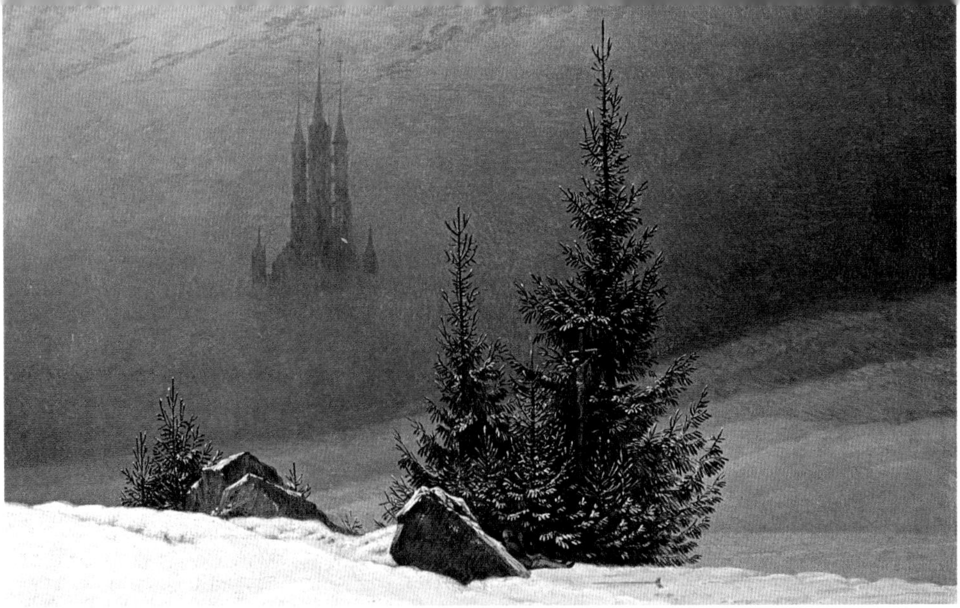

Friedrich, *Winter Landscape with a Church*, 1811,
Museum für Kunst und Kulturgeschichte, Dortmund

"evergreen enduring through all ages, like the hopes of man in Him, the crucified." The silhouette, the mountain top, the setting sun: these were a radical new vision of pure spirituality.

Two years later Caspar returned to this theme with *Morning in the Great Mountains* and *Monk by the Sea*. Both paintings have an intensity seldom seen in religious art. They place belief in isolation, as much a part of nature as apart from it.

Caspar couldn't stay away from winter's beauty and desolation. Much is made of his melancholia, and correctly so, but we may pause a moment over the nearly mystical aspects of his landscapes. "Art serves as a mediator between nature and man," Caspar wrote. "Depicting the most beautiful and the highest and what seizes us the most would obviously be the task of the true artist." The solitary figure in *Winter Landscape* or the cross and abandoned crutches of *Winter Landscape with a Church* illustrate the artist's guiding theme: humanity is dwarfed by nature yet inescapably involved in it.

Caspar often portrayed figures at a distance with their backs turned. When he was fifty, he painted *At the City Wall*. Anyone who has known grief and guilt understands Caspar's gift, or curse, for conveying true isolation. "Close your bodily eye so that you may see your picture first with the spiritual eye," Caspar advised young artists. "Then bring to the light of day that which you have seen in the darkness."

Quietly in the night of our souls, everyone suffers. We are particularly adept at covering our inner wounds, but no wound is ever silent. Only the voice of deep prayer can carry the gentle poultice inwards to these severe crevices and draw out the toxins of hurt. As with all great arrivals in the soul, it comes from a direction that we often could neither predict nor anticipate.

—JOHN O'DONOHUE

"Over all graves grass must grow,
time heals all wounds," such is the solace,
the worst thing to say, as consolations go;
poor heart, not that, not a healed wound.
It is something, at least, this pain;
we amputate the numb and the dead.

—FRIEDRICH RÜCKERT

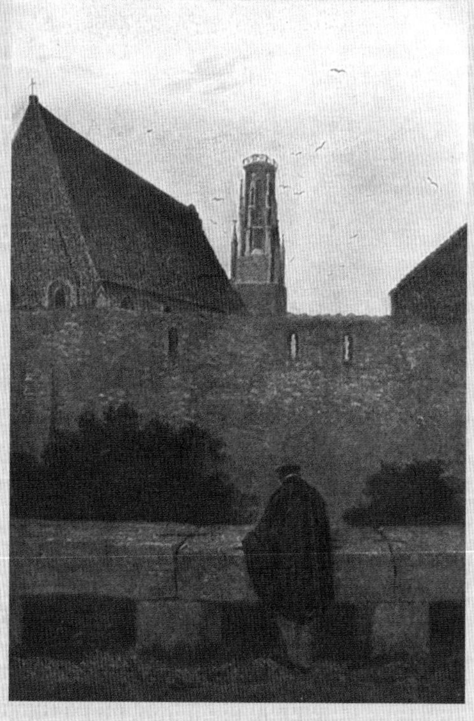

Friedrich, *At the City Wall*, 1824, private collection

Prayer comes to pass in a complete turning of the heart toward God, toward his goodness and power. It is the momentary disregard of our personal concerns, the absence of self-centered thoughts, which constitute the art of prayer. Feeling becomes prayer in the moment in which we forget ourselves and become aware of God.

—ABRAHAM JOSHUA HESCHEL

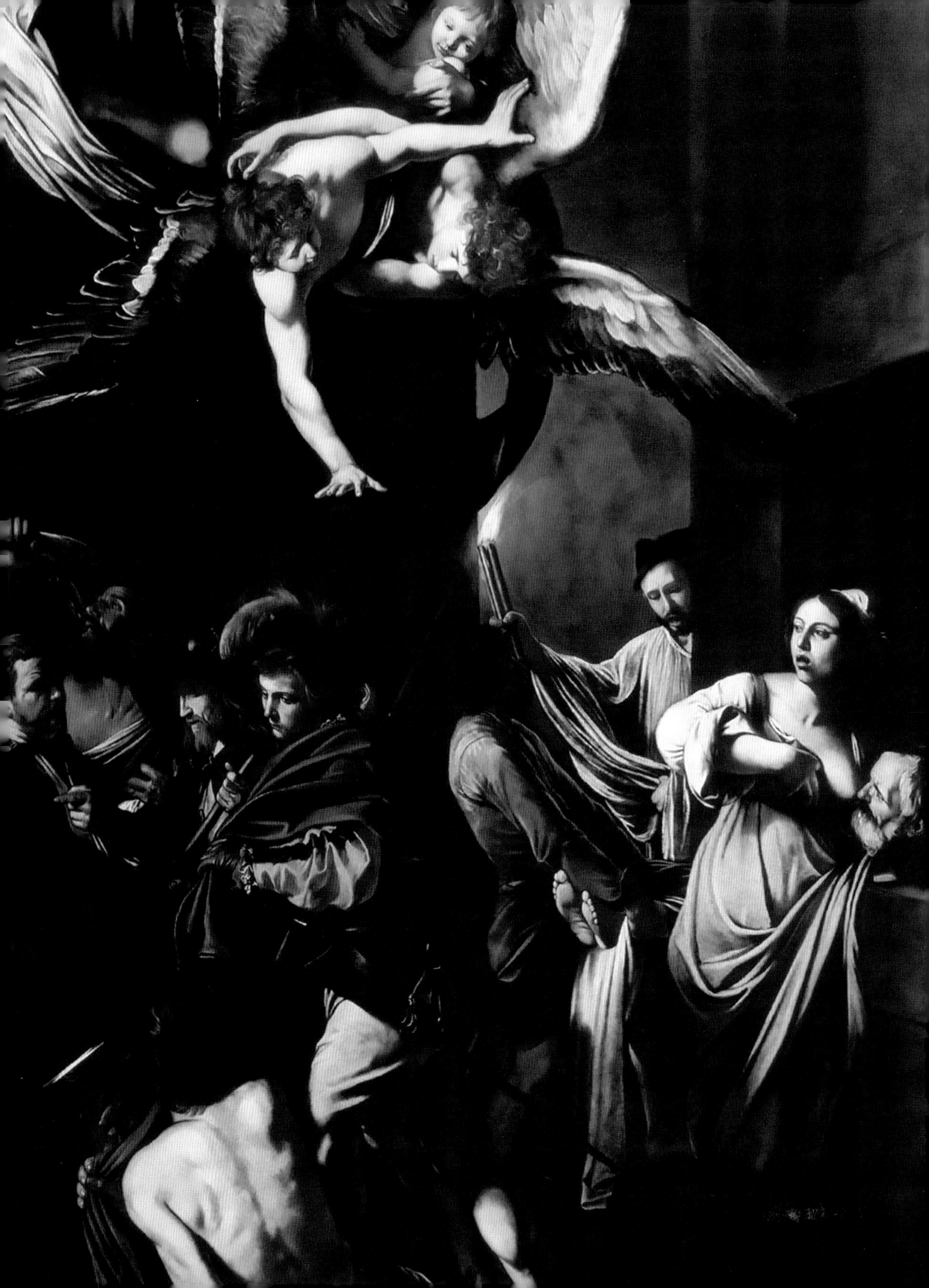

A sinner reaches for the sublime

MICHELANGELO MERISI DA CARAVAGGIO

(1573–1609/10), known as Caravaggio, an Italian painter

> *He has not despised or scorned the suffering of the afflicted one; he has not hidden his face from him but has listened to his cry for help.*
>
> —PSALM 22:24

EVERYTHING ABOUT MICHELANGELO MERISI was wrong. Murderous, licentious, violent, usurious, vain, and intemperate, he had a passion for life surpassed only by—of all things—a devotion to the sacred. His religious paintings are sublime. Before we rush to judge Caravaggio, we may pause to consider David, another troubled artist. David's belief that he mattered to God never wavered, as his psalms of lament, cursing, and praise illustrate.

Caravaggio was voracious in all he did. There are few of the Ten Commandments he did not eagerly break, yet as with David, the First and Third Commandments remained inviolate. His worship, though tainted, seems to have been genuine; it appears he never used the name of God to his own ends.

Caravaggio had a gift for heightened realism. His work is typified by a sense of what is seen and unseen. Consider taking a photo of a breathtaking mountain view: the picture never quite captures what we see. Even if we manipulate the image, increasing depth, contrast, saturation, it remains a pale copy at best. Caravaggio somehow defeats this handicap. His work is rich with what we perceive as well as what we see. His actions were equal to his inner vision—a talent that, alas, was reflected in his life as well as his art.

When the Contarelli Chapel commissioned Caravaggio to paint Matthew in 1602, he produced two somewhat stodgy portrayals of a wise and literate saint. Then he went too far. His *Saint Matthew and the Angel* describes Matthew as an unkempt peasant requiring care and instruction from an angel that was much

◂ Caravaggio, *The Seven Works of Mercy*, 1606–1607, Pio Monte della Misericordia, Naples

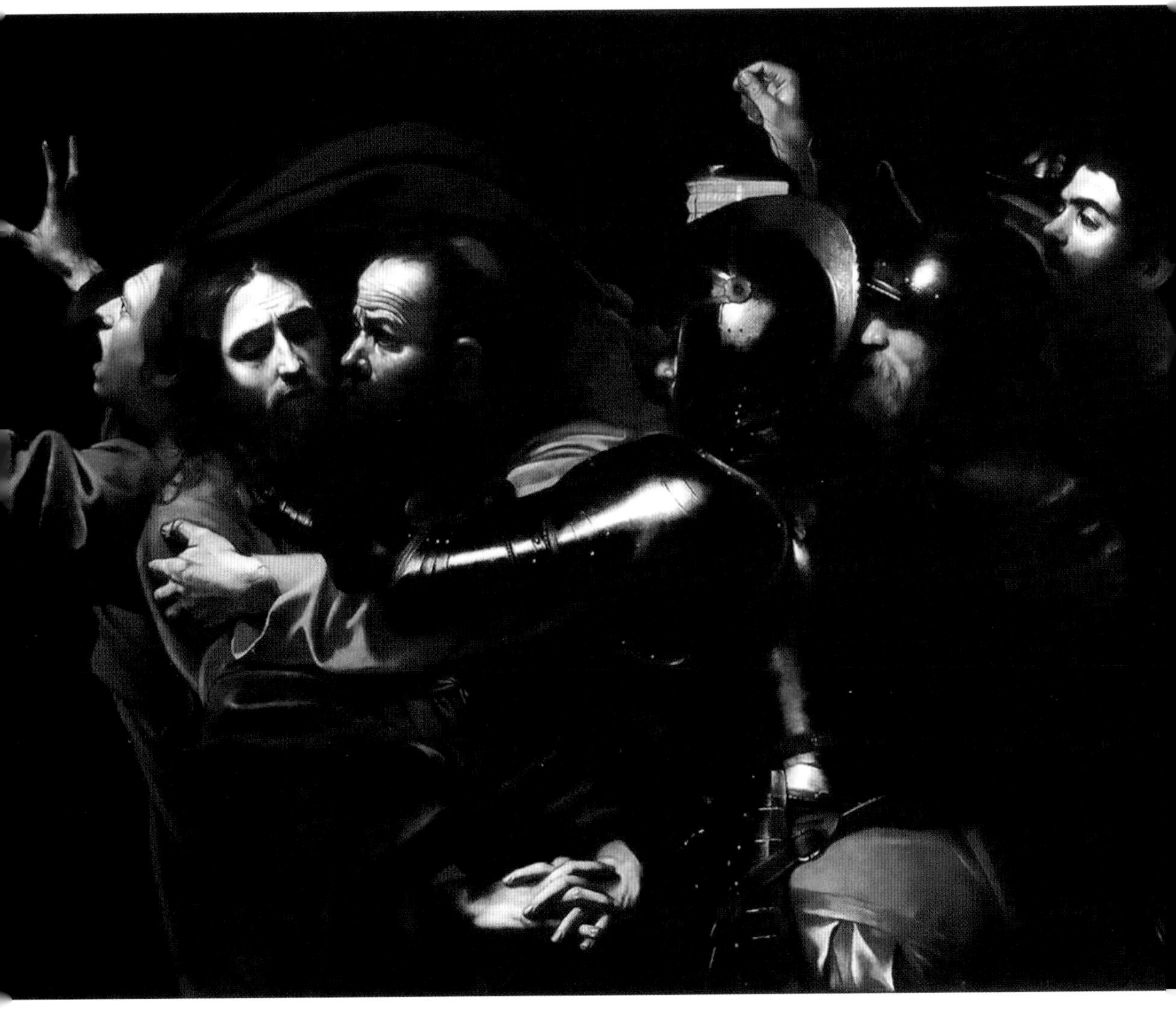

Caravaggio, *Taking of Christ*, c. 1602, National Gallery of Ireland, Dublin too intrusive for the chapel fathers. Caravaggio quickly replaced it with a more traditional *The Inspiration of Saint Matthew*, which empowers Matthew and significantly decreases any sense of helplessness and intimacy that was in the first rendition.

Caravaggio showed this same reckless disregard for tradition in *Death of the Virgin*, commissioned in 1601 by the Carmelites of Santa Maria della Scala. It was on display for only a few days, if that, before the monks quickly removed what they saw as a scandalous and impious representation of Mary. The blood-red cloth, the cast-off body, and apostles more grieving than celebratory all contribute to this painful picture of humanity and loss. Shorn of customary iconography, the painting accomplishes what few others of the period could: we enter the moment and mourn with Mary's friends. Caravaggio likely finished this piece shortly before the crime that forced him out of Rome.

In May 1606, the artist was accused of murder. His many detractors were quick to provide damning accounts: two favorites being a gambling debt or a duel. The facts are somewhat less lurid. The artist and some friends were playing handball, four to a side; a dispute arose over the score, daggers were drawn and Caravaggio was wounded and allegedly killed one of his opponents. The death resulted in Caravaggio's fleeing to Naples, hounded and probably guilty. The subject of his next major work comes as no surprise.

He created *The Seven Works of Mercy* for the Church of Pio Monte della Misericordia in Naples. The medieval church used Matthew 25:35–36 as the text for the six acts of mercy, traditionally adding a seventh, *bury the dead*. Caravaggio chose a Neapolitan street corner to capture each of the works. There is a beggar in the foreground, looked on with compassion by a man of wealth, who shares his robe (*clothe the naked, visit the sick*), probably a reference to a similar tale about Martin of Tours. Above them an innkeeper nods at a desperate pilgrim (*shelter the homeless*); a heat-stricken man eagerly laps at a trickle of water (*refresh the thirsty*), commonly identified as Samson drinking from the jawbone of an ass, though this would represent divine rather than human charity. To the right, we see the feet of a corpse: his pallbearer is in shadow as a sexton recites the funeral office (*bury the dead*). In front of them a harried and fearful woman offers milk from her breast to an imprisoned man, a common motif in Roman stories of charity (*visit the imprisoned, feed the hungry*). Above it all, the Madonna and Jesus look down on the scene, with an angel shedding the light of mercy upon humanity —though, as always with Caravaggio, there are other light sources that are difficult to identify.

In 1609 Caravaggio heard he might be granted a papal reprieve for the murder in Rome. Evading a group of hired thugs for yet another assault, the wounded artist boarded a felucca bound for the Papal States. They met foul weather and put in at Palo. The garrison there had orders to keep an eye out for a known bandit. Caravaggio, with his scars, dagger, rapier, and surly demeanor, seemed a likely suspect. He was immediately detained only to be released two days later after paying a handsome fee to the fort captain. Caravaggio searched frantically for the felucca. His entire stock of unsold art was on board, promised to the papal nephew, Scipione Borghese, as the price of his pardon. But the small craft had been blown north and docked at Porto Ercole, a 100-kilometer journey under the grueling July sun. When Caravaggio reached Porto Ercole, infected and suffering from enteric fever, he collapsed on the beach. He was taken to the Confraternity of Santa Cruz and died within a few days. He was thirty-eight. He was buried in a pauper's grave. Three days later, his pardon arrived.

Returning to 1602, the year of his infamous *Saint Matthew and the Angel*, Caravaggio created one of the great paintings of Judas, *The Taking of Christ*. The composition is enhanced rather than hindered by the lack of a definable light source. The soldiers physically dominate the action, yet it is the pain of Jesus that draws our attention—that and the troubled but resolute face of his betrayer. Perhaps Caravaggio could understand the flaws that led to such terrible treachery. That may be why he painted himself as Peter in the far right: a desperate follower holding up a lamp to the scene, pleading for his Savior.

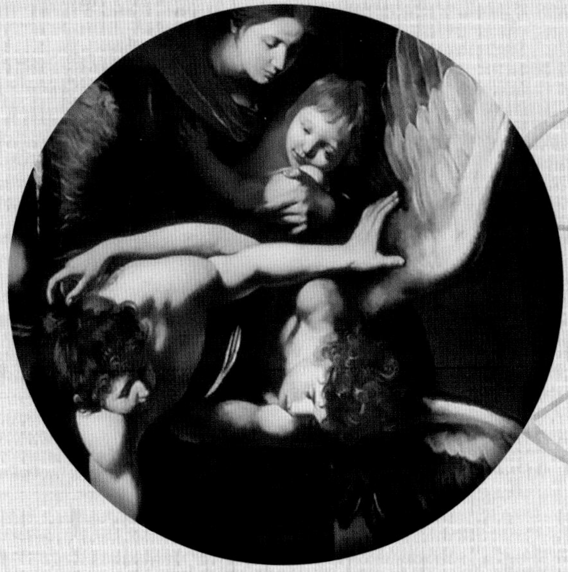

If we believe in God at all we must allow him to bring us his enlightenment and salvation in ways of his own choosing, and it would indeed be surprising if these were not very different from anything that we, from our limited perspective and with our limited wisdom and intelligence, could have foreseen.

—JOHN BAILLIE

Come, bring your sampler, and with art
draw in't a wounded heart.

—ROBERT HERRICK

God creates out of *nothing*, wonderful, you say: yes, to be sure, but he does what is still more wonderful: he makes saints out of sinners.

—SØREN KIERKEGAARD

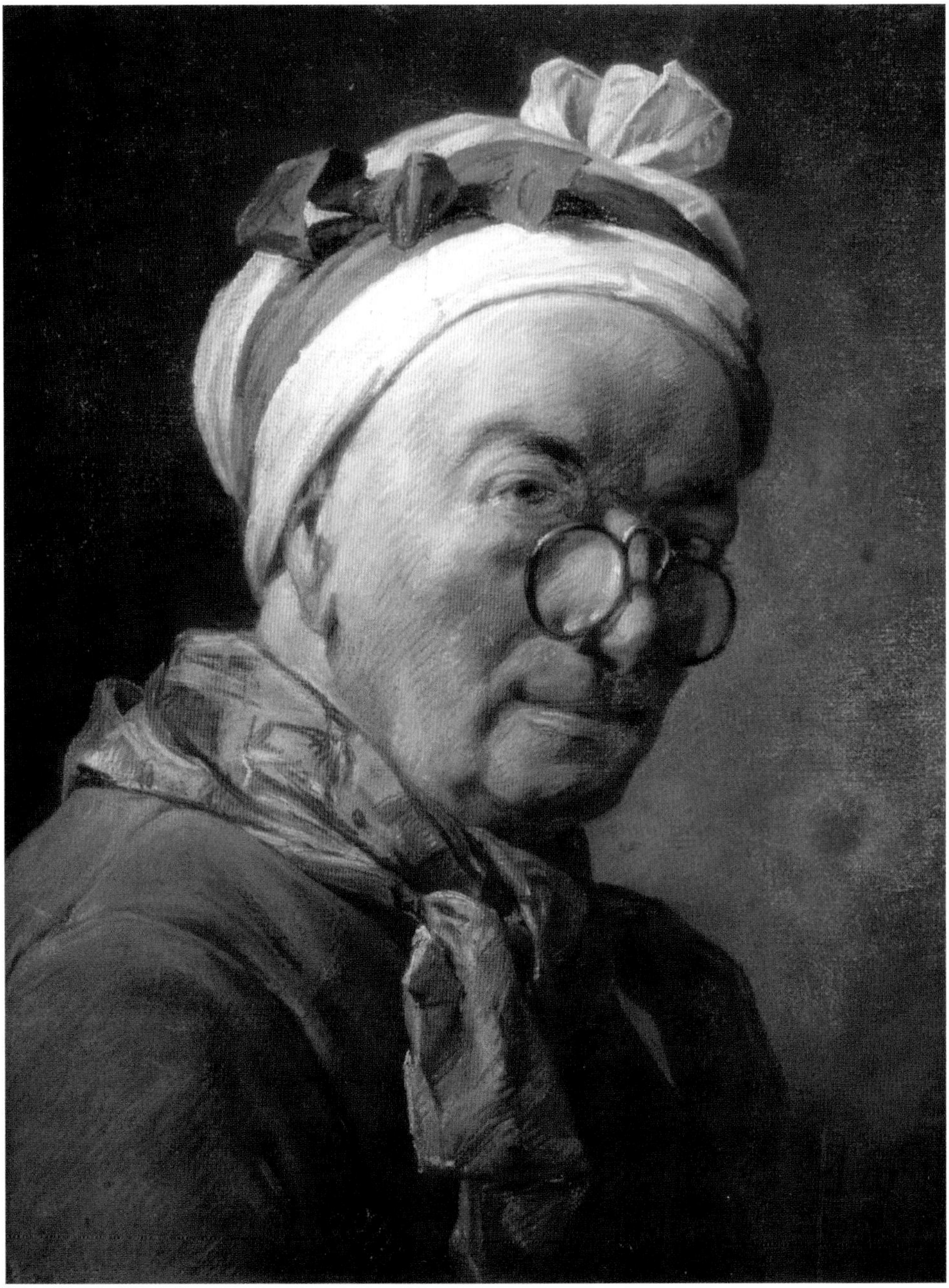

Chardin, *Self-Portrait*, 1771, Louvre, Paris

A heart is transformed

JEAN-BAPTISTE SIMÉON CHARDIN

(1699–1779), a French painter

My grief is beyond healing; my heart is broken.
—JEREMIAH 8:18 (NLT)

JEAN-SIMÉON CHARDIN loved his wife. During their long engagement he painted many of his great still lifes. Like his best work, Jean-Siméon was guileless, loyal, a perfectionist, and often a bit too plainspoken.

Over time his fiancée's health declined along with her family's finances. Jean-Siméon's father urged him to negate the contract. The artist refused. He cared little for what Marguerite could bring to a union. She was enough. They were married in February 1731; nine months later their son, Jean-Pierre, was born. The boy was a toddler when the Chardins welcomed another child to the family, Marguerite-Agnès, in 1733. The two years they were together stayed with Jean-Siméon and Jean-Pierre the rest of their lives.

The artist's father had died shortly after their marriage. Marguerite died in 1735. Marguerite-Agnès died one year later, at age three. Jean-Siméon and his five-year-old son were alone.

For the next few years the artist focused almost entirely on genre paintings of caring women and the children in their charge. They are uncomplicated and sparse, conveying a sense of deep quiet. Jean-Siméon continued to produce similar scenes after his mother died in 1743 and well into his second marriage the following year. His new wife, Françoise, was a widow. The couple knew loss and the value of each moment. If God is love, as he surely is, then perhaps we need look no further for the spiritual nature of this artist.

Jean-Siméon was a modest man. He took pains to ensure that his work had the most unassuming locations at gallery shows, frequently giving lesser artists pride of place. His associates found him puzzling. Vanity and ambition seemed alien to him. He was more uninterested than saintly.

Jean-Siméon preferred a white pigment in his oil paintings. He used it to great effect, giving his still lifes a particular sheen. By the time he was seventy-two, the lead-based paint had damaged his eyes. He turned to pastels. The French art world was amused that a man his age was trying something new. They were astonished at the results. The master's touch was not lost. His pastels are works of genuine pathos; Jean-Siméon's *Self-Portrait* (1771) describes an artist who is robust and alert.

Jean-Pierre, who lost his mother so young, never quite lived up to his father's talent or gift of concentration. The young man won prestigious prizes but failed to complete his commissions. There was tension and estrangement between him and his father. In 1772, he threw himself into a canal in Venice. Jean-Pierre was forty-one when he ended his life.

Imagine for a moment his father's overwhelming sense of guilt. Suicide was even more a stigma in eighteenth-century France than it is across the world today. Studies show that some 70 percent of parents take three to four years to put a child's death into perspective. It can take even longer when exacerbated by the loneliness, ostracizing, and condemnation that often accompany what is labeled and dismissed as a "bad death." Researchers have found that suicide and drug-related death survivors are consistently more troubled by grief than those who lost someone to accidental and natural causes. This is not to suggest that any specific group mourns more. One difference lies in the guilt they feel. Another seems to lie in the grace of others.

Studies indicate that the challenges in grieving are "of immense proportion" for these parents. They find less compassionate responses from their significant others and the public-at-large due to the intense stigma against drug use and suicide. The former is an addiction, the latter mental illness. In both cases, parents would prevent the deaths if they could. Yet they continue to be subject to social censure. The children are blamed and the parents are held at fault by others and themselves. These losses are seldom publicly mourned or socially supported. The relationship with the dead person is poorly recognized: their grief is rarely acknowledged in any meaningful way.

Three years after Jean-Pierre's death, Jean-Siméon painted *Self-Portrait Wearing Glasses* (1775). Gone are the glittering eyes of the artist. His previous unrivaled

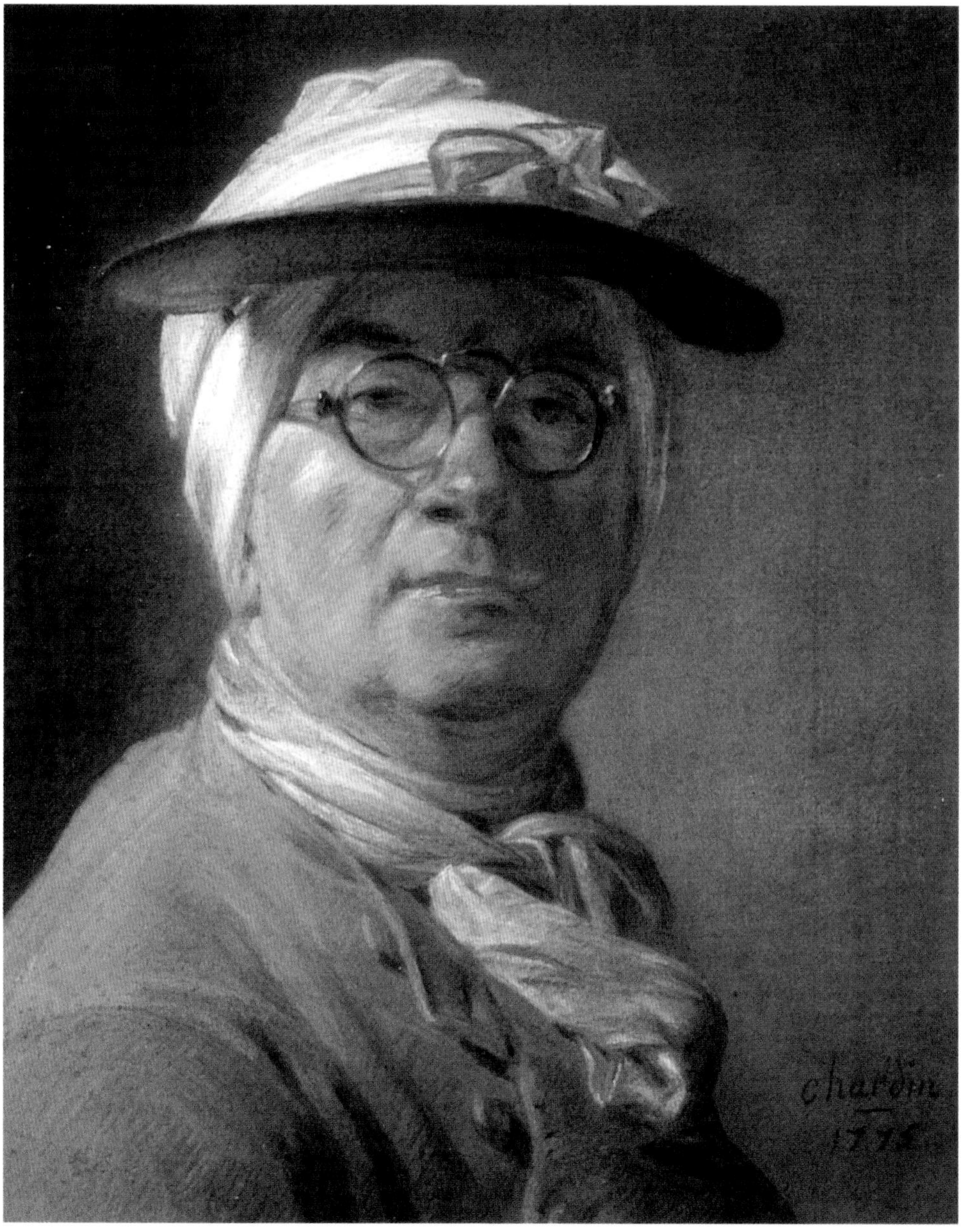

Chardin, *Self-Portrait Wearing Glasses*, 1775, Louvre, Paris

technical proficiency is matched by a new warmth, elegance, and patience. He painted only a dozen or so pastels before his death in 1779, but they remain some of the most important in the medium. Pastels enhanced the artist's gift for truth. "One uses color," Jean-Siméon often said, "but paints with the heart."

Whatever the facts of his son's death, the truth of his life cannot be lost, for we see that life in each brushstroke from his father's hand. His artist's heart was not dimmed over time; it was transformed—never more so than in the final homage to his son, painted five years after Jean-Pierre's death: *Portrait of a Young Boy* (1777).

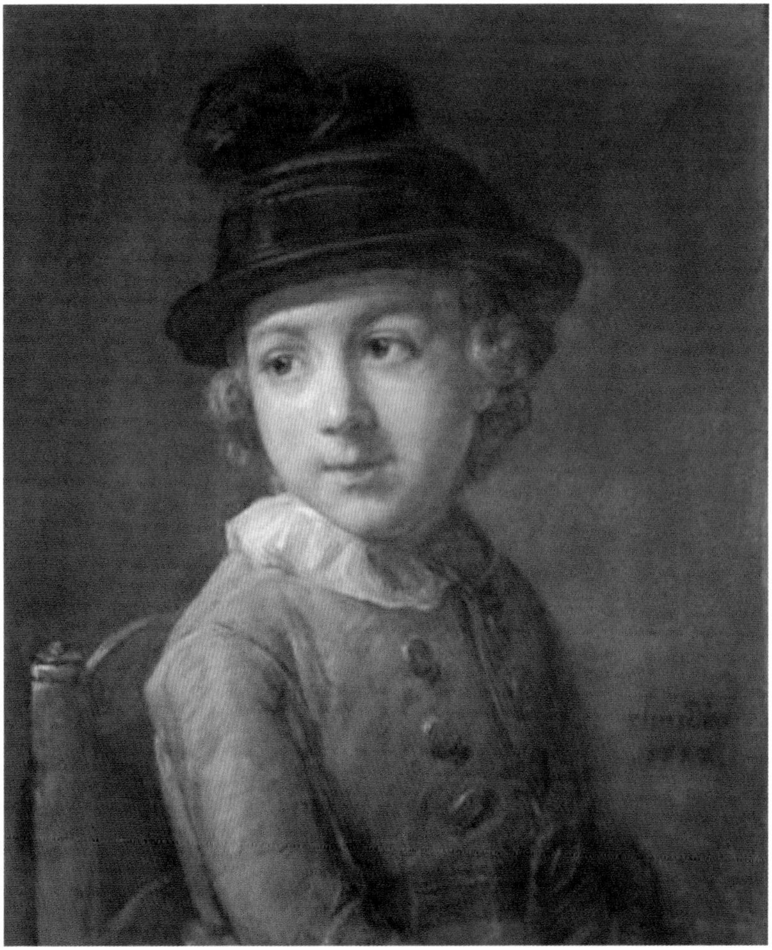

Chardin, *Portrait of a Young Boy*, 1777, private collection

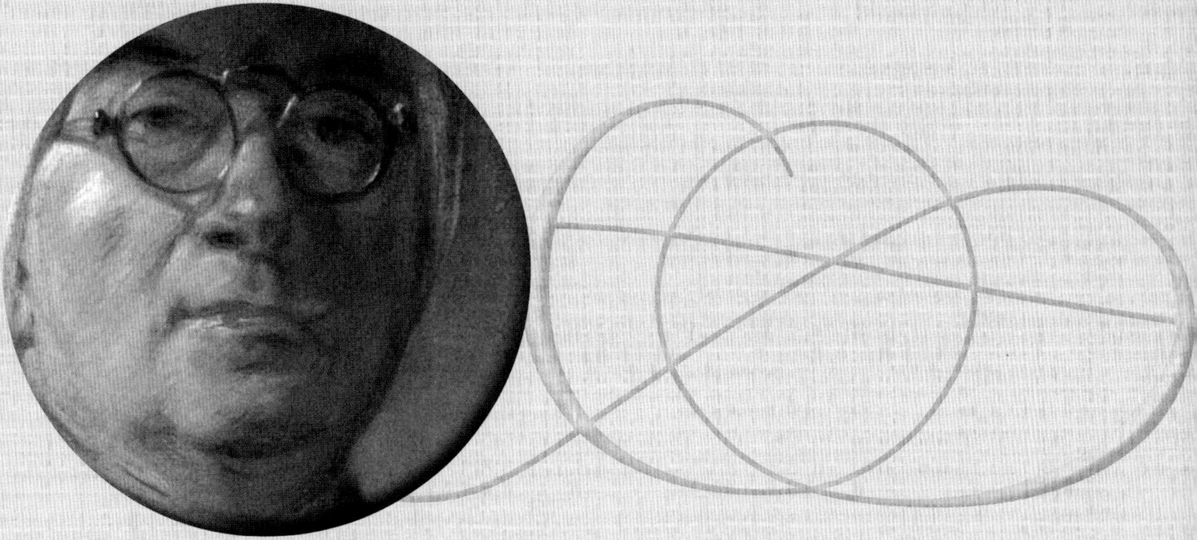

Beauty springs from within, from the inner need of the soul.
—WASSILY KANDINSKY

I live, and bear
The aspect and the form of breathing men.
But grief should be the instructor of the wise;
Sorrow is knowledge: they who know the most
Must mourn the deepest o'er the fatal truth.
—LORD BYRON, *Manfred*

The great secret of death, and perhaps its deepest connection with us, is this: in taking from us a being we have loved and venerated, death does not wound us without, at the same time, lifting us toward a more perfect understanding of this being and of ourselves.
—RAINER MARIA RILKE

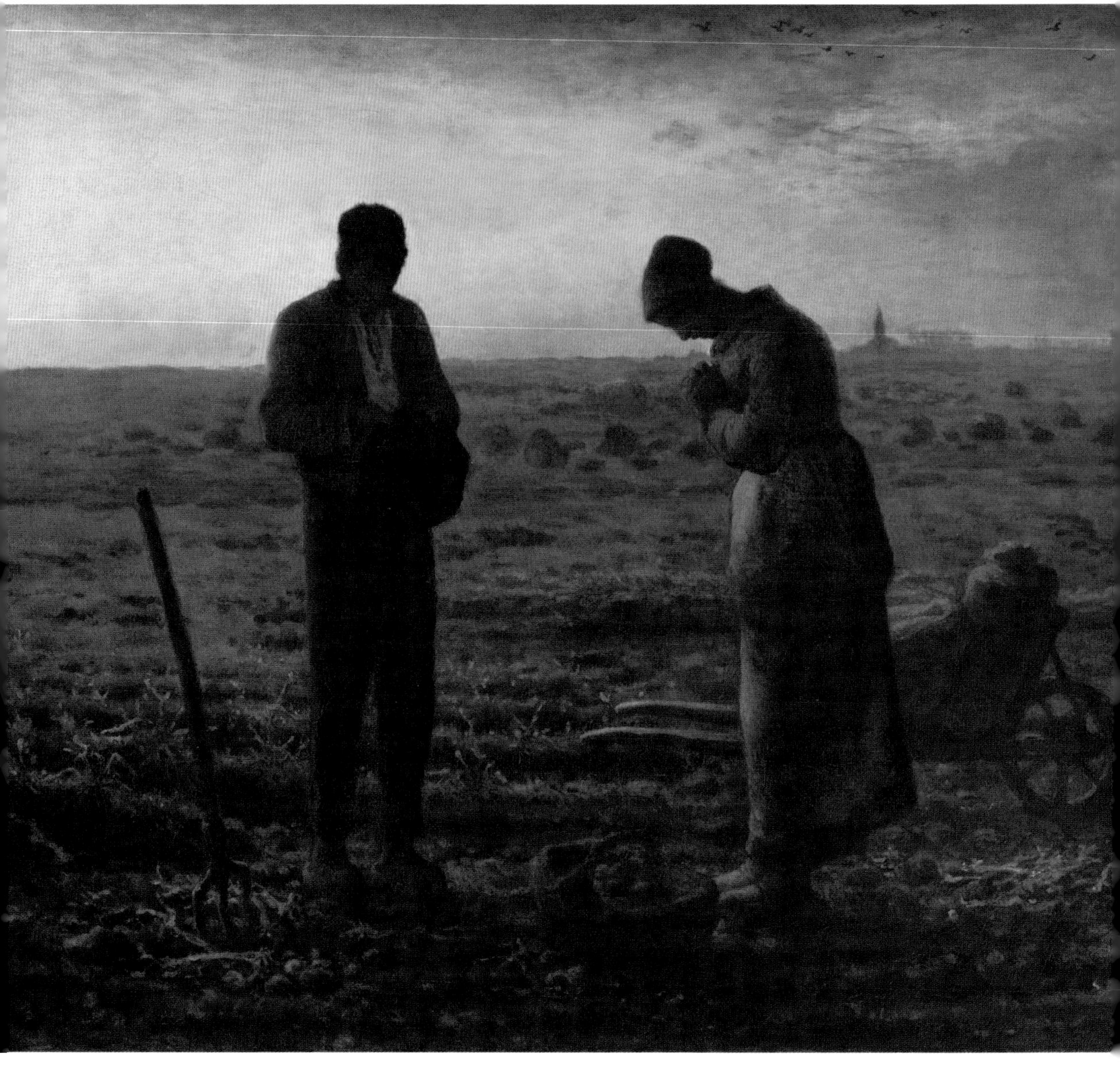

Millet, *The Angelus*, 1859, Musée d'Orsay, Paris

Truth is often hidden

JEAN-FRANÇOIS MILLET

(1814–1875), a French painter

The secret things belong to the Lord *our God, but the things revealed belong to us and to our children forever.*
—DEUTERONOMY 29:29

Jean-François Millet put life into his paintings. It was a life he knew as a child, one he observed, but not one he led. Or perhaps he never quite left that life behind. It remained hidden in his finest painting, waiting for an X-ray to discover.

Jean-François grew up in a small village. As the eldest son, he was expected to help his family in the fields. It was there that he experienced the simple moment captured so eloquently in his most famous piece. "The idea for *The Angelus* came to me," Jean-François wrote, "because I remembered that my grandmother hearing the church bell ringing while we were working in the fields, always made us stop work to say the Angelus prayer for the poor departed very religiously and with cap in hand." For years there seemed no reason to doubt this explanation—though artists are as guilty as anyone of providing versions for public consumption that keep certain aspects private. It is an elegant work, rich with pathos and simplicity: a poor couple praying over a basket of potatoes at twilight, church bells tolling in the distance. But the artist's comment may give a clue to his original intent, a "prayer for the poor departed."

Salvador Dali loved and hated *The Angelus*. He insisted that the light and the figures were representative of mourning, that the potatoes were nothing if not suggestive of the small coffin of a child. His insight was dismissed, but Dali would not leave it alone. Ultimately, and mainly due to Dali's persistence, the Louvre submitted the painting to X-ray analysis. It revealed the clear outline of a child's coffin under the basket of potatoes. The original version had no steeple in the distance.

Jean-François never said why he changed the painting. In fact, he never commented on an earlier version at all. It was the last of his famous trio of harvester paintings: *The Sower* (1850), a somewhat forced work; followed by two unquestioned masterpieces, *The Gleaners* (1857) and *The Angelus* (1859). All three show the toil of an unheralded and often oppressed class of people—a message dear to the artist's heart.

While much of his work is spiritual, Jean-François produced few overtly religious pieces. Even the best known, painted in 1853, started with the title "Ruth and Boaz" but prior to exhibition was changed to *Harvesters Resting (Ruth and Boaz)*. He worked on it for three years and would always consider it his most important work. In choosing a contemporary setting, Jean-François described the dignity and backbreaking labor of the harvesters. We notice Ruth's meager gleanings compared to generous stacks of grain belonging to an absent landowner. Boaz is a sharecropper in this version. We can nearly step into the scene, or recoil, thankful that such is not our lot.

But it had been Jean-François's lot, and that of his family, a personal history the artist left at age eighteen but could not leave behind. His first wife, Pauline, died in 1843 after two years of marriage. In 1845, he met and lived with the woman who would become his second wife, Catherine. They had eleven children. Who, then, was the child in the forgotten coffin of *The Angelus*? A sibling? An acquaintance? The children of laborers? A metaphor? Or Jean-François himself, covering a life never truly forgotten with nostalgia-tinged hues? We likely will never know; but we *do* know that many of us carry silent grief and loss.

Important reality operates on a different level of things—it is not in the overt subject, but in the little brush strokes, all the little, everyday events and *things* that make up our lives. They may be past in a historical sense, but they are nonetheless present, each one of them, on the canvas, and it is they, taken together, that make up our painting. Each of us gets to paint one, and when it is done it is ours forever—it is all that *is* ours, on into howling eternity.

—JAMES KUGEL

The crucial question is one of personal "history"; in it lies the human story, the human suffering.

—CARL JUNG

The time draws near the birth of Christ:
  The moon is hid; the night is still;
  The Christmas bells from hill to hill
Answer each other in the mist.

This year I slept and woke with pain,
  I almost wish'd no more to wake,
  And that my hold on life would break
Before I heard those bells again:

But they my troubled spirit rule,
  For they controll'd me when a boy;
  They bring me sorrow touch'd with joy,
The merry merry bells of Yule.

—ALFRED LORD TENNYSON

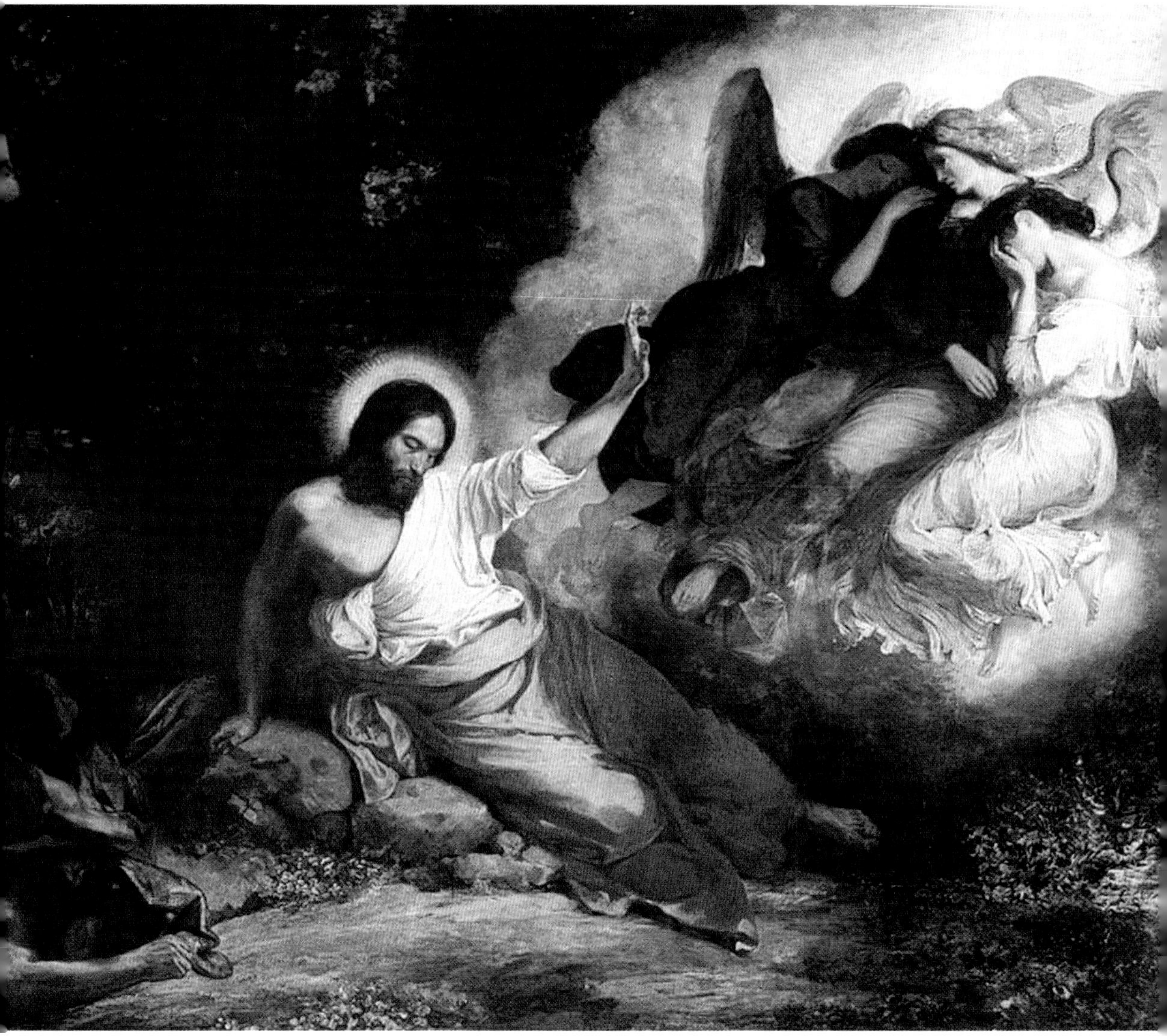

Delacroix, *Christ in the Garden of Olives*, 1827, Church of Saint-Paul-Saint-Louis, Paris

An orphan struggles with God

EUGÈNE DELACROIX

(1798–1863), a French painter

> *You have taken away my companions and loved ones.*
> *Darkness is my closest friend.*
> —PSALM 88:18 (NLT)

EUGÈNE DELACROIX eschewed traditional Christmas paintings. He had little interest in nativities or colorful wise men. Struggle was his inspiration: in it he found redemption. Eugène could not stay away from *Christ on the Sea of Galilee.* He returned to the subject many times from 1841 to 1854. Art historians separate the paintings by those with sails and those with oars—but it is the figure of Jesus in each that resists classification.

Eugène's first foray, in 1841, is more human than later attempts. Jesus seems truly at peace; the apostles seem agitated and overcrowded in a tiny rowboat. By the 1850s Eugène had made many visits to Dieppe. His seascapes are masterpieces, as in the 1854 rendition: the storm itself is conspiring against the helpless sailboat. Why the Sea of Galilee, whether in a boat unequal to the task or in a storm few crafts could weather?

Eugène's father died in 1805, when the artist was seven years old. His siblings were much older than he and had lives of their own. One brother was a general; his sister married a diplomat. Another brother died in battle in 1807; his mother died in 1814. By age sixteen Eugène was an orphan.

Eugène's sister died in 1827 while he was working on his first major religious piece, *Christ in the Garden of Olives.* This is a study in solitude: soldiers arrive in the background while the half-seen apostles sleep; Jesus seems to wave off the grieving angels. When the piece was exhibited in 1827–1828, it was hailed for its religious fervor and condemned for its impiety. Critics felt it lacked faith. The angels had no reason to weep, they said; Jesus no cause to resist their ministrations.

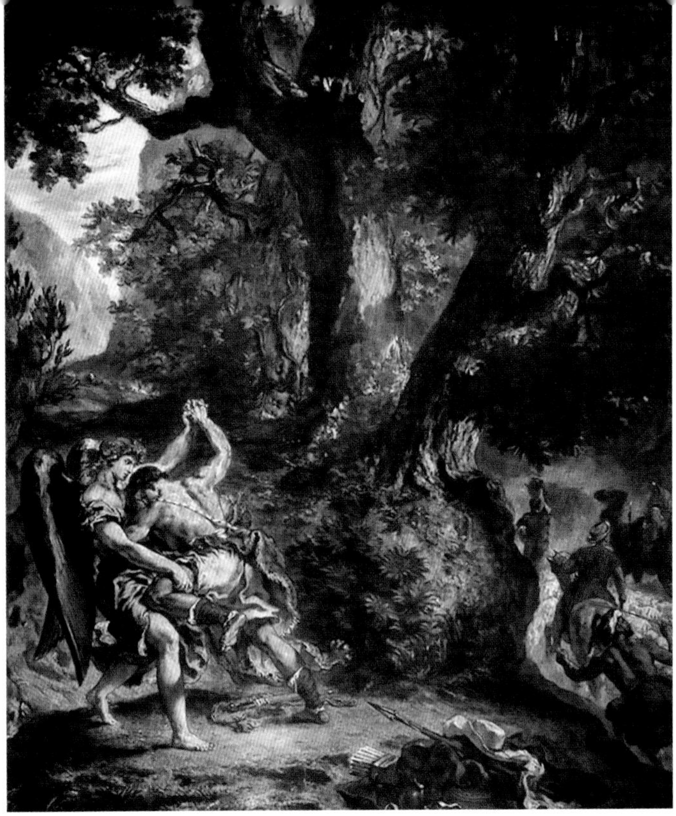

Delacroix, *Jacob Wrestling with the Angel*, 1856–1861, Church of Saint-Sulpice, Paris

"The effect must be for the soul and not the eye," Eugène wrote. "In a painting, a mysterious bridge seems to exist between its painted subjects and the spectator's spirit." Perhaps, after so much death and loss, Eugène saw something of himself in Christ's extremity. He was on his own.

These themes of stubborn resolve and solitude typified much of Eugène's religious work, but it was *powerlessness* that seemed to fascinate him. He returned to it over and over in settings of unforgiving landscapes, seascapes, and harsh weather.

"This struggle is regarded, by Holy Scripture, as a sign of the ordeals that God sometimes visits upon his chosen ones," Eugène wrote of his mural *Jacob Wrestling with the Angel.* Man fights alone with God in a beautiful but uncaring land. Our attention is drawn to its vivid background. The artist has cleared away any excess. Consider the detailed still life in the foreground: Jacob has set aside his scarf, spear, arrows, and a hat that is noticeably similar to those favored by artists of Eugène's day. "A stubborn struggle," Eugène wrote, "which ends only when Jacob, wounded in the tendon of the thigh by his opponent, is made powerless."

Man must be alone to listen, to feel and even to fight God, for God engages only those who, paradoxically, are both threatened and protected by solitude. From his contest with God, Jacob emerged triumphant but limping; he was never to be the same again.

—ELIE WIESEL

A Dirge

Rough wind, that moanest loud
  Grief too sad for song;
Wild wind, when sullen cloud
  Knells all the night long;
Sad storm, whose tears are vain,
Bare woods, whose branches stain,
Deep caves and dreary main,
  Wail, for the world's wrong!

—PERCY BYSSHE SHELLEY

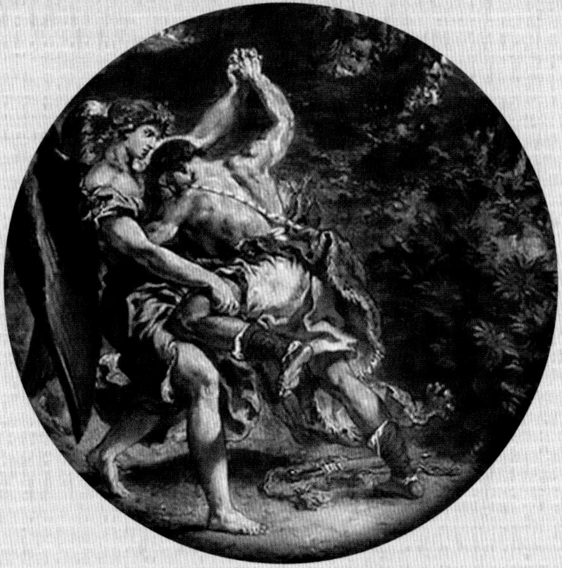

He's a mysterious, terrifying, wounding Adversary against whom we all struggle. The God Whom Jacob confronts terrifies him. Encounters with God are very serious experiences, and we will come away wounded—but believing. The story isn't about morality, though. It's about grace—the unexpected and unearned. It's about free gifts given to the most undeserving people.

—JOHN KSELMAN

Thayer, *Mount Monadnock*, 1911, National Gallery of Art, Washington, DC

An ideal is realized

ABBOTT HANDERSON THAYER

(1849–1921), an American artist

> *ADONAI is good to all;*
> *his compassion rests on all his creatures.*
> —PSALM 145:9 (CJB)

ABBOTT THAYER loved nature—not as a visitor, but as an inhabitant. The last twenty years of his life were spent in Dublin, New Hampshire, among the hills and animals. His family lived in a summer home, poorly equippd for harsh winters that reached forty degrees below zero. The children didn't seem to mind. Each night they slept in nearby lean-tos. Owls, rabbits, dogs, and guinea pigs wandered freely in and out of the house, including a porcupine that daintily cleaned off the dinner plates. Abbott was fond of carrying kittens in his pockets.

They had a breathtaking view of Mount Monadnock, the subject of a poem by Abbott's favorite author, Ralph Waldo Emerson. The artist painted it from the same vantage point throughout the year. To him and his children it was the realization of an ideal. Abbott spent his life in search of "unsullied purity; spiritual truth." *Mount Monadnock* is precisely that.

Abbott is famous for his paintings of angels. They are difficult to avoid in his work. Thayer angels appear in prints, greeting cards, bookmarks, stickers, even on the cover of *TIME Magazine*. But these seldom capture the attention of critics. Too romanticized, they insist, no expression of the soul. Abbott may have been searching for something more. "For *men*, the dawn, girls, mothers and children, and brave kind men," he wrote, "all these things in their most familiar form are more ravishing every day come over again, through all time by virtue of their ever-deepening layers of heavenly connotations which they accumulate." As with many artists, words were a poor rambling copy of his inner vision. Abbott may not have been idealizing his subjects; perhaps he simply saw them that way.

A week after getting married in 1875, Abbott and his wife, Kate, left for Europe. They stayed in Paris some four years while Abbott studied art. Their daughter, Mary, was born there, in 1876; a son, Harry, was born in 1878. The young family returned to America the following year. In 1880, Harry died; a year later another son, Ralph Waldo, died at three months old. "It is a comfort to think that his dear life was more beautiful on earth than those who didn't know could believe," Abbott wrote, adding that even in the agony of his grief, "the horror of dying is changed forever, and an unspeakable delight of greeting shines back through the obscure future." The family began to travel, rarely staying in one location for more than a season. They had another son, Gerald, in 1883 and a daughter, Gladys, in 1886.

Kate's father died in 1887. It was all too much. The restless moving, grief, losing two children and now her father—Kate slipped slowly into a depression from which she would never recover. Abbot and his children's true pilgrimage had begun.

That year Abbott painted his first *Angel*, using his eldest daughter as a model. It is different from later renditions. Mary makes for a sad angel, unsure and vulnerable. Her toddler brother died when she was four years old. Another brother died soon after that, and now her mother seemed lost. The portrait says as much about the eleven-year-old child as it does her father's attempt to capture the unseen on canvas.

Kate was diagnosed with melancholia and institutionalized in 1888. She died three years later. *Virgin Enthroned* was painted shortly afterwards. It is a work of sorrow. Mary seems desolate; Gladys and Gerald, the other models, are gentle but dependent. Over the next few years, Abbott's portraits of his children changed. They grow more and more formidable. We see in Mary a stern protectiveness of her siblings.

Abbott soon remarried. In 1901, he and his second wife, Emma, packed up the children and moved to New Hampshire. Two years later he painted a tribute to another favorite author, Robert Louis Stevenson, buried atop Mount Vaea in Samoa. In *Stevenson Memorial*, Mary is a thoughtful but resolute angel. The twenty-seven-year-old model was no longer a child. By this time the artist and his hardy family had found a new source of inspiration and solace: the hills around them.

The Thayer clan had been in Dublin for ten years when a group of developers made plans to purchase swaths of Mount Monadnock. Abbott rallied the community to successfully save the land. That same year, 1911, he began work on his masterpiece, *Mount Monadnock*, a shadowy, stark vision of dawn in winter. Abbott died in 1921. Mary and the others scattered his ashes on the summit of what their father had often called "this dear mountain."

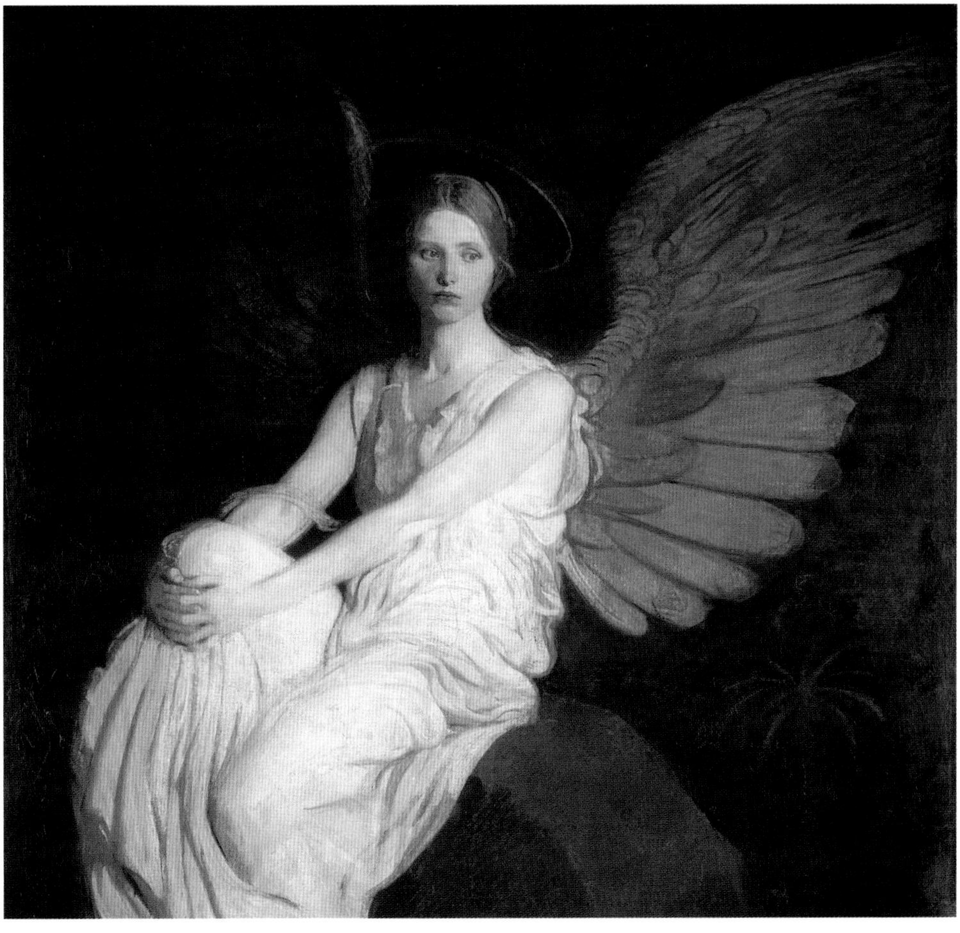

Thayer, *Stevenson Memorial*, 1903, Smithsonian American Art Museum, Washington, DC

When we run from darkness, how much do we really know about what we are running from? If we turn away from darkness on principle, doing everything we can to avoid it because there is simply no telling what it contains, isn't there a chance that what we are running from is God?

—BARBARA BROWN TAYLOR

Thousand minstrels woke within me,
"Our music's in the hills":—
Gayest pictures rose to win me,
Leopard-colored rills.
"Up! If thou knew'st who calls
To twilight parks of beech and pine."
I heard, and I obeyed,—
Assured that he who made the claim,
Well known, but loving not a name,
Was not to be gainsaid.

—RALPH WALDO EMERSON,
"Monadnock, the Mountain, N.H."

Angels often come without being called. I have never needed them and they were not there. Many times they come among Christians and are unseen. I myself, many times, have seen them among Christians.

—ST. JOAN OF ARC

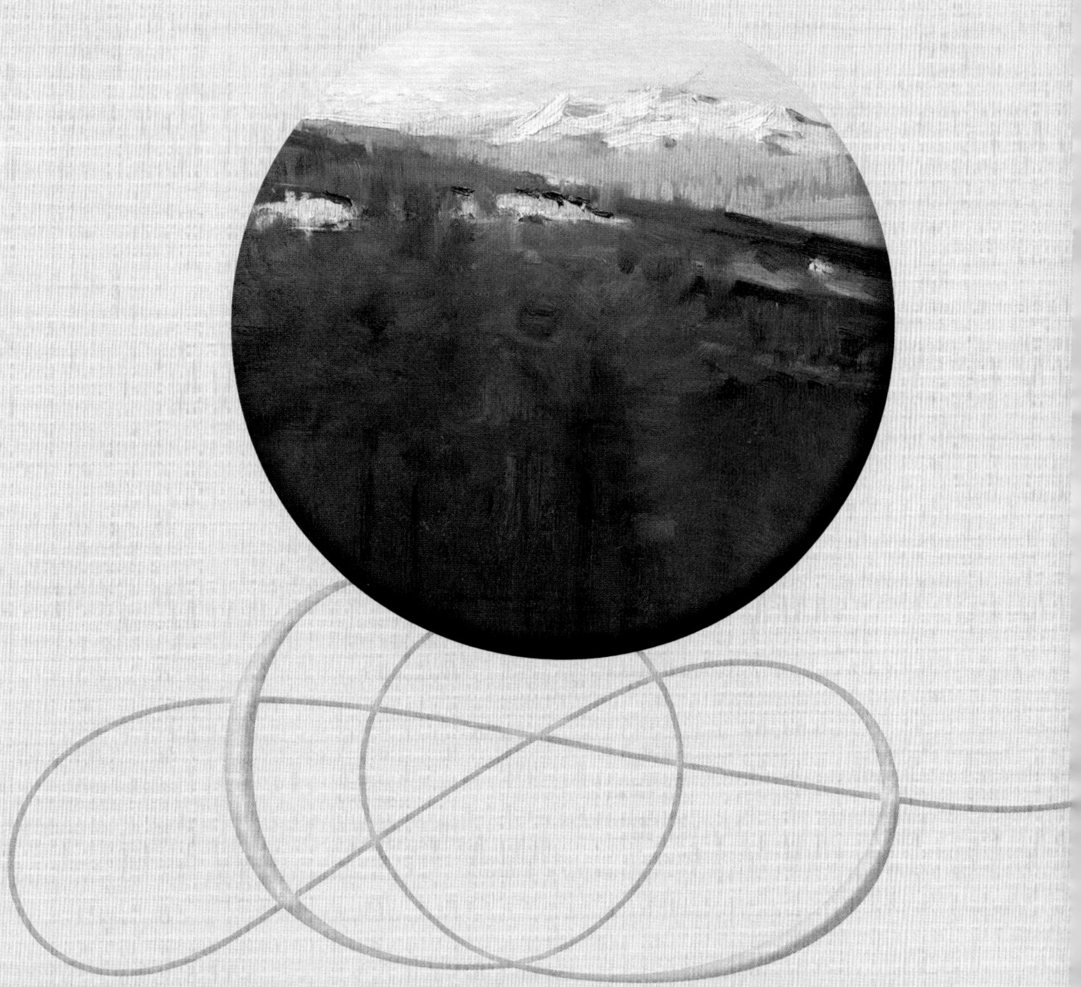

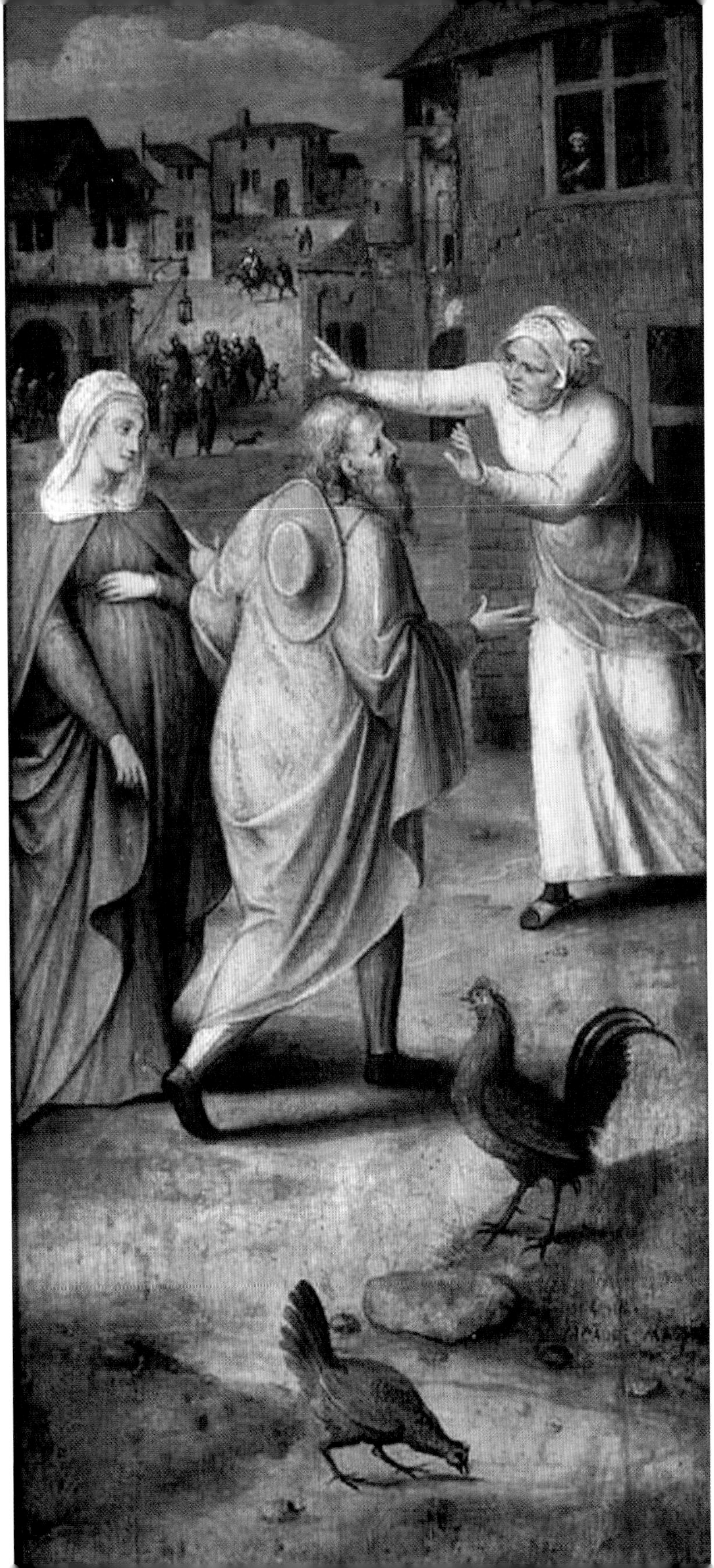

The pain of injustice
JAN MASSYS
(c. 1510–1575), a Flemish painter

I was a stranger and you invited me in.
—MATTHEW 25:35

JAN MASSYS'S father, Quentin Massys, was a true master. He died in 1530, praised for his talent and piety. Jan was twenty years old. He had trained under his father and continued his studies over the next decade. But the family lacked Quentin's knack for fitting in.

Jan's aunt Catherine and her husband were found guilty of reading the Holy Bible in the vernacular—a capital offense at the time. Why they risked official censure in this way is unclear, but the penalty was severe. In 1543, Jan's uncle was decapitated; his aunt was buried alive in a church square in Leuven. The next year, Jan and his brother, Cornelius, were banished from Antwerp: presumably for speaking out, though it is probable they were guilty of the same crime as their aunt and uncle. In later years Jan would paint scandalous and often disturbing scenes from the Old Testament: Lot and his daughters; Susanna; Bathsheba. The pieces suggest a thorough knowledge of the Bible, which might have come from reading it, as well as a certain glee in tweaking the nose of a structure that murdered his family members and exiled him for eleven years.

The brothers returned to Antwerp in 1555. Three years later, in 1558, Jan received a commission to paint a nativity from the same city fathers who had banished him. He honored their request in a way uniquely his own. The rejection of Mary and Joseph was all but ignored by artists until the sixteenth century. Jan changed that. In the cruelties heaped upon Mary and Joseph, he may have glimpsed his own yearning for a world free of injustice.

This was an unconventional subject for him, but the result is far more intimate and personal than many of his famous nudes. The elements may offer clues to

◂ Massys, *Hospitality Refused to the Virgin and Saint Joseph*, 1558, Royal Museum of Fine Arts, Antwerp

how Jan perceived his family's treatment by the church: a bedraggled and pleading Joseph, refused room where even chickens have shelter; onlookers observing the scene from shadowed windows; and, most telling, an innkeeper at once resolute and slightly fearful—of public censure?

The painting is steeped in pain, helplessness, and the sting of injustice and rejection. Is it any wonder Jan chose the title he did? *Hospitality Refused*.

The immanent God in us becomes wounded with us, suffers, struggles, hopes, and creates with us, shares every drop of our anger and sadness and joy. We should not be dismayed that God's being surpasses understanding, for it is precisely through this mystery that God incarnate can both lovingly share our condition and powerfully deliver us from it. It is through this mystery that grace remains absolute, permanent, and victorious.

—GERALD MAY

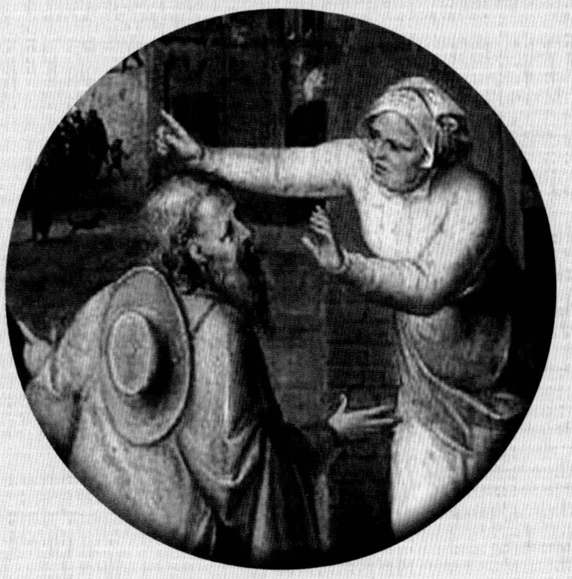

For my particular grief
Is of so flood-gate and o'erbearing nature
That it engluts and swallows other sorrows
And it is still itself.

—WILLIAM SHAKESPEARE, *Othello*

We can never struggle too much with God in our genuine search for truth.

—SIMONE WEIL

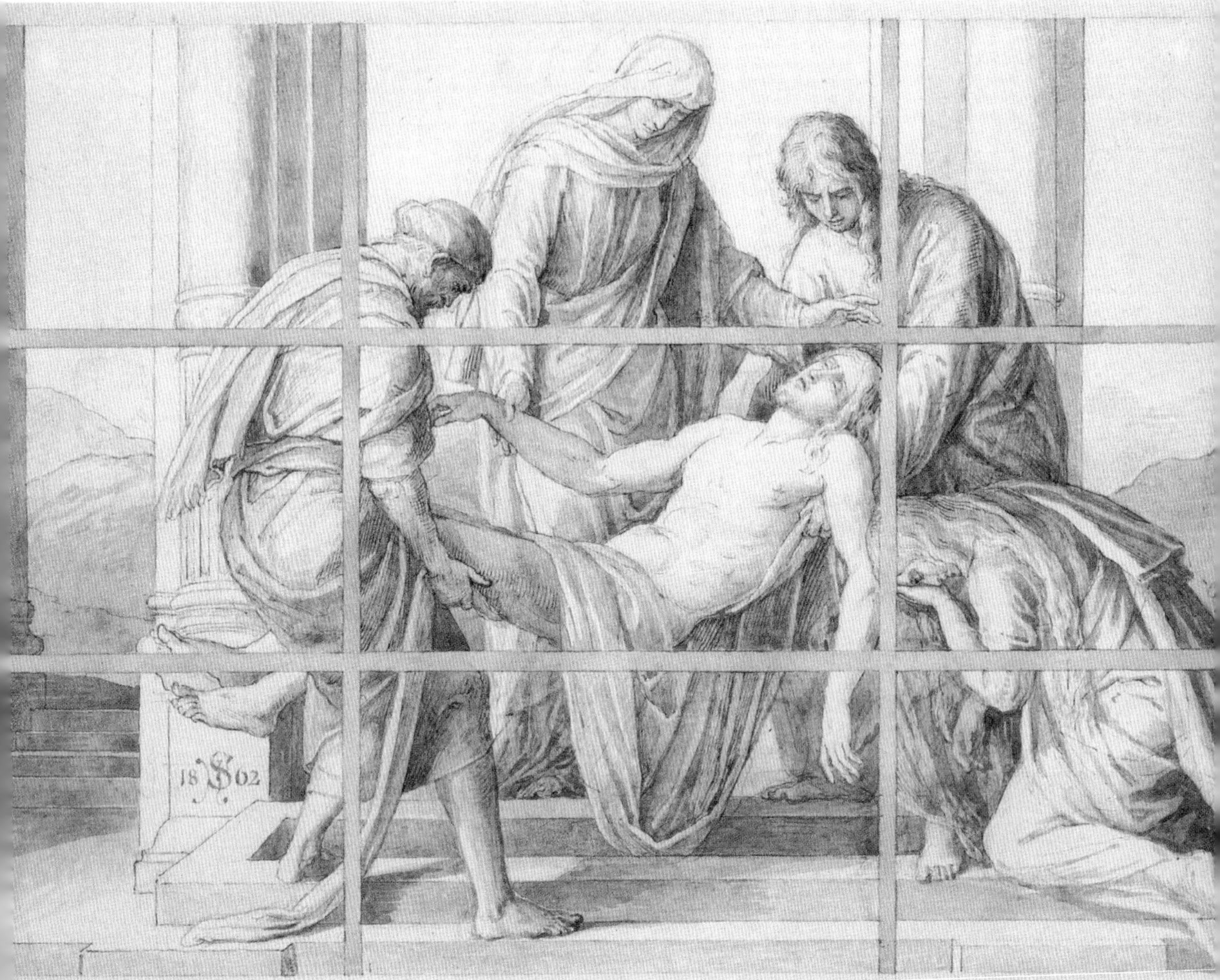

Carolsfeld, *The Entombment of Christ*, 1862, Saint Paul's Cathedral, London

A father finds the space between

JULIUS SCHNORR VON CAROLSFELD

(1794–1872), a German painter

The Spirit helps us in our weakness. We do not know what we ought to pray for, but the Spirit himself intercedes for us through wordless groans.
—ROMANS 8:26

JULIUS SCHNORR VON CAROLSFELD is famous for his *Picture Bible*, published in installments between 1852 and 1860. It was the highlight of his artistic career and a source of considerable income. Critics then and now find his work somewhat tedious. More workmanlike than inspired, they sniff, more illustration than art. Still, there are moments of brilliance—bold strokes and angular lines hidden within his traditional compositions that hint at a passion for his subject.

The Entombment, part of the *Picture Bible*, exemplifies the artist's often cluttered work. Although the body of Jesus is the focus of the piece, it evokes little emotion. The two men interring the body, balanced on either side, betray a hint of their loss; but it is only the woman, clutching the hand of Jesus, that breaks up the composition and adds tension and pathos. Julius later designed an *Entombment of Christ*, in 1862, for St. Paul's Cathedral in London. Again, the framing feels staged, though considerably more involving—two aspects that may have a simple explanation. Julius had spent the intervening years watching his son perform opera in the finest houses of Germany.

Ludwig Schnorr von Carolsfeld was married the same year his father's *Picture Bible* was finished. Ludwig already had a promising career as a tenor. A favorite of Richard Wagner, Ludwig and his wife created the title roles of *Triston und Isolde* to mixed but overall positive reviews. On July 9, 1865 Ludwig performed the lead in *The Flying Dutchman*. Twelve days later he died of complications arising from apoplexy. He was twenty-nine.

Julius died seven years later, in 1872. Very little is known about how he reacted to his son's death. But the handful of sketches he created offers a hint—and left the world what could have been one of its great masterpieces.

Studies show that parental bereavement is a particularly persistent and overwhelming grief. To lose a child is to change every aspect of who and what we are. "Bereaved parents do not 'recover' in the sense of returning to who they were before the death," wrote Ida Martinson in the professional journal *Death Studies*. "Instead, they appear to change as they integrate the loss into their lives." Parents deal with the exhaustive mourning and extreme, long-term stress in different ways, but one common thread is a marked neurological change. This can happen as early as three weeks after the loss with measurable biochemical components persisting throughout the first eight months. Over the first five years of grief, bereaved parents show demonstrable differences in how they fashion sentences and in basic motor skills. These are not hindered, just different. Julius, an artist, seems to have undergone similar shifts in how his hands found expression.

Ten months after his son's death, Julius attempted *The Parable of the Lost Sheep*. It is desultory, routine, and a far cry from his earlier work. However, a few years later, as late as 1868, Julius began another *Entombment of Christ*. The strokes are round, rich, and bold. Where his earlier illustrations seemed a bit rushed—the pressure of deadlines?—this piece exudes patience. It captures a single moment in ways much of Julius's work did not. The body is not the center of the piece; rather, the focal point is clearly *the space between* the mourners and the dead Jesus.

To modern thinking it may seem a shame to leave what could have been a masterpiece unfinished. But Julius may not have seen it that way. Friends of bereaved parents often despair that they seem to have given up when actually the opposite is true. Many parents say they have come to appreciate life in ways they did not before: its preciousness and transience. They experience each day in itself. The old expression "one day at a time" is for them a fact of existence and survival.

This may provide a clue to Julius's last *Entombment of Christ*. He chose the subject of Christ's burial with care. It is not a work of despair. The completed mourners stand out in contrast to the unfinished portion: their grief is immediate and stark; a future reunited with the dead is only a sketched-in hope. Yet it is *the space between* that draws our attention. Julius surely knew how the story ends: the advent of all joy, when despair turns to hope and parting to reunion. Perhaps the work is not unfinished. It is merely waiting.

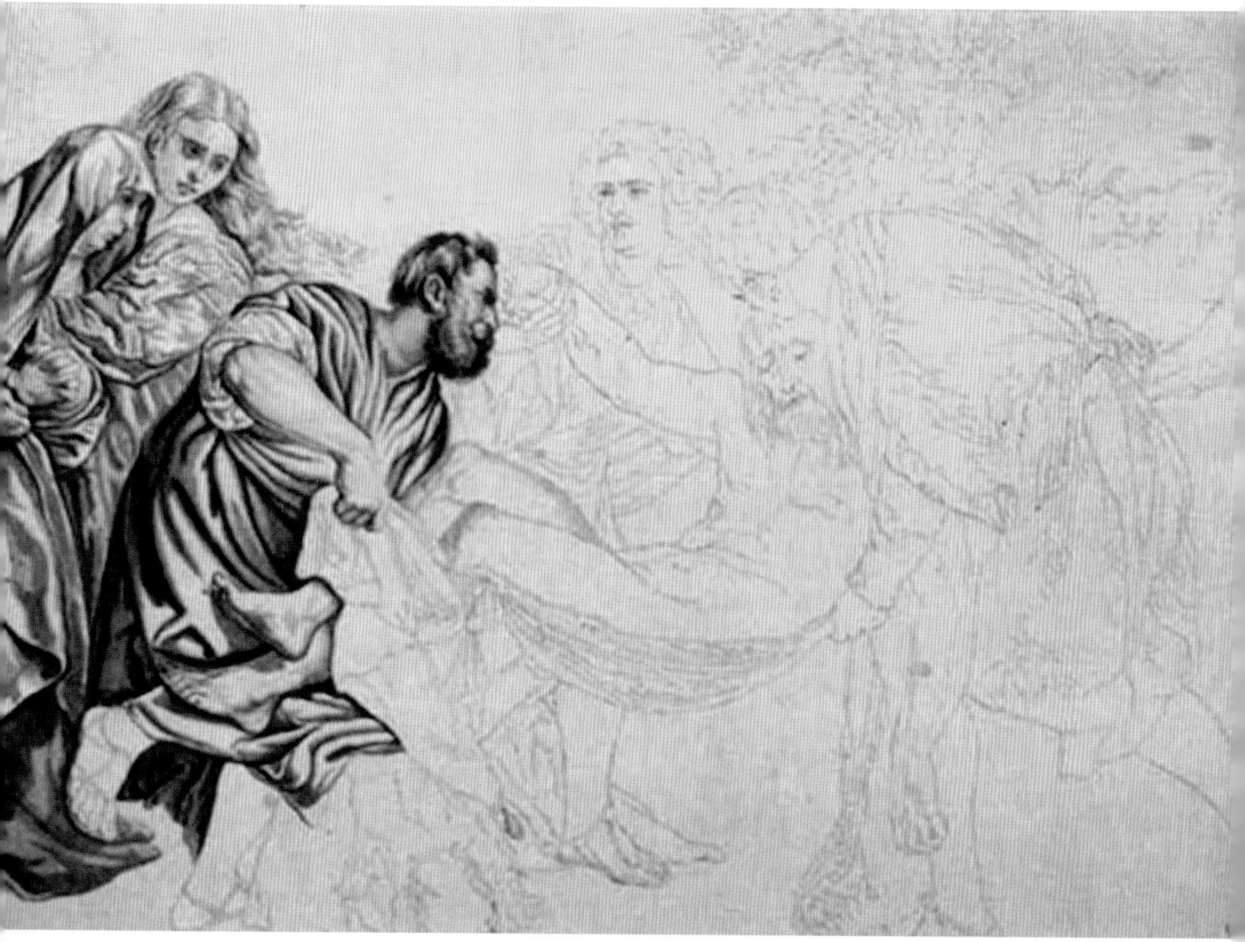

Carolsfeld, *The Entombment of Christ*, 1868–1872, private collection

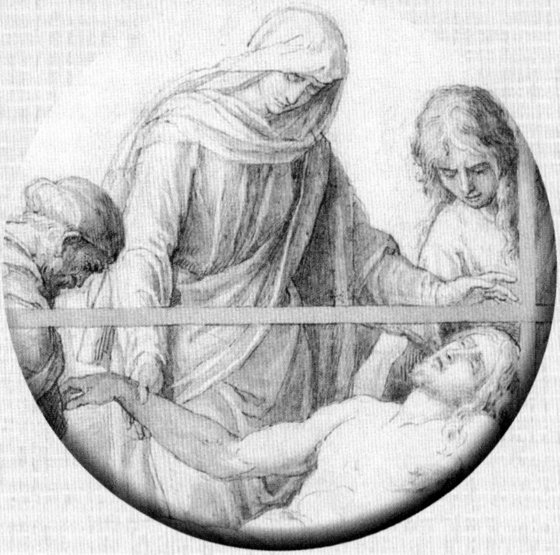

Every great loss demands that we choose life again.

—RACHEL NAOMI REMEN

Modes of aesthetic experience are divine gifts to us. Aesthetic transcendence, beauty, and sublimity are routes to the understanding of who and what we are in relation to God.

—PAUL CROWTHER

What is dying? What is dead?
So he asked, my son, so full of life.
How should I answer?
"Without color, no longer red."

What is dying? What is dead?
Oh, so he asked of me!
As does my heart, weak, weeping!
"Decay, its threat and dread?"

Was it a message, an ill breath?
Yes, a premonition, perhaps.
And so no longer asking, you died:
"What is dying? What is death?"

What is dying? What is death?
And so I ask, as you asked me;
and you answer, as if to say:
"To leave this earth, to be free."
—FRIEDRICH RÜCKERT

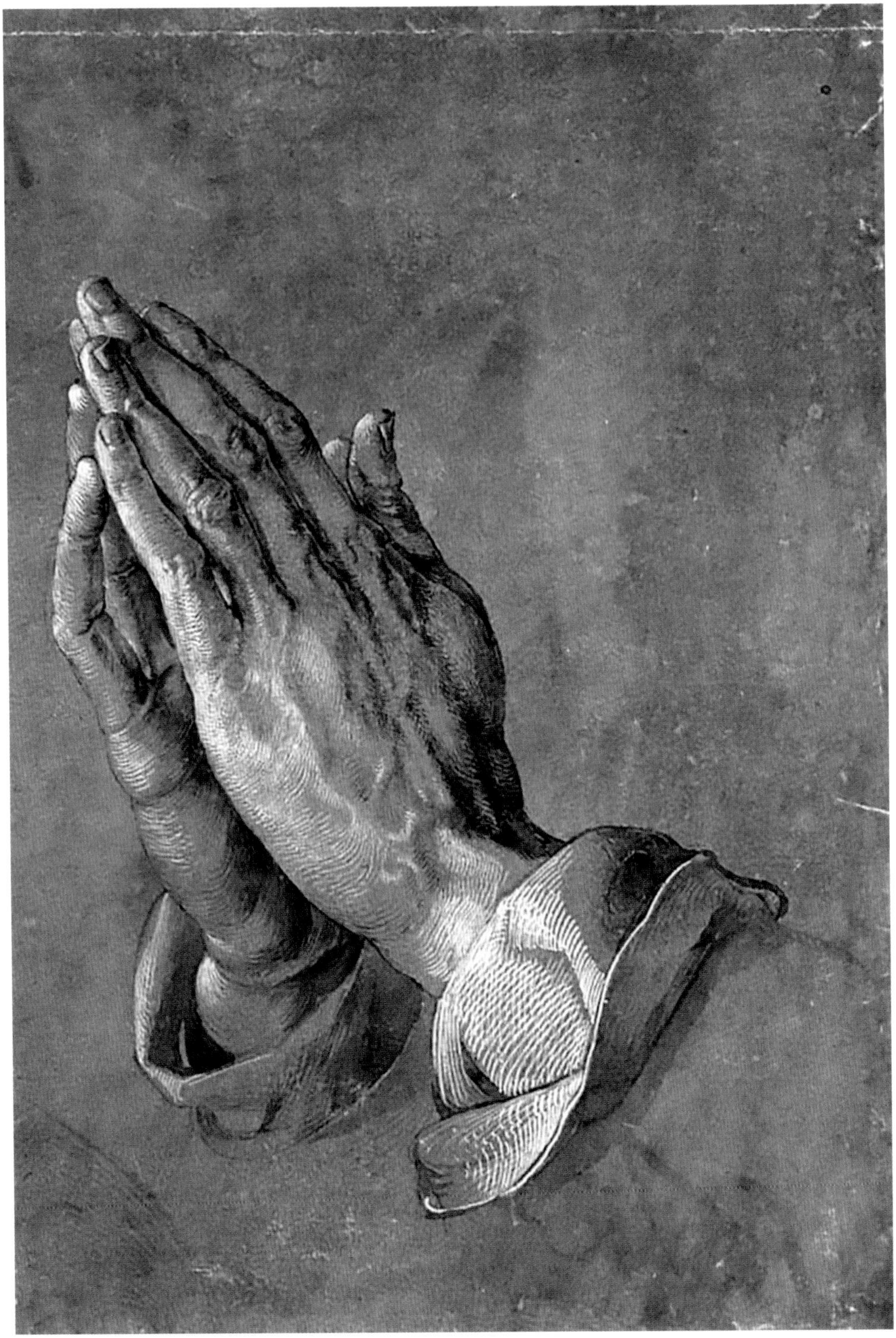

Dürer, *Praying Hands*, 1508, Albertina, Vienna

A sick artist sorrows

ALBRECHT DÜRER

(1471–1528), a German painter

The Lord is close to the brokenhearted and saves those who are crushed in spirit.
—PSALM 34:18

Albrecht Dürer painted himself as Christ. In the sixteenth century it was common for artists to place themselves and their patrons in religious pieces. They were as ubiquitous as faces on billboards today, or authors and singers posing on the covers of modern books and music. A different time, to be sure, but before we scoff, we may pause to look closer at Albrecht's face. There seems to be more than vanity at work.

Albrecht came from a large and prosperous family. The second son of eighteen children, Albrecht began studying art early, as did his brother Hans. Albrecht was prone to exaggerating the harsh conditions of his parent's lives, either out of devotion or simply as part of the classical "modesty topos" of the age, when it was deemed prudent to underestimate one's net worth. The record paints a slightly different picture. His father, Albrecht the Elder, was a favorite of the emperor, who called him "my goldsmith." The family could easily afford the two artists' educations. Still, there is no doubt that Albrecht's father "endured much grief": fifteen of his eighteen children died before him.

Young Albrecht was named after his father, a singular honor and responsibility in Germany at the time. Although Albrecht was sympathetic to Martin Luther's views, he remained Catholic like the rest of the Dürer family. Albrecht the Elder died in 1502. His memorial day would naturally hold emotional and religious significance to the family. Studies show that such anniversaries have a very real physical effect on the bereaved even years after the death—whether they are acknowledged or not.

In 1508, Albrecht was commissioned to paint the altarpiece of the Dominican Church of Saint Thomas in Frankfort, *The Assumption and Coronation of the Virgin.* It took the artist thirteen months to complete. *Praying Hands* was one of a plethora of Albrecht's customarily detailed preliminary studies. More accurately entitled *Hands of an Apostle*, it was drawn in gray and white brush on blue-grounded paper. The veined, gnarled hands are Albrecht's own, posed in a Gothic arch. They are the tapered fingers of an artist, yet we sense a weariness in the sketch that has resonated with believers for centuries.

In 1521 Albrecht contracted malaria. By this time, Albrecht had lost his father (1502), his mother (1514), and fifteen of his seventeen siblings. He suffered from continuous bouts of fever, chills, and sweats throughout the following year and sporadically for the rest of his life. He was likely recovering from such an attack when he drew himself as *The Man of Sorrows* in 1522—the twentieth anniversary of his father's death. In the painting, Jesus is surrounded by the instruments of the Passion. Consider Albrecht's pose, his taut frame weakened by illness, his eyes wild and haunted by an old grief. What seemed an artistic conceit may offer some clue to a profound truth: God is with us in our deepest despair.

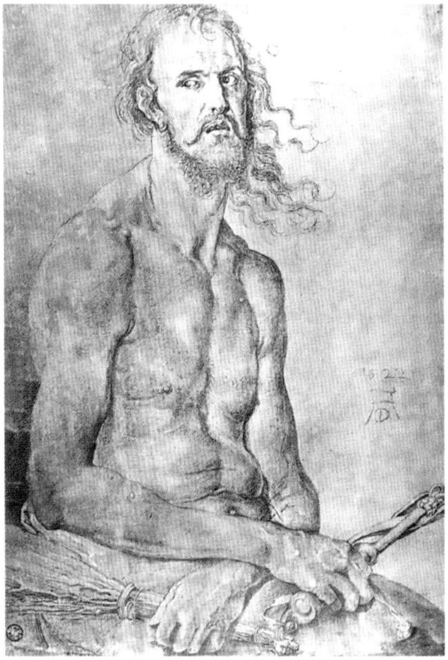

Dürer, *Man of Sorrows*, 1522, Kunsthalle, Bremen

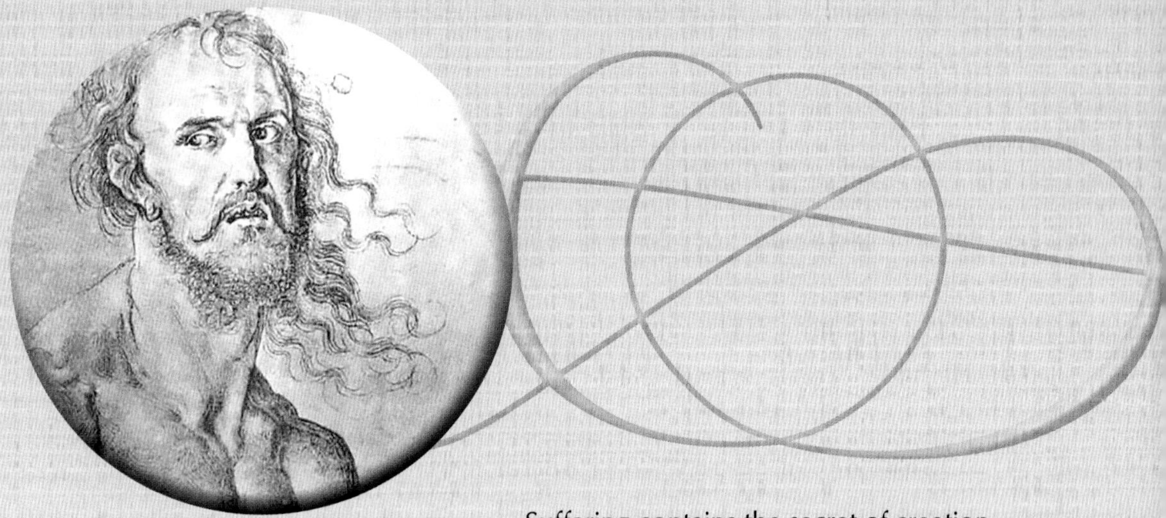

Suffering contains the secret of creation and its dimension of eternity; it can be pierced only from the inside. Suffering betters some people and transfigures others. At the end of suffering, of mystery, God awaits us.

—ELIE WIESEL,
The Gates of the Forest

In the midst of life we are in death:
to whom may we turn but you, Lord?
—GREGORIAN CHANT

Shut out suffering, and you see only one side of this strange and fearful thing, the life of man. Christ saw both sides. He could be glad, he could rejoice with them that rejoice; and yet the settled tone of his disposition was a peculiar and subdued sadness. That gave the calm depth to the character of Christ; he had got the true view of life by acquainting himself with grief.

—FREDERICK ROBERTSON,
"Typified by the Man of Sorrows, the Human Race"

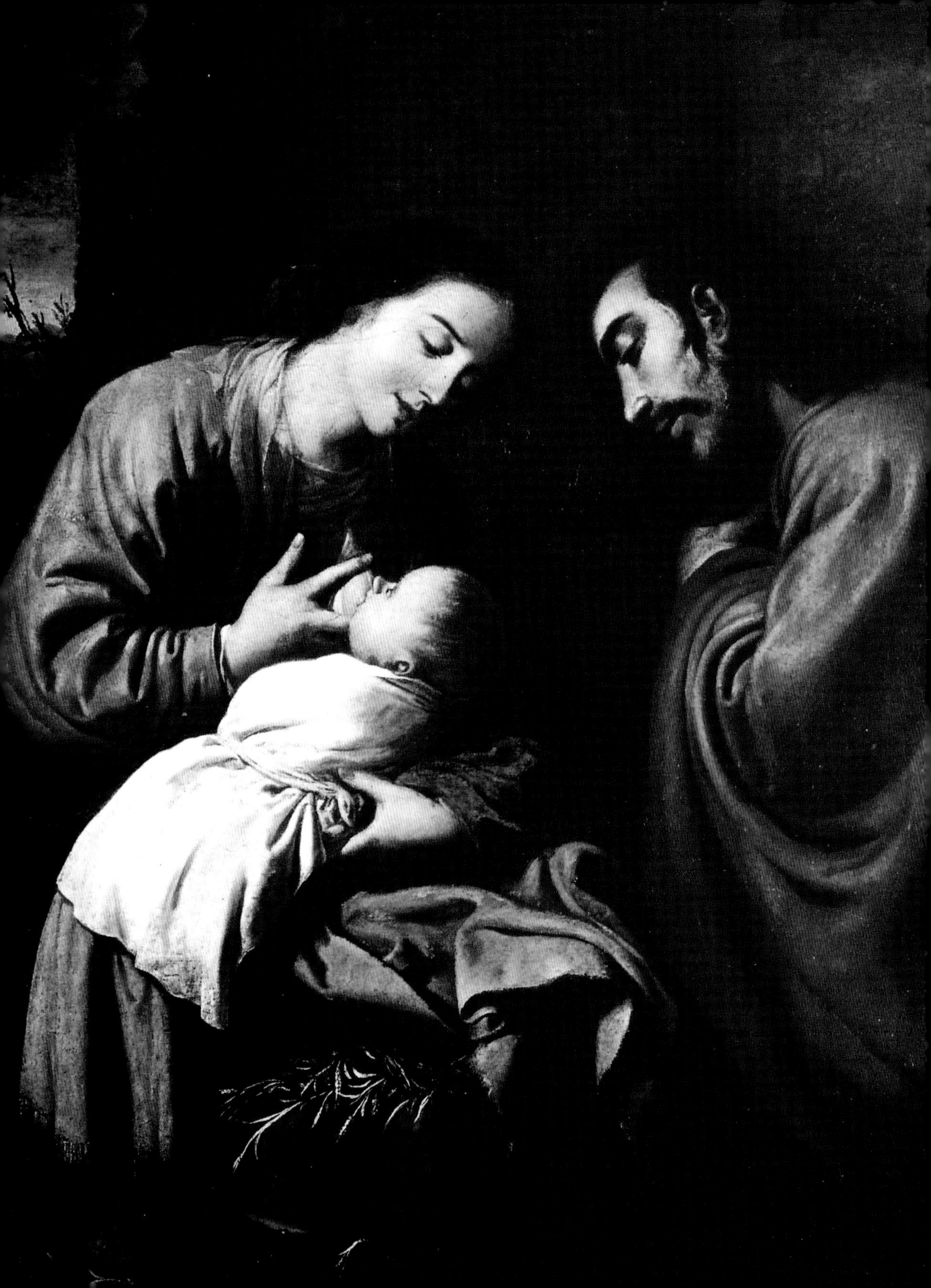

The face of compassion

FRANCISCO DE ZURBARÁN

(1598–1664), a Spanish painter

> *They urged him strongly, "Stay with us, for it is nearly evening; the day is almost over."*
> —LUKE 24:29

FRANCISCO DE ZURBARÁN is justifiably famous for his commissioned work. Over the years he was hired to paint scenes from the life of Christ, sprawling life-size portraits of Jacob and his twelve sons and dozens of famous saints. He did not hold back; many are true masterpieces. He compensated for his inability to capture depth by focusing on the foreground elements and his remarkable gift for flowing robes and curtains. Yet despite the fine attributes of his commercial pieces, it is in his personal work that we catch glimpses of Francisco's true artistry.

Francisco was widowed twice. His first wife, Maria, was twenty-eight when they married. Francisco was nineteen. Maria died within seven years, in 1624. They had three children. He remarried the next year. His second wife, Beatriz, died fourteen years later, in 1639.

That same year he began *Christ and the Virgin in the House at Nazareth*, which was finished in 1640. Tales of the childhood of Jesus were popular at the time and usually found a willing audience. Francisco may have begun the work with that in mind. It has many of the hallmarks of his commercially successful pieces: tight, aggressive brushstrokes and sharp, startling contrasts. But there are differences, hints at his sorrow and the artist he would become.

Unlike his other work, in *House at Nazareth* Francisco did not use a biblical tale or even one of the legends surrounding the Holy Family. Instead he invented a domestic scene. Young Jesus pricks himself while fashioning a crown of thorns. Mary is weeping. This is the first real example of what would come to characterize Francisco's later paintings: a looser, softer style of quiet intimacy.

◂ Zurbarán, *The Holy Family*, 1659, Museum of Fine Arts, Budapest

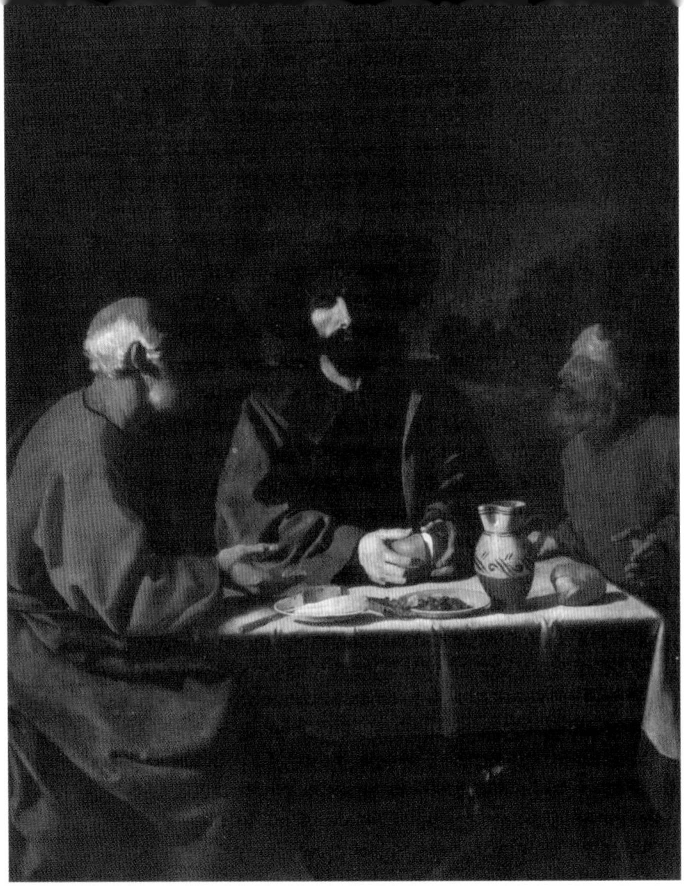

Zurbarán, *Supper at Emmaus*, 1660, Museo Nacional de San Carlos, Mexico City

Francisco married for a third and last time in 1644. His commissioned pieces grew less strident over time. His personal work reflected an atmosphere of calm and resignation. His *The Holy Family* from 1659 is a study in love, the parents for each other and both for their child. This attention to kindness is characteristic of those who have grieved for many years. Studies show there is often a sense of transcendence or transfiguration in the hearts of the bereaved: in their search for meaning they turn outward, commiserating with the suffering of others.

A year later Francisco finished *Supper at Emmaus*. The scene itself is well known. We note Francisco's careful attention to the foreground. It is the guest that surprises us: his patience with the two men, the genuine care he gives the simple act of breaking bread. This is the face of compassion, truly "God with us," from the hand of an artist who knew its value.

Let us think too of the two disciples on the way to Emmaus: their sad faces, their barren journey, their despair. But Jesus does not abandon them: he walks beside them, and not only that! Patiently he explains the Scriptures, which spoke of him, and he stays to share a meal with them. This is God's way of doing things.

—POPE FRANCIS

The two disciples whom Jesus joined on the road to Emmaus recognized him in the breaking of the bread. It is the most human as well as the most divine gesture.

—HENRI NOUWEN

Jesus answered with these words, saying: *"All shall be well, and all shall be well, and all manner of thing shall be well."* This was said so tenderly, without blame of any kind toward me or anybody else.

—JULIAN OF NORWICH

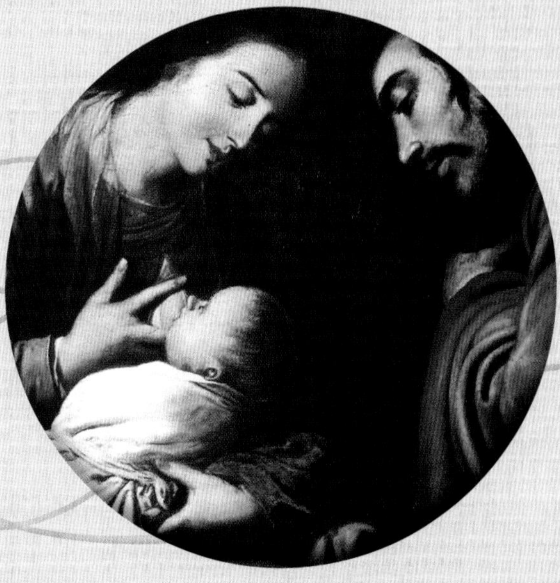

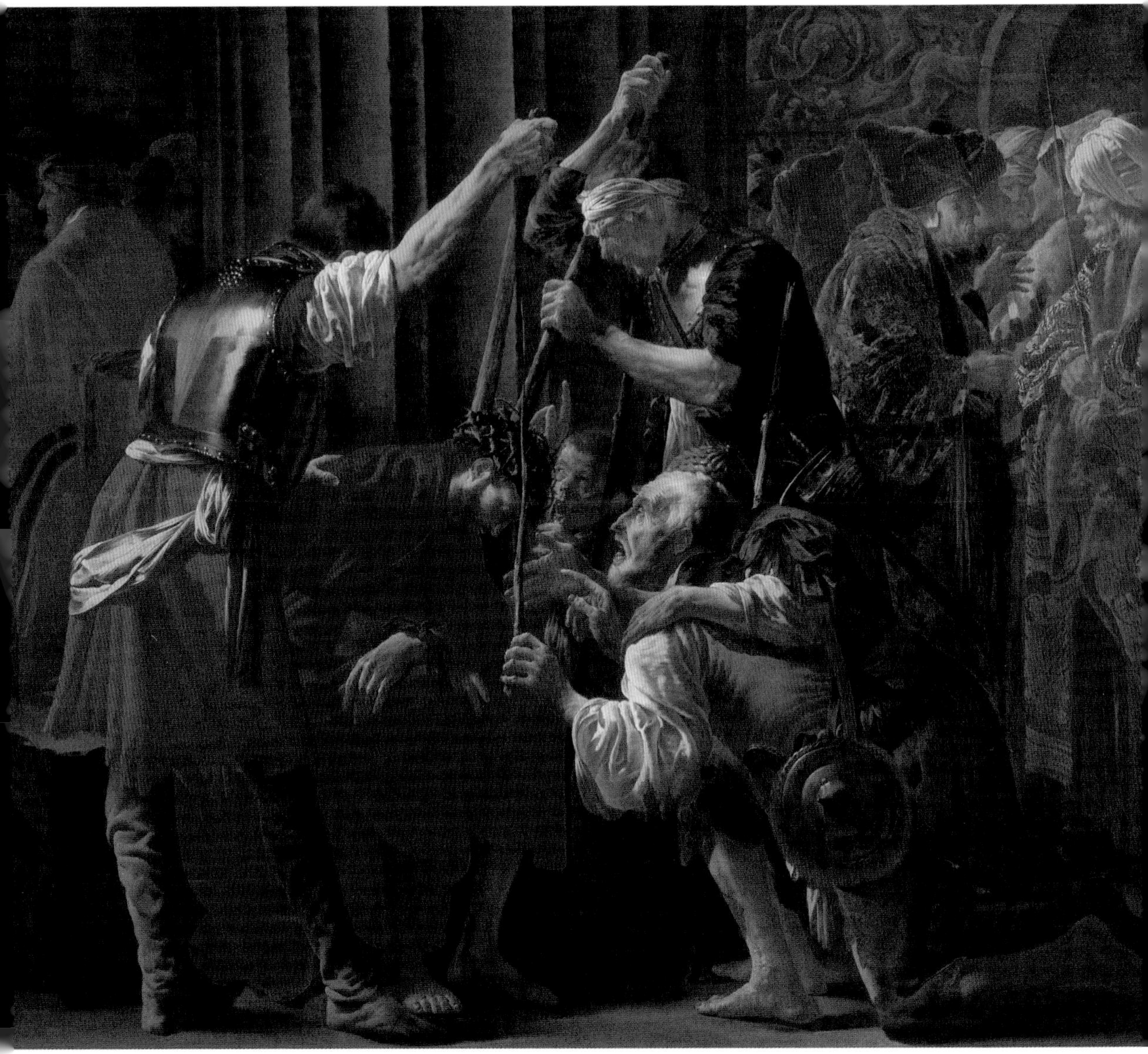

Brugghen, *Christ Crowned with Thorns*, 1620, National Gallery of Denmark, Copenhagen

Repentance has no age limit

HENDRICK JANSZ TER BRUGGHEN

(c. 1588–1629), a Dutch painter

> *I live in the high and holy place but also with the broken and humble, in order to revive the spirit of the humble and revive the hearts of the broken ones.*
> —ISAIAH 57:15B (CJB)

MUCH IS MADE OF HENDRICK TER BRUGGHEN and Michelangelo Merisi da Caravaggio. Did they know each other? historians ask. Might they have met? Art experts grant Hendrick the dubious distinction of being the leading Dutch Caravaggist. But in rushing to classify and label the Dutch artist's work, we may miss his own unique style and a more poignant influence.

Hendrick was an illegitimate grandson. His father, the first bailiff of the States of Holland, was the bastard child of a Catholic priest. Such a situation was uncommon but not unheard of in those days. Hendrick's brother and sister both became Protestants. Hendrick was married in 1616 in a Dutch Reformed Church; four of his eight children were baptized in Reformed churches. We know little of Hendrick's feelings about his paternal grandfather. It does not strain credulity to imagine a number of conflicting emotions for a man he may have wanted to love—as any grandson might—but could not openly acknowledge. We have hints, however. The artist remained Catholic till his death. Many of his religious paintings feature one elderly man, oddly out of place and partially obscured from view.

The Adoration of the Magi, painted in 1619, has the Holy Family surrounded by visitors. The one man allowed to approach the child is elderly. Traditionally this was Caspar, thought of as somewhere around sixty, the senior member of the party and the first to kneel. By the seventeenth century it was something of a trope that he had a white beard; this in itself is not remarkable. Caspar's decrepit posture and appearance, however, makes him seem a bit too old for the arduous

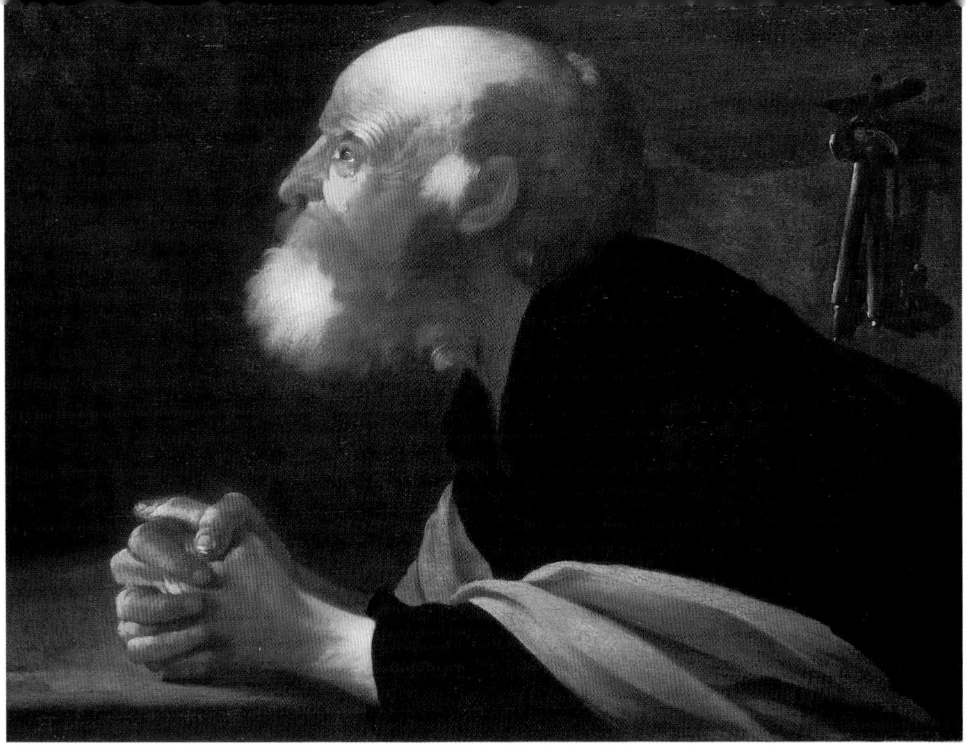

Brugghen, *The Repentant Peter*, 1616, Centraal Museum, Utrecht

journey associated with the wise men. The old magi is more realistic than many representations but not entirely likable. The next year, 1620, Hendrick used similar framing in *Christ Crowned with Thorns*. This time an elderly man is not worshiping the infant; he is taunting Jesus. In both paintings their behavior seems uncharacteristic with their age and station. It is a question of artistic choice. Why men of such age when most artists skewed slightly younger or at least more robust?

The Repentant Peter, painted in 1616, may provide a clue. We see Peter in profile with the symbolic overlapping keys physically present on the wall. Representations of Peter as an elderly man were quite common. Hendrick's choice is not surprising. But the paradox catches our attention: tears pour from eyes of stern resolve. It is a work of beauty that, like Peter and some grandfathers, requires patience to appreciate.

You can kiss your family and friends good-bye and put miles between you, but at the same time you carry them with you in your heart, your mind, your stomach, because you do not just live in a world but a world lives in you. You are a world.

—FREDERICK BUECHNER

We would be quite surprised if we knew what the soul sometimes says to God.

—BROTHER LAWRENCE

God is nearer to us than our own soul.

—JULIAN OF NORWICH

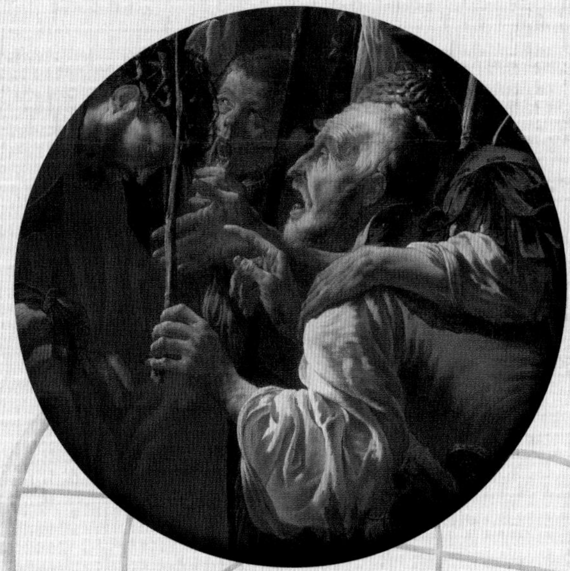

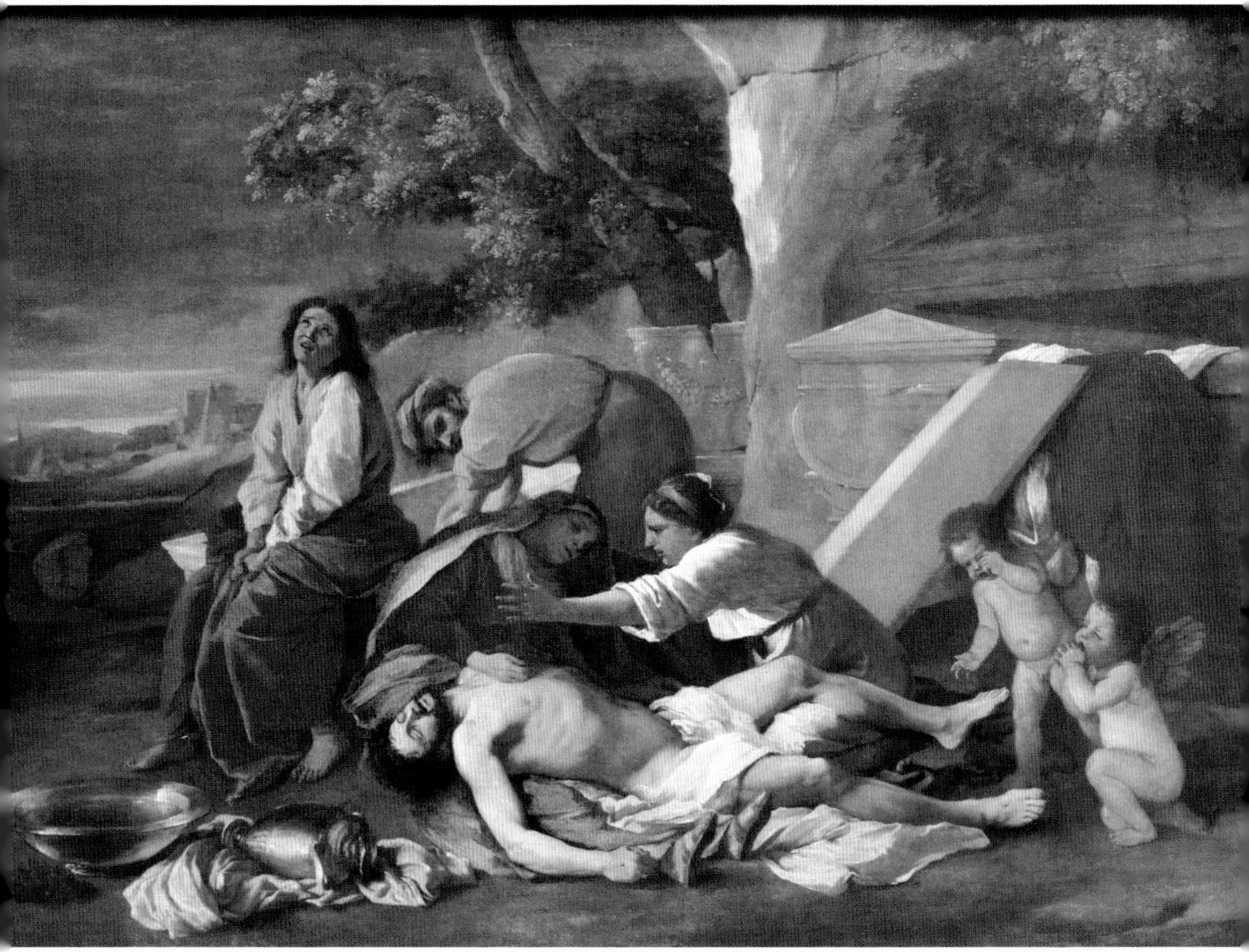

Poussin, *Lamentation of Christ*, 1628–1629, Alte Pinakothek, Munich

A quiet man

NICOLAS POUSSIN

(1594–1665), a French painter

I have been an alien residing in a foreign land.
—EXODUS 2:22B (NRSV)

NICOLAS POUSSIN was the stereotypical distracted artist. Meticulous and thorough, he created paintings displaying concentration and exhaustive attention to detail. As often happens with people who excel in one area, other aspects of his life suffered. He was constantly one step ahead of his creditors. This led to serious difficulties in France, where debtor's prison was still law. Nicolas moved again and again between Paris and Rome. He ultimately settled in Italy, a more congenial country for debtors, particularly when one has powerful and wealthy patrons.

Nicolas was terrible with money. This forced him to accept commissions at the greatest possible profit. Most of his paintings show the trends of the age. He was skilled with *affetti*, facial expressions, a popular way to illustrate many points of view—and points in time—in a single painting. His paintings were produced on commission and, as suited his personality, Nicolas delivered precisely what was required with very little artistic intervention. This is not a criticism, merely an observation. After all, creating masterpieces to order is no small thing.

Still, there are moments when Nicolas let his personality intrude. *Spring, or the Garden of Eden*, one of four seasonal pieces, describes the moment when God leaves Adam and Eve to their own devices. The retreating back of God may offer a subtle but important clue to how Nicolas saw the world.

The feeling of being an onlooker, even unwelcome, is not uncommon with creative artists, particularly those perceived as shy or reserved. There is little question Nicolas was just such a man. He married at thirty-six, somewhat late in life for his time, had no children, and seemed unable to do much of anything other than paint—and that with astonishing focus.

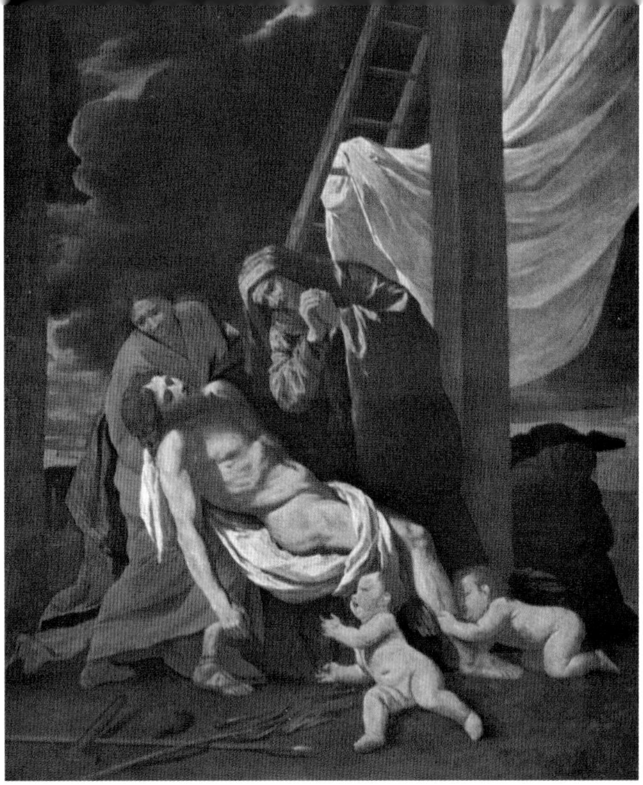

Poussin, *Descent from the Cross*, c. 1630, Hermitage Museum, Saint Petersburg

Nicolas may have known how intense concentration could lead to distraction. *Lamentation of Christ* is a tragic example of this motif. Jesus is dead. The angels weep; the women are keening. The only person not openly grieving is the man, the onlooker, distant yet not unaffected.

This is not to say Nicolas was without passion. Introverts can be highly sensitive. Acutely aware of others, they cannot help feeling, often too much, and so they turn inward out of self-preservation. Inside Nicolas burned the heart of an artist.

Descent from the Cross eschews the panoramic for an immediacy that leaves us heartbroken. There is no male onlooker, unaware of the proceedings. We see the women, the body of Jesus, and very little else. The weeping angels and perfect subtlety of the background emphasize this terrible moment.

These are the artist's most involving works. His delightful *affetti* are fun to locate and decode, but those vast story-paintings seem distant somehow. In *Descent* we see the hand of the master. He is still an onlooker, yes, but not distant and distracted *inside* the painting. He observes from the other side of his brush, so closely we can feel every tear.

Bear in mind that appearance is not reality. So the next time you see a person with a composed face and a soft voice, remember that inside her mind she might be solving an equation, composing a sonnet, designing a hat. She might, that is, be deploying the powers of quiet. Introverts are offered keys to private gardens full of riches.

—SUSAN CAIN

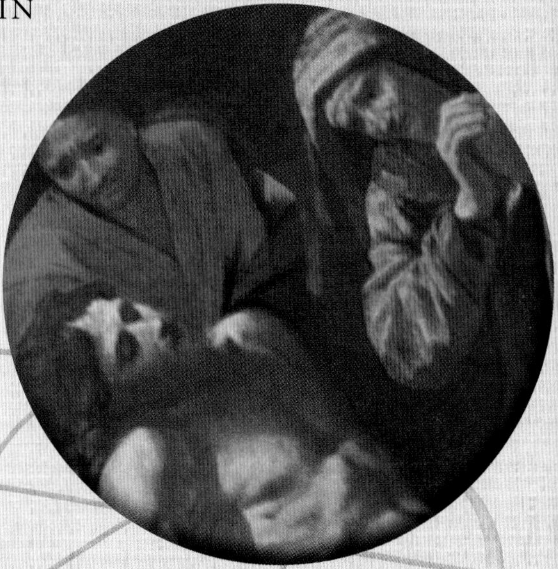

All of us are called to meditate deeply on our own true selves, to embrace the reality of our vocations, and to let God transform our true selves into sources of new life for others.

—JAMES MARTIN, SJ

God still speaks today as he spoke to our forefathers in days gone by. What is the secret of how to find this treasure? There is none. It is available to us always, everywhere. It is God who must decide what we shall do and when, and not ourselves. When we walk with God, his will directs us and must replace every other guidance.

—JEAN-PIERRE DE CAUSSADE

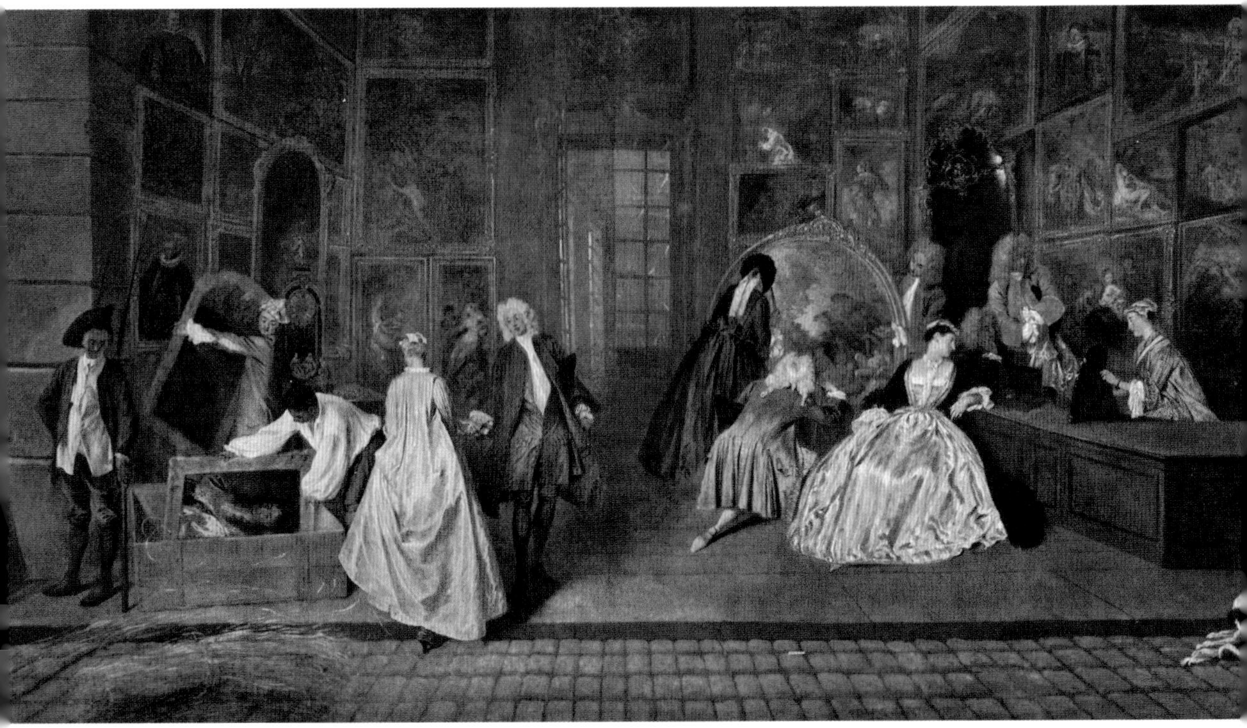

Watteau, *The Shop Sign of Gersaint*, 1720, Charlottenburg Palace, Berlin

A dying artist gives life

JEAN-ANTOINE WATTEAU

(1684–1721), a French painter

Turn to me and be gracious to me,
for I am lonely and afflicted.
—PSALM 25:16

ANTOINE WATTEAU never felt at home. He observed life from the same shadows that added melancholy to his paintings. Despite being born in Valenciennes six years after it became part of France, Antoine was always called a Flemish artist. This twist of thoughtless labeling may have been an irritant; his tuberculosis, on the other hand, weakened him to the point that all life seemed vexing, distant, and precious.

Antoine's paintings are enchanting: garden parties, social events, love among the young and foolish. His famous *Pilgrimage to Cythera* is a masterpiece of color and staging. The capering Cupids and playful couples seem more frivolous than fulfilled, illustrating just how shallow the delightful comedies of life can be. Much of Antoine's work has this hidden spiritual quality. The wasting effects of his disease were a constant companion; we see it in each painting, irrespective of their celebratory subjects.

Antoine grew up in poverty. At age twenty-five he received a commission to return to Valenciennes to paint scenes of the Duke of Marlborough's campaigns. Here we see what is otherwise subtle in the artist's more festive works. Antoine had an acute eye for everyday life. He painted few battles, choosing instead to describe camp existence, with its boredom and small joys. *The Bivouac* reflects Antoine's compassion for those who suffer in squalor. The glory of war is stripped away.

One overtly religious work, *The Holy Family*, shows Mary, Joseph, and Jesus resting on the flight to Egypt. Its themes are common enough and show the influence of Peter Paul Rubens: angels, a loving mother, and a squirming toddler.

Antoine was a master of depth, yet Joseph is in shadow, oddly shrunken, not quite in proper perspective, an observer more than a participant. This scene of repose on an arduous journey has an undertone of foreboding and sorrow.

In 1719, Antoine sought the help of Richard Mead, a famous London physician. Any benefits of Mead's remedies were offset by the English weather. The artist got worse, but that did not still his restless nature. Antoine returned to France in the winter of 1720. He asked shop owner Edme François Gersaint if he might paint a sign for his store. The cold was affecting him, Antoine said. He worked for eight mornings in a row "to limber up his fingers," according to Gersaint.

The Shop Sign of Gersaint was Antoine's final masterpiece. He saw it as his one genuinely acceptable work. It invites us into genteel society while hinting at the disturbing natures of its subjects. Just left of center, a young woman enters the shop, eyeing a portrait of the late Louis XIV while her companion assists her. Directly behind them are works of seduction and motherhood, clues to the couple's true motivations. Right of center, an older pair is studying a scene of hedonism. Behind their helpful clerk is a portrait of the licentious Pan. The red of the clerk's hand and cheeks matches Pan exactly. But here the scene shifts. The painting above them is of a man in white kneeling at prayer. This juxtaposition of outer and inner realities is repeated to the far right.

A young sales girl is assisting three customers. The polite men's faces have a reddish tone that is repeated in scenes of excess and sensuality above them. Observe the bored, unladylike posture of their female friend. In contrast, the sales girl sits beneath the Holy Family. She is separate, contained, encircled by the same shades of light as those which bathe Mary and the infant Jesus.

To the far left we see yet again an onlooker, lending genuine pathos to a scene that is at once beautiful, ennobling, and pathetic. The artist's scenes of pleasure often held deeper meaning: dark and tawdry or shining with inner purity, artifice cannot hide the reality behind our facades.

Watteau, *The Shop Sign of Gersaint* (detail) ▶

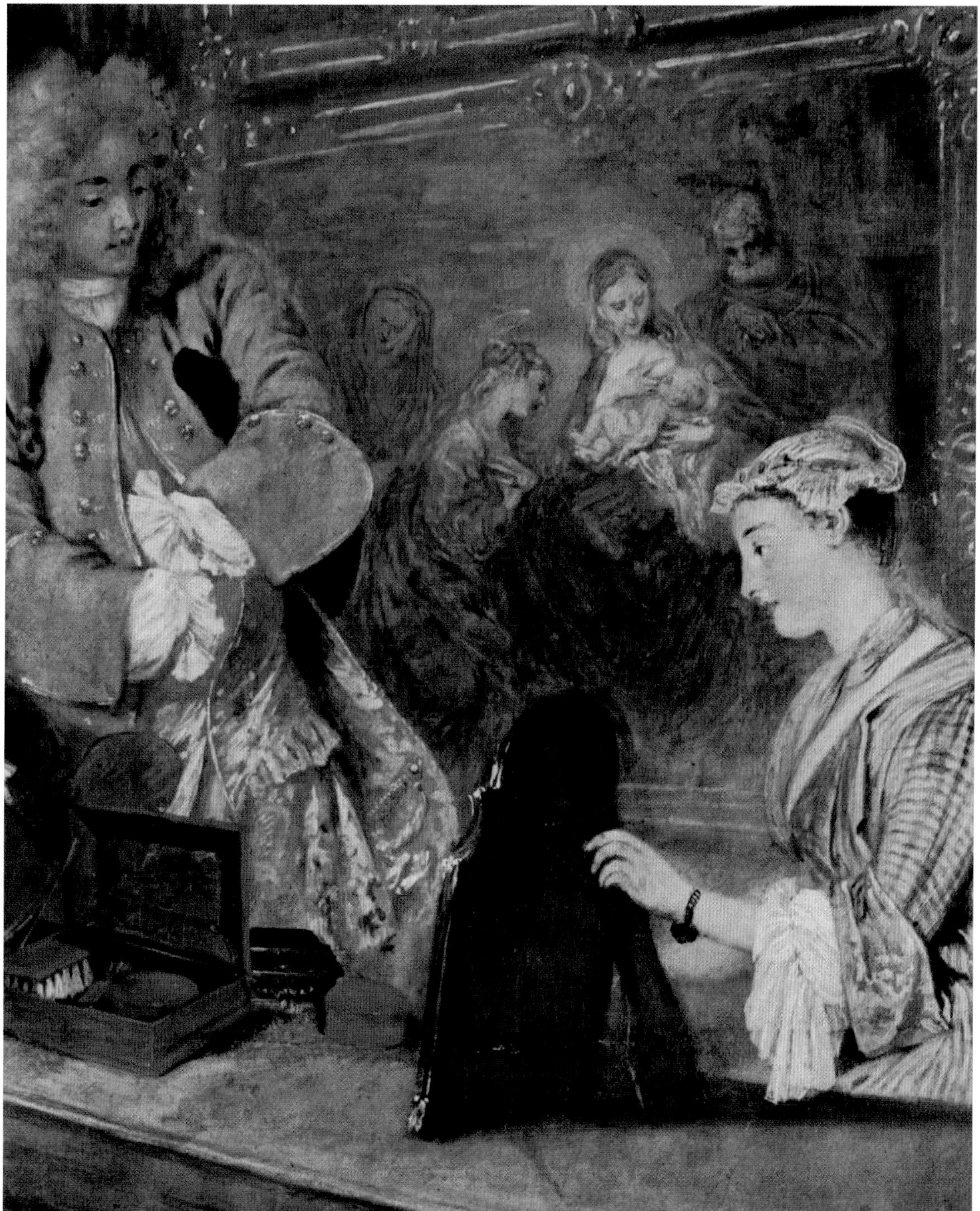

Antoine captured the whole of life on canvas but seems to have lacked the health or temperament to enjoy it himself. In his final days he could not speak. He lay in bed, delirious, creating paintings in the air with an imaginary brush. Antoine was thirty-six when tuberculosis took his life.

A priest from the Nogent-sur-Marne commune attended the artist at his bedside. "Take away that crucifix," Antoine said, refusing to kiss it, "it makes me feel sorry." The priest took this to be a dismissal of its crude carving, but to the end Antoine had a penchant for double meanings, verbal or artistic. "Is it possible that my Master should have been so badly treated?"

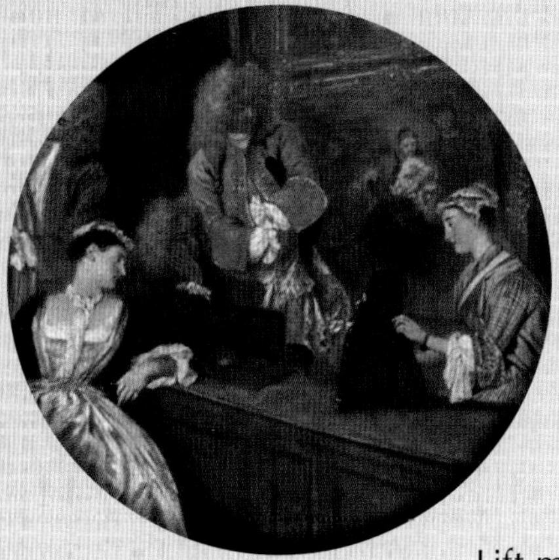

To talk of accepting death when its approach is inevitable is not mere resignation or submission. Accepting death's coming is the very opposite of doing nothing.

—CICELY SAUNDERS

Lift me above
this dull cloud cover,
up to where it is clear,
to waxing stars,
the waning moon,
and the sun in its splendor.

For in the sun- and moonshine,
in the quiet wreath of stars
smiling upon me;
I do not hear
as they ask:
"Is the Eternal Light in our light?"

—FRIEDRICH RÜCKERT

You can *keep* forever only what you *give up*: beginning with the thing it is hardest to give up—one's self. What you grab you lose: what you offer freely and patiently to God or your neighbor, you will have.

—C. S. LEWIS

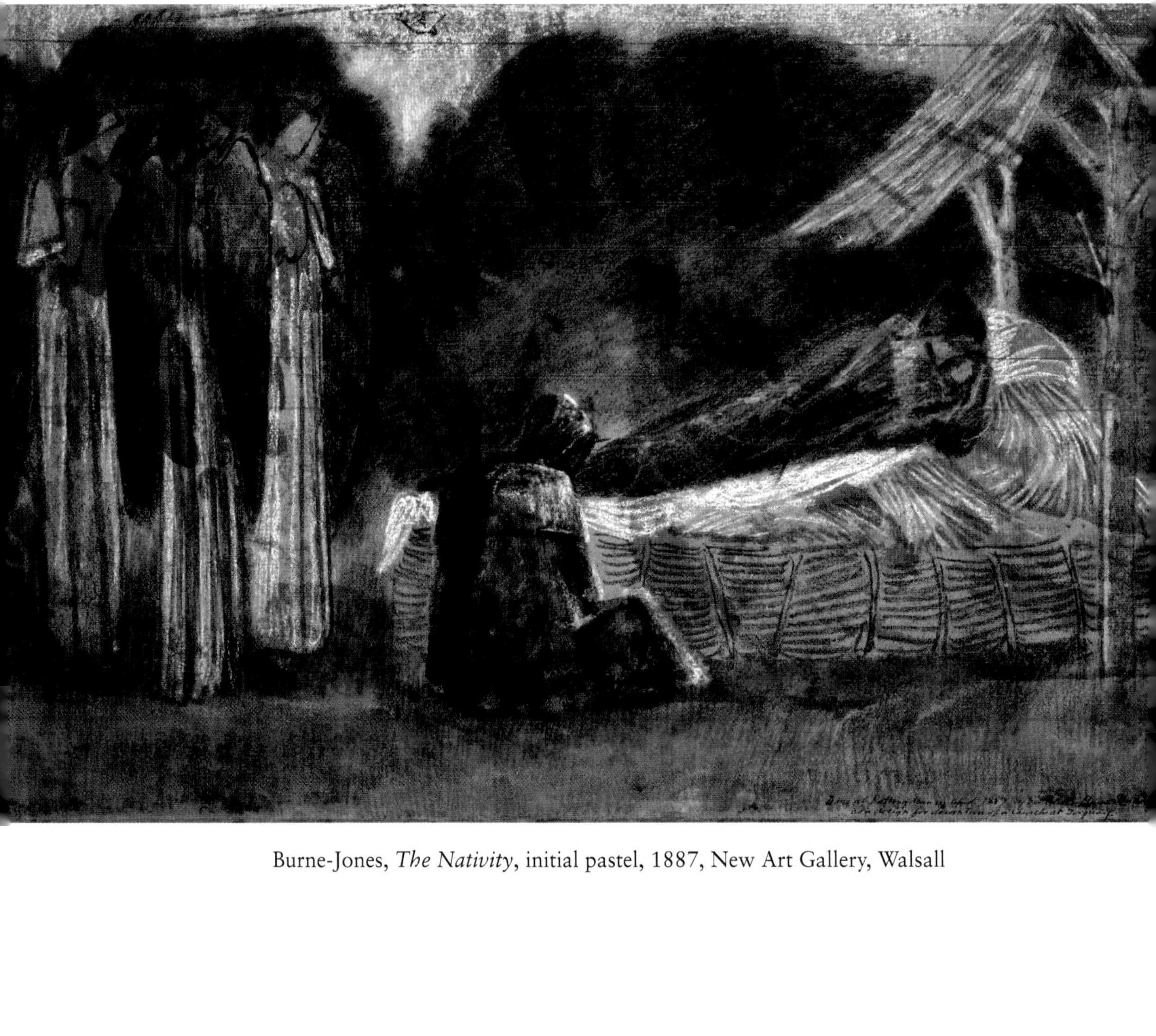

Burne-Jones, *The Nativity*, initial pastel, 1887, New Art Gallery, Walsall

A bereaved father sees hope and grief in the Nativity

EDWARD COLEY BURNE-JONES

(1833–1898), an English painter

> *The deepest thoughts of many hearts will be revealed. And a sword will pierce your very soul.*
>
> LUKE 2:35 (NLT)

EDWARD BURNE-JONES knew the joy of childbirth and its potential for lifelong grief. His mother died shortly after his birth in 1833. Edward's first child was a healthy boy. While carrying their second son in the winter of 1864, Edward's wife, Georgiana, contracted scarlet fever. The infant died within days. There is little doubt that Edward felt both losses his entire life.

In 1887 the Church of Saint John in Torquay, England, commissioned Edward to paint a nativity. It is not known if he consciously recalled the deaths of his mother and son in childbirth as he prepared the work, but it would be odd if he did not. Studies in parental bereavement indicate that the death of an infant is as profound a loss as the death of an adult child. After all, a parent's love is not measured by years spent with a child; nor is a parent's grief measured by the years without a child. Researcher Robert Weiss observed that parents "develop very strong investment in newly born children, in children still in gestation," adding that the sense of continued connection to the child never abates. Parental bonds are usually immediate, persistent, and absolute. "We know little about what triggers attachment to children," wrote Weiss. "Nor do we understand fully why parental grieving so regularly persists indefinitely."

Lewis Smedes and his wife lost their child within a day of the infant's birth, yet years later he dedicated an entire chapter of his memoir to the death. "Doris and I cried a lot," Smedes wrote, "and we knew in our tears that God was with us, paying attention to us, shedding ten thousand tears for every one of ours."

Such tears are nearly palpable in Edward's *The Nativity*, particularly in his initial pastel of 1887: a seated Joseph, Mary lying on a bed of hay caressing the child, and angels that seem to be at once sorrowing and worshipful. Edward's later sketch added the crown of thorns, a chalice, and an urn of myrrh—symbols of the Passion and Crucifixion that surely call to mind loss and pain to a grieving parent. The final painting has the same somber tone, shrouded garments and bier-like setting. It was not uncommon in nativity scenes to see a supine Mary, facing upward or to the side, but the combination of elements in Edward's work is more suggestive of a funeral than a celebration.

Edward saw in art a chance to capture something beyond the physical world, to communicate a spiritual aspect to which many of us may at times be blind. "I mean by a picture a beautiful romantic dream of something that never was, never will be—" he wrote, "in a light better than any light that ever shone—in a land no one can define or remember, only desire—and the forms divinely beautiful." His insight gives us a glimpse of something beyond the usual nativity. There is joy, yes, and glory and celebration, but it is muted by the reality of this moment when God chose to step into history. He is an infant, vulnerable, subject to death that is, alas, inevitable. Writing of his own child's death, Lewis Smedes observed: "It seems to me that the privilege of being the delicate organisms we are in the kind of world we live in comes at price. The price is that things can go wrong, badly wrong sometimes, which should come as no surprise." This was a price Edward knew all too well.

What Christ came to do was not to convince us even that God is love, but to be with us and in us as the loving God forever and ever. He came not to preach the living God but to be God our life; yes, not to preach even the loving God but to be the love that God forever is.

—P. T. FORSYTH

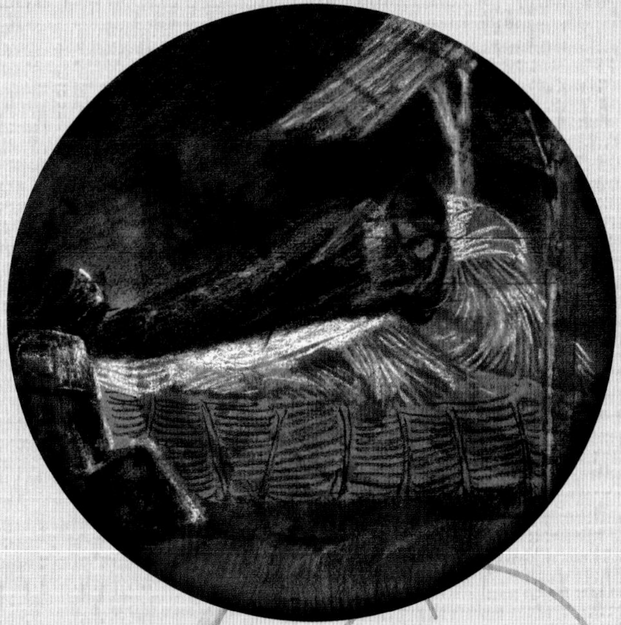

What can I give Him
Poor as I am?
If I were a shepherd
I would bring a lamb,
If I were a Wise Man
I would do my part, —
Yet what I can I give Him,
Give my heart.
—CHRISTIAN ROSSETTI

Nothing irredeemable has happened to us or can happen to us on our way to our destiny in God's full world. Irredeemable harm does not befall those who willingly live in the hand of God.
—DALLAS WILLARD

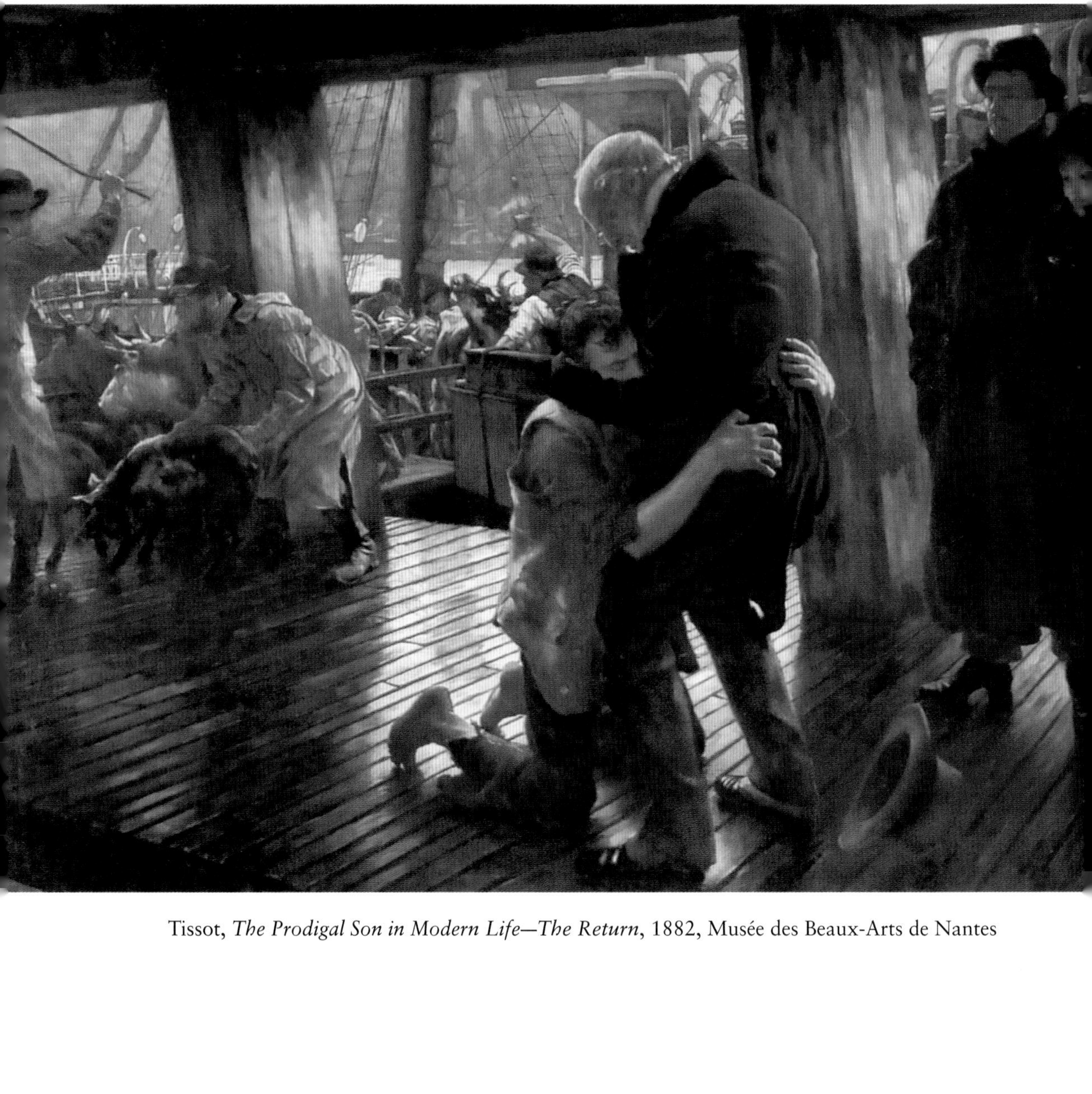

Tissot, *The Prodigal Son in Modern Life—The Return*, 1882, Musée des Beaux-Arts de Nantes

A grieving man sees Christ and returns to his faith

JACQUES JOSEPH TISSOT

(1836–1902), anglicized as James Tissot, a French painter

> *If I say, "I will not mention him, or speak any more in his name," there is in my heart as it were a burning fire shut up in my bones, and I am weary with holding it in, and I cannot.*
>
> —JEREMIAH 20:9 (ESV)

JACQUES TISSOT painted *The Prodigal Son in a Modern Setting: The Return* (1882) at an irreligious but spiritual time in his life. In the painting, the father's hat falls to the ground, reflecting the reckless joy Jacques himself felt as he sat painting on his stool at the Port of London.

The source of this "domestic bliss," as Jacques called it, was the woman in the far right of the painting: Kathleen Newton. A divorcée and single mother of two, Kathleen was something of a scandal—already a famous beauty, a social pariah who was publicly condemned by leaders of her church. This last aspect of her personality fascinated Jacques, who had turned away from his belief years before. They met in 1875. She had another child a year later, and they set up house soon thereafter. Jacques felt his dreams of family life had come true.

It was not to last. In 1882 Kathleen contracted tuberculosis; her eyes in *The Prodigal Son* already show the wasting effects of the disease. The joyous celebration of the painting carries within it a foreboding of sorrow. Kathleen died that same year. She was twenty-eight.

Jacques sat with her coffin for four days. The next morning he took the children and moved away. But his sorrow remained. Three years later, in May of 1885, Jacques believed he saw Kathleen at a séance, which he memorialized in his infamous painting, *The Apparition*. The medium was later exposed as a fraud, but Jacques maintained to his death that his experience, at least, was indeed authentic. "Peace, let it be," Kathleen said in Jacques's account. "The dead are not dead but alive."

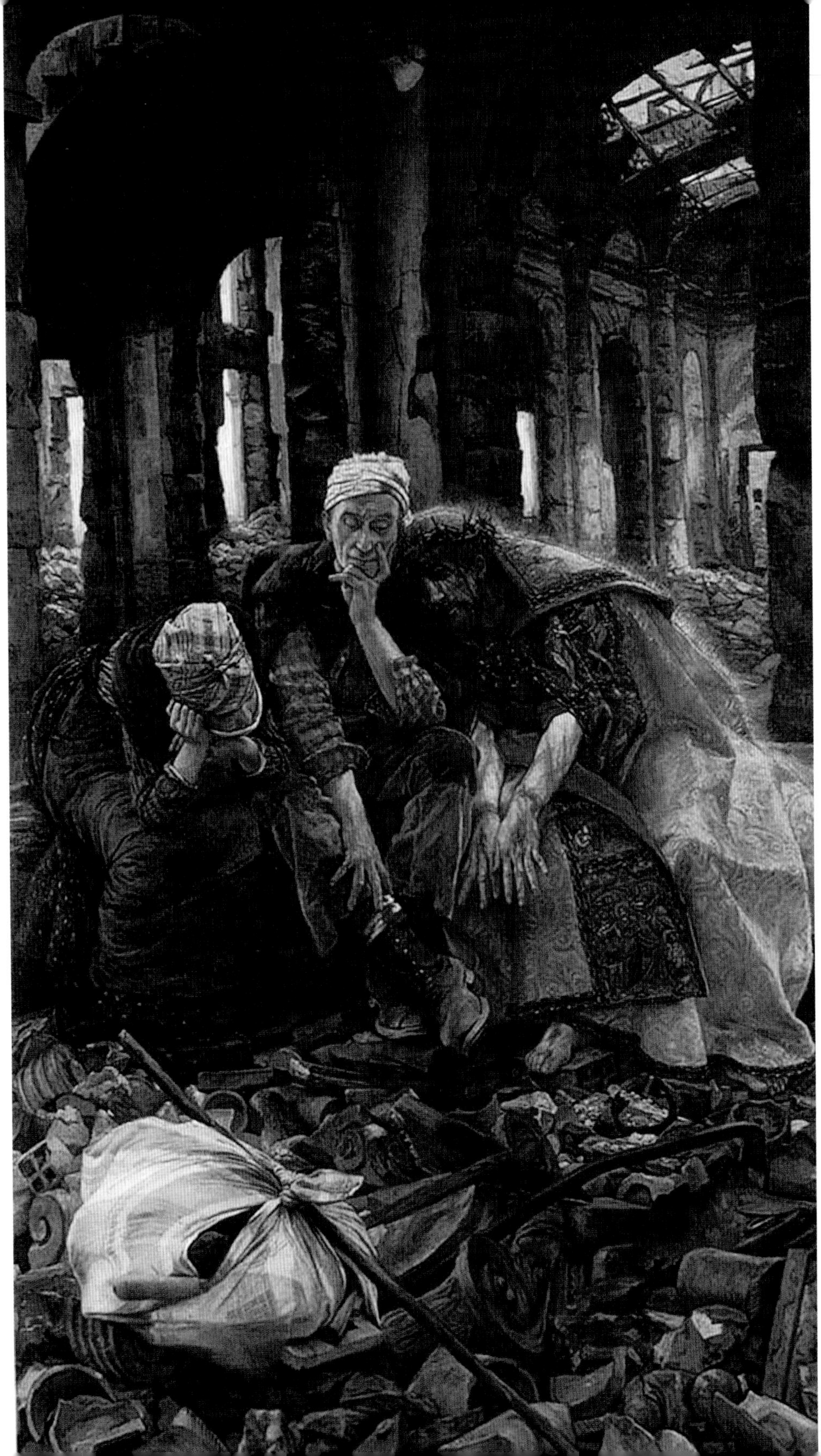

We may reasonably question Jacques' methods if not his desperation. He had turned from his religion, but something of his faith seems to have remained. The possibility of visions was commonplace among Christians in the early first century, as it was during Jacques's lifetime. Most major religions speak of a reunion with loved ones after death. Researchers have found that belief in a soul provides the bereaved with a hope that they may somehow sense the deceased.

Such experiences are not without precedent. C. S. Lewis was certain he experienced his father after his death, not as a visitation but in a real way nonetheless. The famous Bible translator J. B. Phillips swore he interacted with Lewis shortly after he died. Frederick Buechner related a dream and tangible expression of a friend who had passed a few months earlier. Norman Vincent Peale frequently told the story of how at his father's funeral, Peale saw him walking down the aisle. After his daughter died, Martin Luther knew and approved of one story about a mother's encounter with her dead son. Thousands of bereaved parents relate similar stories. Without exception, even among atheists, they insist that they know they will see their loved ones again. They relate stories of experiencing them in a fallen leaf, a bird, a presence, a knick-knack, a random word, an unexpected wind or scent.

Jacques was probably the victim of cruel chicanery, yet the experience gave him hope and renewed purpose. That same year he received a commission from the Church of Saint-Sulpice. While working on the painting, Jacques wrote later, he experienced a vision of Jesus. He saw Christ comforting two poor Parisian women who remained unaware of his presence. He set this scene to canvas in *The Ruins (Inner Voices)*.

This experience led to a return to his Catholic faith. In the years that followed, Jacques's series of Bible paintings drew worldwide acclaim that continues to this day. But somehow, after years of seeking wealth, the artist remained untouched by his fame. In sorrow and desperation, the prodigal son had truly returned home.

◀ Tissot, *The Ruins (Inner Voices)*, 1885, private collection

I feel very strongly (and I am not alone in this) that some great good comes from the dead to the living in the months or weeks after the death. I think I was much helped by my own father after his death: as if our Lord welcomed the newly dead with the gift of some power to bless those they have left behind. Certainly, they often seem just at that time, to be very near us.

—C. S. LEWIS

Is it not at least conceivable, therefore, that around us now in this mysterious universe are those we have loved and lost for a while, but that between us is a barrier through which we can see only in rare moments when for some reason the frequency in them corresponds with some higher frequency in ourselves? I think so.

—NORMAN VINCENT PEALE

With a slow and noiseless footstep
Comes the messenger divine,
Takes the vacant chair beside me,
Lays her gentle hand in mine.
Uttered not, yet comprehended,
Is the spirit's voiceless prayer.

—HENRY WADSWORTH LONGFELLOW

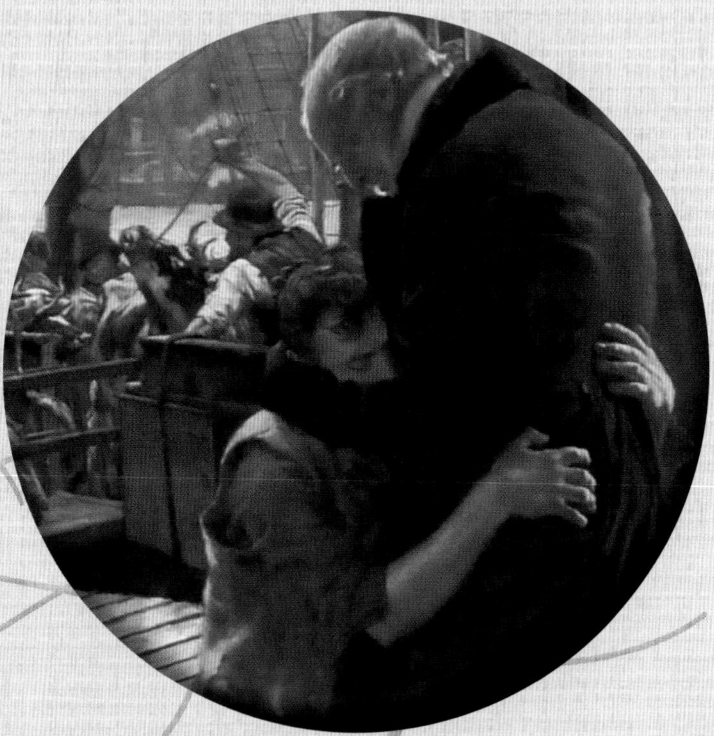

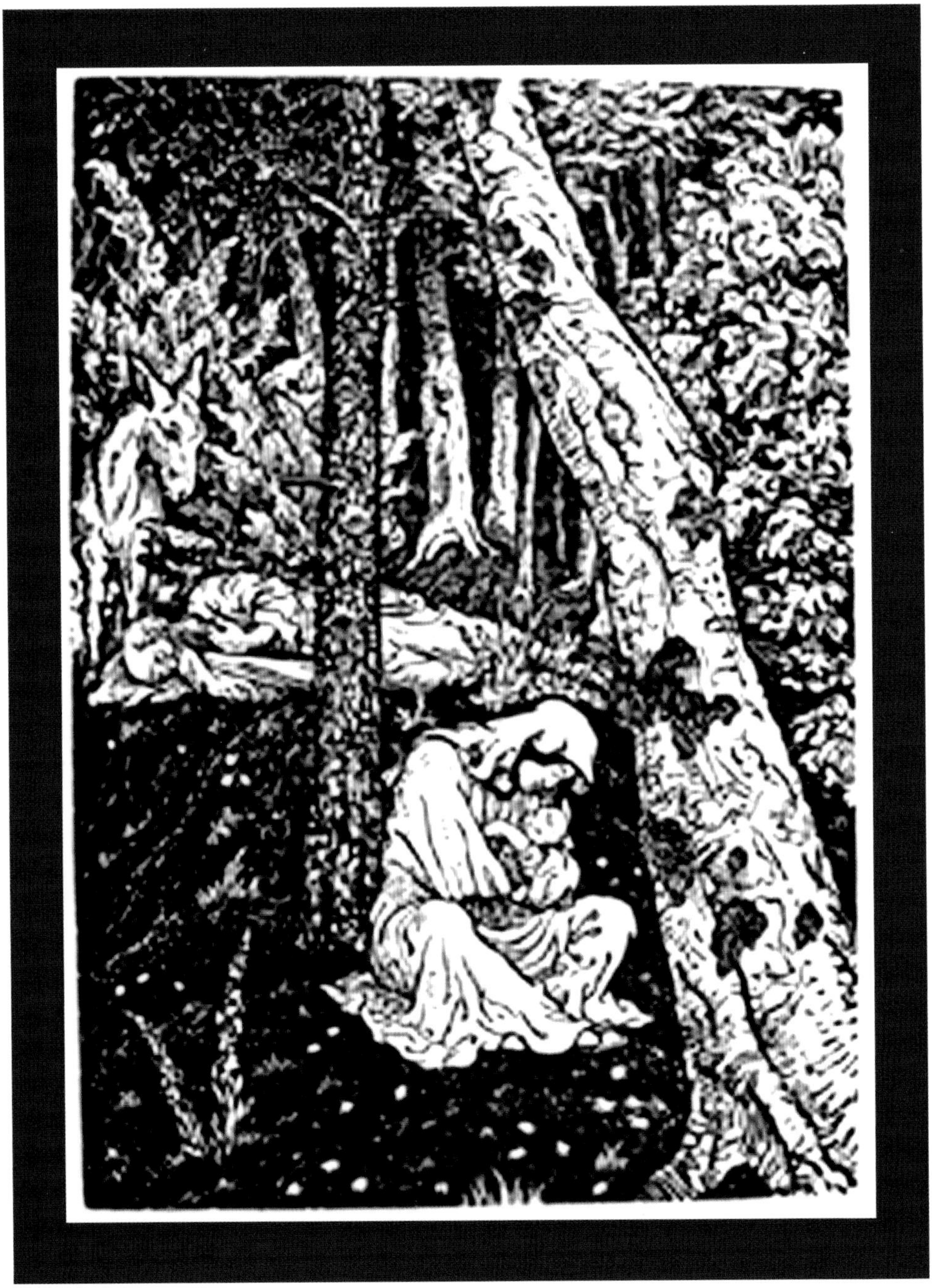

Thylmann, *Mary and Joseph in the Wilderness*, 1915–1916

The blind can see

KARL THYLMANN

(1888–1916), a German artist

Remember, Lord, your great mercy and love, for they are from of old.
—PSALM 25:6

KARL THYLMANN wanted to be a painter, but his father encouraged more practical pursuits. The boy persisted.

His childhood attempts were garish and disjointed. The tones were right, but the colors never quite worked. When Karl was fifteen he found out why. While on an outing, his friends commented on the beauty of some red poppies against the green grass. Karl saw little difference between them. He was color blind.

Karl tried to follow his father's advice and study architecture. He went to Italy in 1911. There he met his future wife, the Dutch actress Joanna Koops, known as Jo.

With Jo's help, Karl discovered his gift for woodcuts. They are at times harsh and challenging, but in them we sense the artist's spiritual pilgrimage. He had dabbled in Eastern beliefs and philosophy. Jo could be taken with charismatic leaders; Karl considerably less so. He was not fond of organizations. He felt that the spiritual and the real were not as separate as we might think—that an invisible world exists within reach. Yet his religious woodcuts reflect a surprising lack of romanticism.

Karl and Jo were married in 1914. The following year he was drafted to serve in World War I. That autumn, Karl worked obsessively on Christian woodcuts, often playing light against dark. *Mary and Joseph in the Wilderness* is a study in darkness and solitude. If the artist could not contrast colors, he most assuredly could contrast ideas.

"It is terrible; it is always the same," Karl wrote to Jo. "Nostalgia, desire, agony, something crashes down upon me, cracks and bends. It is like the pool of Bethesda, its frenzied swells and foam when an angel stirs it up." It was around this time that the artist produced his best-known woodcut. Even in its worst reproductions, *Christ Healing the Leper* stuns us with its excruciating candor. Karl continued to work on religious pieces through the summer of 1916. His infantry regiment was ordered forward on the morning of Friday, August 4. "I was wounded by the very first grenade that hit us," he wrote. While in Montmédy hospital, Karl composed this poem:

Awakening
The laughter of convalescents
rips me back into my body.
Through the frosted glass
I see the shadow of a sparrow,
leaving sharp forms,
tiny tracks, crooked black stars.
I fall back into dream,
my couch spinning,
spiraling away.
O black stars, escort me!

He died soon thereafter. He was twenty-eight. Karl had produced some seventy woodcuts in all. "On the morning of August 29, after days of visions," Jo would write later, "Karl died in humility and godliness." She was six months pregnant.

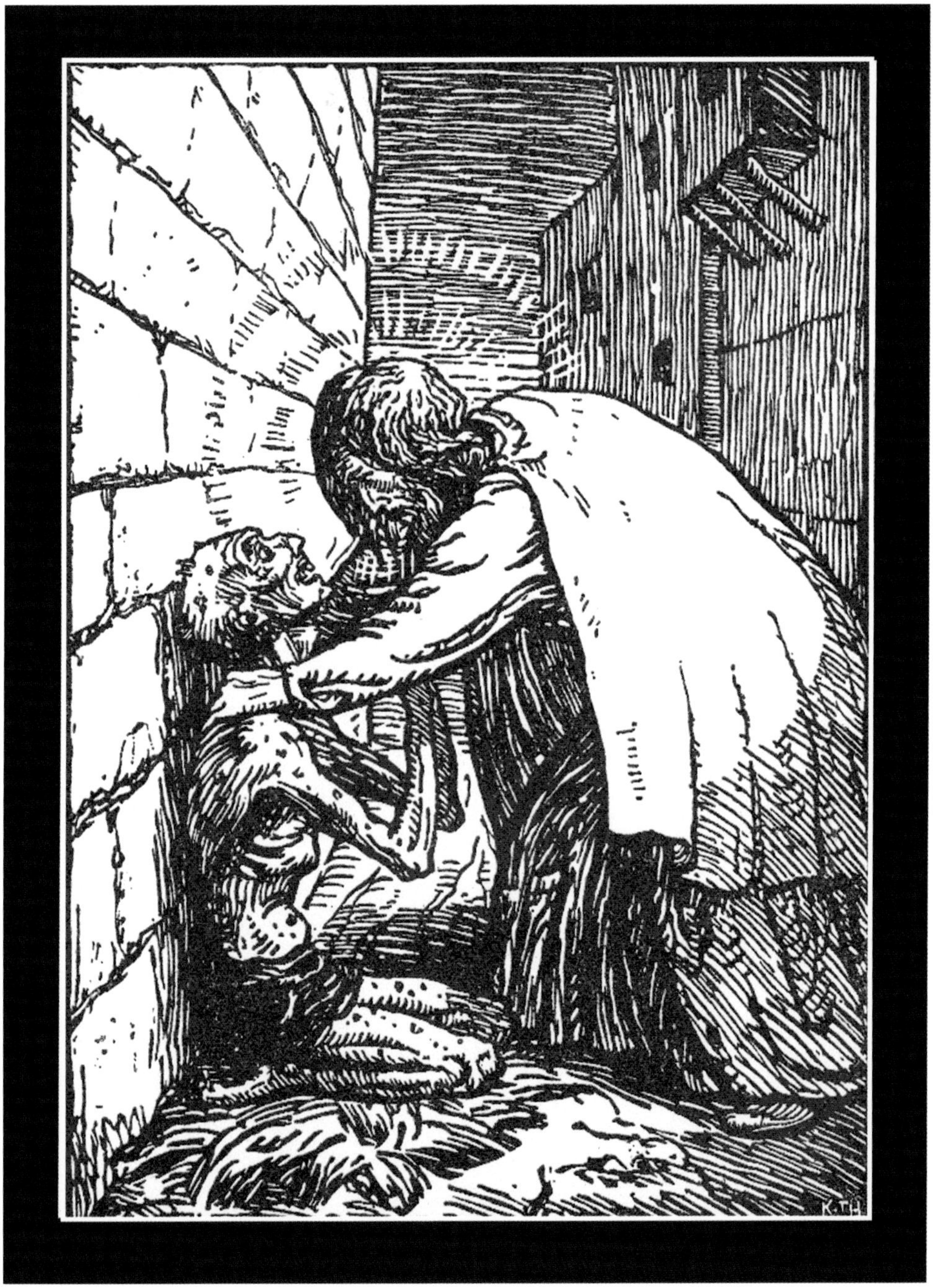

Thylmann, *Jesus Healing the Leper*, 1915–1916

This is a road I must travel bleeding.

—ISABEL ALLENDE
in 1992 as her daughter lay dying

The ache of loss sinks down and down, deep beyond all telling. How deep do souls go? My wound is an unanswered question. Life eternal doesn't depend on getting all the questions answered; God is often as much behind the questions as behind the answers. But never had the unanswered question been so painful. Can I live this question with integrity and without stumbling?

—NICHOLAS WOLTERSTORFF

I realize that suffering is a condition of life; we have come into this world to lose everything, including awareness and life itself. That's how we grow up, that's how the soul matures, and that's also how we learn happiness.

—ISABEL ALLENDE
in 2002, ten years after the death of her daughter

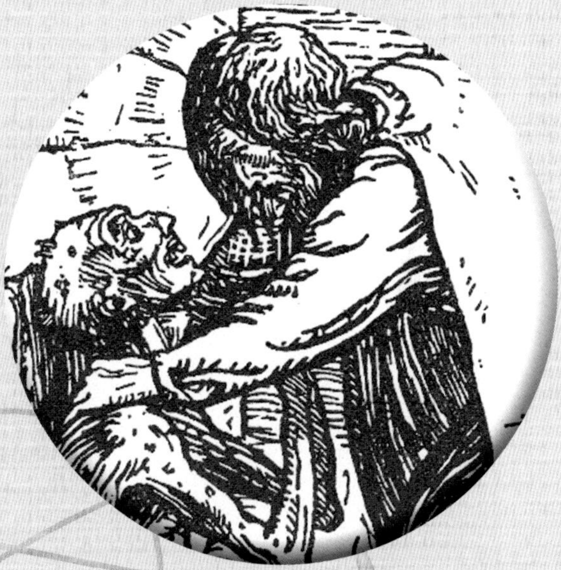

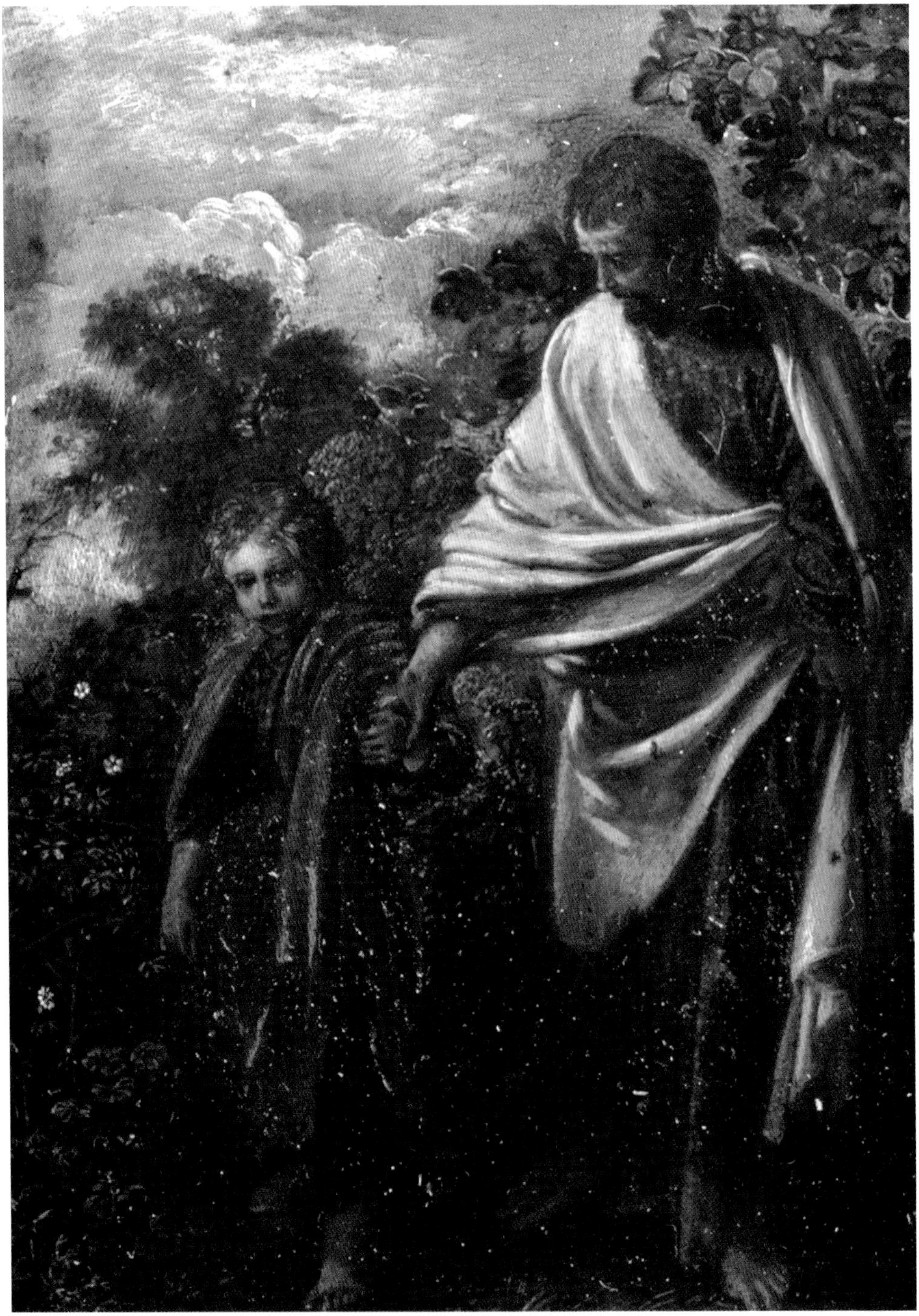

Elsheimer, *Saint Joseph and the Christ Child*, 1605, Petworth House, West Sussex

The Milky Way lights the way

ADAM ELSHEIMER

(1578–1610), a German painter

> *He alone has spread out the heavens and marches on the waves of the sea. He made all the stars—the Bear and Orion, the Pleiades and the constellations of the southern sky. He does great things too marvelous to understand.*
>
> —JOB 9:8–10A (NLT)

ADAM ELSHEIMER was a reserved, melancholic man. He left few paintings, but those we have tell of deep feelings and desperate hopes.

Much of Adam's early work has a sense of delight and anticipation. *Holy Family with Saint John the Baptist*, painted in 1599 when Adam was twenty-one, shows Joseph holding the rod associated with him in legend, from which a dove flew to indicate he was to be Mary's betrothed. It is a celebration of form and light.

Around the same time, Adam finished his first *Flight into Egypt* (1605). In some ways it is uninteresting: the background is traditional and banal, Mary is exhausted, the child playful; Joseph looks more like a hired hand than a father. Adam was one of ten children. It is not uncommon for children in a large family to see their parents in just such a light.

Shortly after finishing the piece in 1605, Adam met his future wife, Carola. During their courtship he created *Saint Joseph and the Christ Child.* Apparently, Adam's dreams of domestic life may have been quite different from what is portrayed in the 1605 *Flight into Egypt.* Adam and Carola were married in 1606. Three years later, in 1609, they had a son. The child died that same year. Shortly afterward, Adam created his final painting.

The Flight into Egypt (1609) is a small, delicate work: it is no more than a foot high and sixteen inches wide, painted with oil on copper. These "cabinet pieces," as they were called, were intended to be displayed in parlors or private rooms. They were hailed for their attention to detail. This was Adam's masterpiece.

Consider the nocturnal setting, unique among traditional paintings of a daytime flight; the dark landscape, at once threat and shelter; and the four distinct light sources: the moon, its reflection, a friendly campfire, and Joseph's torch. The artist's sky is a revelation. Rather than mere background, as in his earlier work, it is an accurate depiction of the Milky Way—the first realistic representation of a night sky in Renaissance art. We can spot Ursa Major to the left, with the bright star, Regulus or Little King, directly over the Holy Family. At the time, the Milky Way was popularly considered a symbolic Jacob's Ladder; here it is shown as a lighted path to heaven that guides Mary and Joseph as much as the shepherds' fire.

Observe Joseph's tender concern for his son. Mary's expression is a mixture of exhaustion and mourning. Even the child, looking at his earthly father, seems somehow compassionate and sorrowing. Most striking, Joseph's iconic rod is now a slender reed, held in the exact angle and position of an artist at work with his brush.

Adam died a year later, in 1610. He was thirty-two. *The Flight into Egypt* was hanging on his bedroom wall.

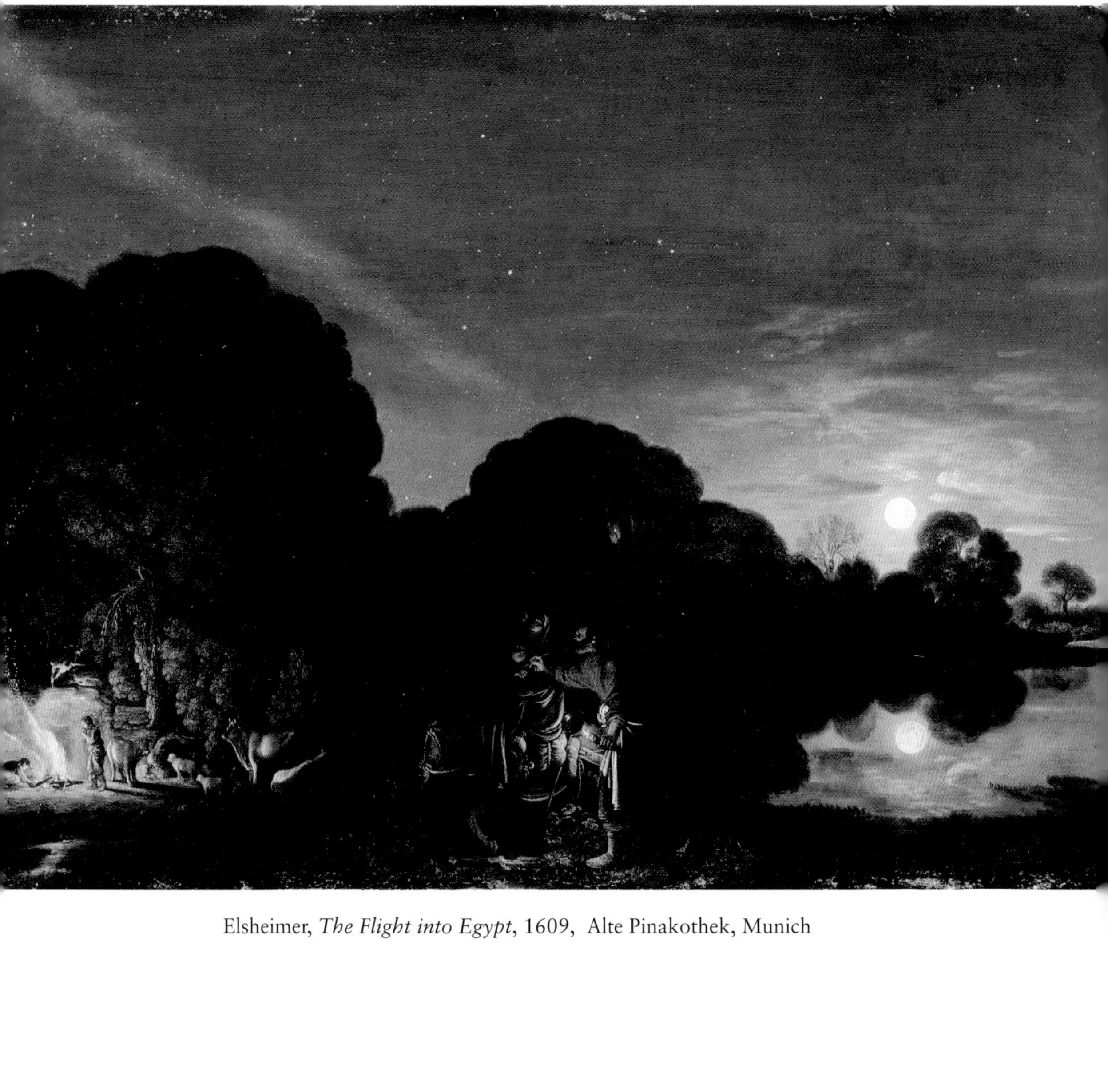

Elsheimer, *The Flight into Egypt*, 1609, Alte Pinakothek, Munich

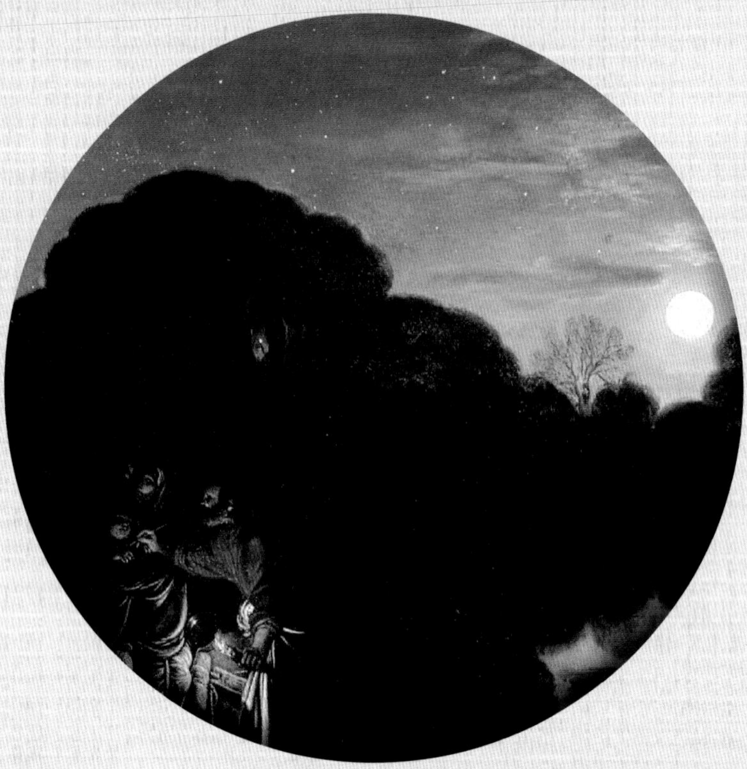

It *is* bad, it tears us apart. There are many things in life which one just has to say, "This is terrible." To give an easy answer at that point I think is just very bad news. To try to say, "Oh, well it's all right because . . ." There is no *all right because*. It's just this is part of the groaning of creation, and all we can do is groan and weep and somehow hope and pray that God the Spirit is groaning within us, and will, through that groaning, bring God's new world to birth.
—N. T. WRIGHT, on officiating at the funeral for a young couple's infant son

Nature is unsettled,
as is my heart;
outdoors, it is merely the spring,
in me, there is other harm.

Spring knows its pain,
the outdoors born anew;
but for me, o broken heart,
what was born is lost.

—FRIEDRICH RÜCKERT

A messenger comes to the mourner's house. "Come," says the messenger, "you are needed." "I cannot come," says the mourner, "my spirit is broken." "That is why you are needed," says the messenger.

—LEON WIESELTIER

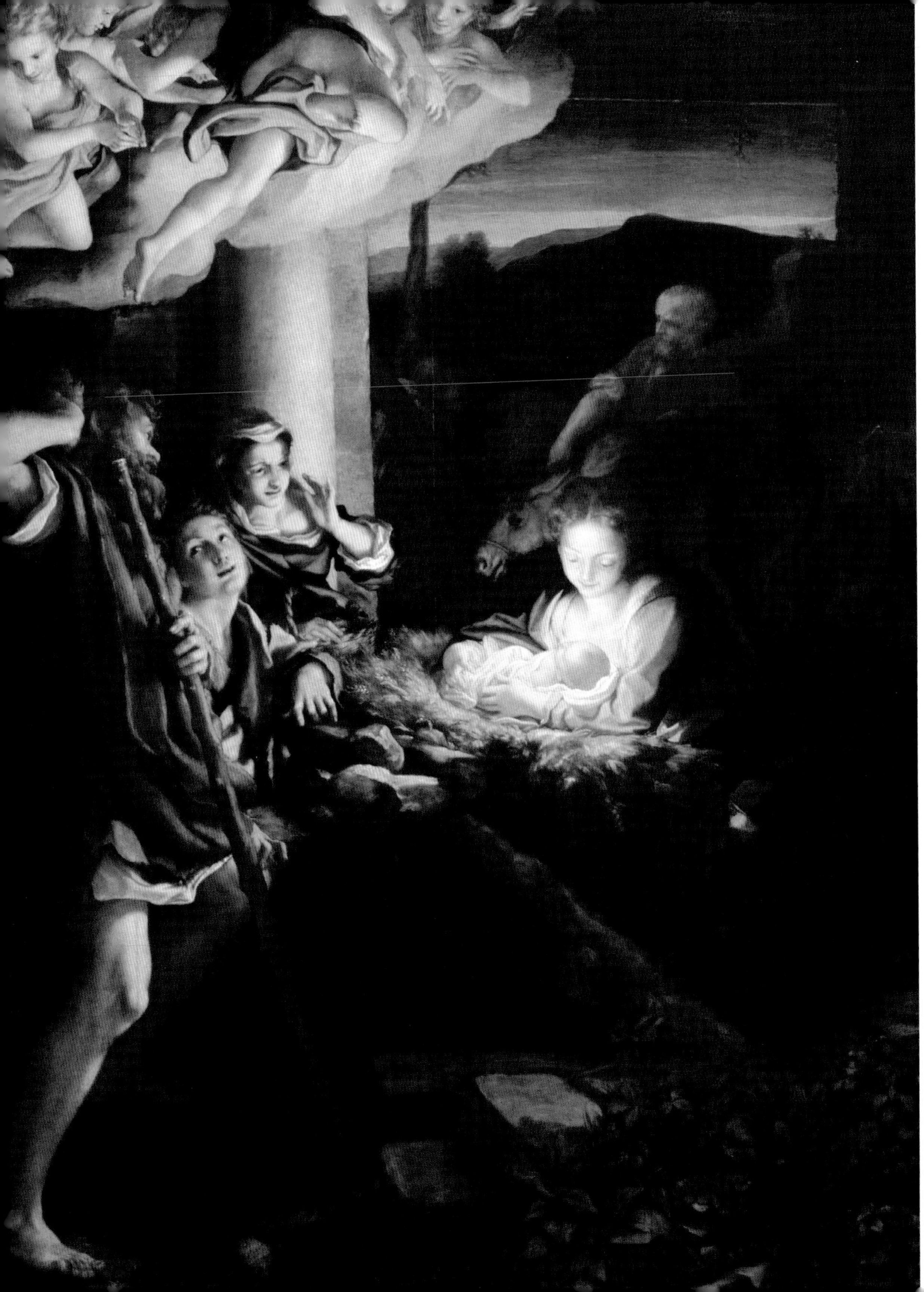

Bathing in light

ANTONIO ALLEGRI DA CORREGGIO

(c. 1490–1534), known as Correggio, an Italian painter

As a mother comforts her child, so will I comfort you.
—ISAIAH 66:13A

IT TOOK NEARLY one thousand years for Christmas to catch on. It was recognized as a separate holiday in 336, but Epiphany continued to be the main observation for the nativity, combined with celebrations marking the wise men's visit and Jesus's baptism. Then, in the thirteenth century, sparked by St. Francis of Assisi, the Franciscans all but adopted Christmas, creating small crèches of the Holy Family and dramatizing the birth in minor theatricals. Over the next three hundred years these reenactments grew in popularity until by the sixteenth century they had spread across most of Europe. Christmas had come into its own. Savvy artists saw a market for realistic nativity scenes.

Antonio Allegri was a working painter, attuned to the needs of his patrons. His first *Nativity*, painted in the 1510s, capitalized on a certain conventional sentimentality for his subject. His next foray, *The Adoration of the Magi* (1516–1518), has hints of the artist's signature tonal contrasts, but again the Holy Family fails to elicit more than a passing interest.

Antonio was married in 1520. He and his wife, Girolama, had a son one year later. The young family then moved from Correggio to Parma. That was where, in 1522, Antonio accepted a commission for another nativity that took him eight years to complete.

Art scholars generally agree that Antonio's lack of enthusiasm may have been due to the paltry fee promised for the painting, though the births of three more children during the intervening years may have had something to do with it. Antonio and Girolama had three daughters: Francesca, Caterina, and Anna. Caterina and Anna died in infancy a year apart during what we now call the holiday season. There can be little doubt that the couple felt a deep and crippling grief. Heartbroken and in failing health, Girolama died in 1529. She was twenty-six.

◄ Correggio, *The Night*, 1530, Gemäldegalerie Alte Meister, Dresden

In recent decades some historians have embraced an odd but influential hypothesis of "parental indifference," first published by Philippe Ariès in 1960. Death was so common prior to the seventeenth century, Ariès posited, that parents distanced themselves from their children—the better to mourn less when a few of them inevitably died. He pointed to art from before the Renaissance that depicted children as small-scale adults to illustrate that *childhood* as we know it is a modern construct. The suggestion gained ground through repetition, if not study. By the 1970s it was repeated as fact in journals and popular magazines, encompassing all children across the globe. The supposition that parents in other eras were callous to their children does not bear scrutiny. It seems unlikely that Joseph and Mary considered life, in one historian's words, "too harsh to bother overmuch about an infant who probably would not survive anyway," or that Mary mourned less at the cross than bereaved mothers do today. Consider David's cry at the death of his son, Absalom, "If only I had died instead of you!" Surely Job and his wife were not unmoved at the loss of ten children; the next ten might bring joy but never consolation. The hypothesis was nonsense, of course, as modern scholarship has confirmed.

After losing his wife and two daughters, Antonio at last turned to the eight-year-old commission. He seems to have worked on nothing else from the time Girolama died until the painting was finished a year later. Known in English as *Nativity (The Holy Night)*, the artist entitled it simply, *The Night*. It was placed in the Church of San Prospero of Reggio Emilia in late 1530. Antonio moved back to Correggio with his two young children. His output was considerably diminished until his death four years later.

The Night is at once prosaic and profound. Much of it was new for the artist and the art world. It is known as the first nocturnal piece of note in Europe; it certainly displays Antonio's knack for asymmetry. But this is trivial. Using the dark of night as contrast, Antonio painted a light that seems to shine upon and radiate from the infant Jesus. It nearly blinds one shepherd, pleasing and astonishing the others. It reaches out to illuminate Joseph (reining in a donkey) and the angels above. Significantly, Mary is not stunned. The light seems to bathe, console, and assure her. Jesus is a comfort and a guide.

You will not awaken one morning miraculously filled with a joy of life. You will not leave your sadness behind; to be told you could is neither realistic nor truthful. But, instead, your sadness will no longer pull you down. You will now carry it with you, inside you. Remember this: you will carry it. It will not carry you!

—HARRIET SARNOFF SCHIFF, *The Bereaved Parent*

Never did I see you wake
with other than a joyous laugh;
as if in a dream you picked blossoms
from the Tree of Life.

And so I hope, with a joyous laugh
you will now wake
from this brief dream of life
under the tree of Paradise.

—FRIEDRICH RÜCKERT

(The Paradise Tree, or Tree of Life, was part of medieval holiday celebrations, a precursor to the modern Christmas tree)

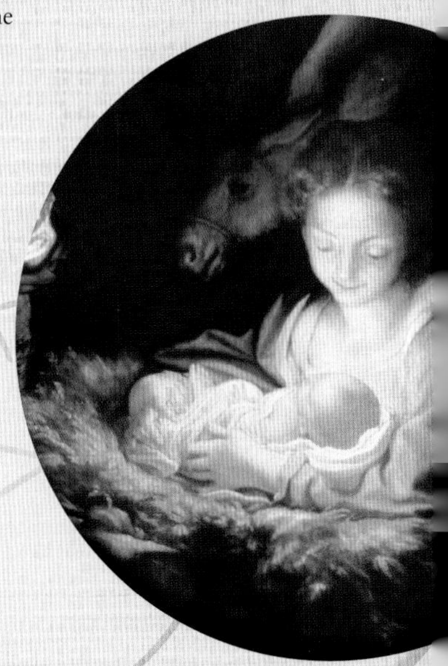

The passing joys of human life do not have to disappear forever. This Child will show us how to see them all in the mystery of endless day. Most precious of all joys are those that come from love. More than all else we do not want to be separated forever from those we love. He came that we may be forever with Him—and with them.

—BENEDICT GROESCHEL, CFR

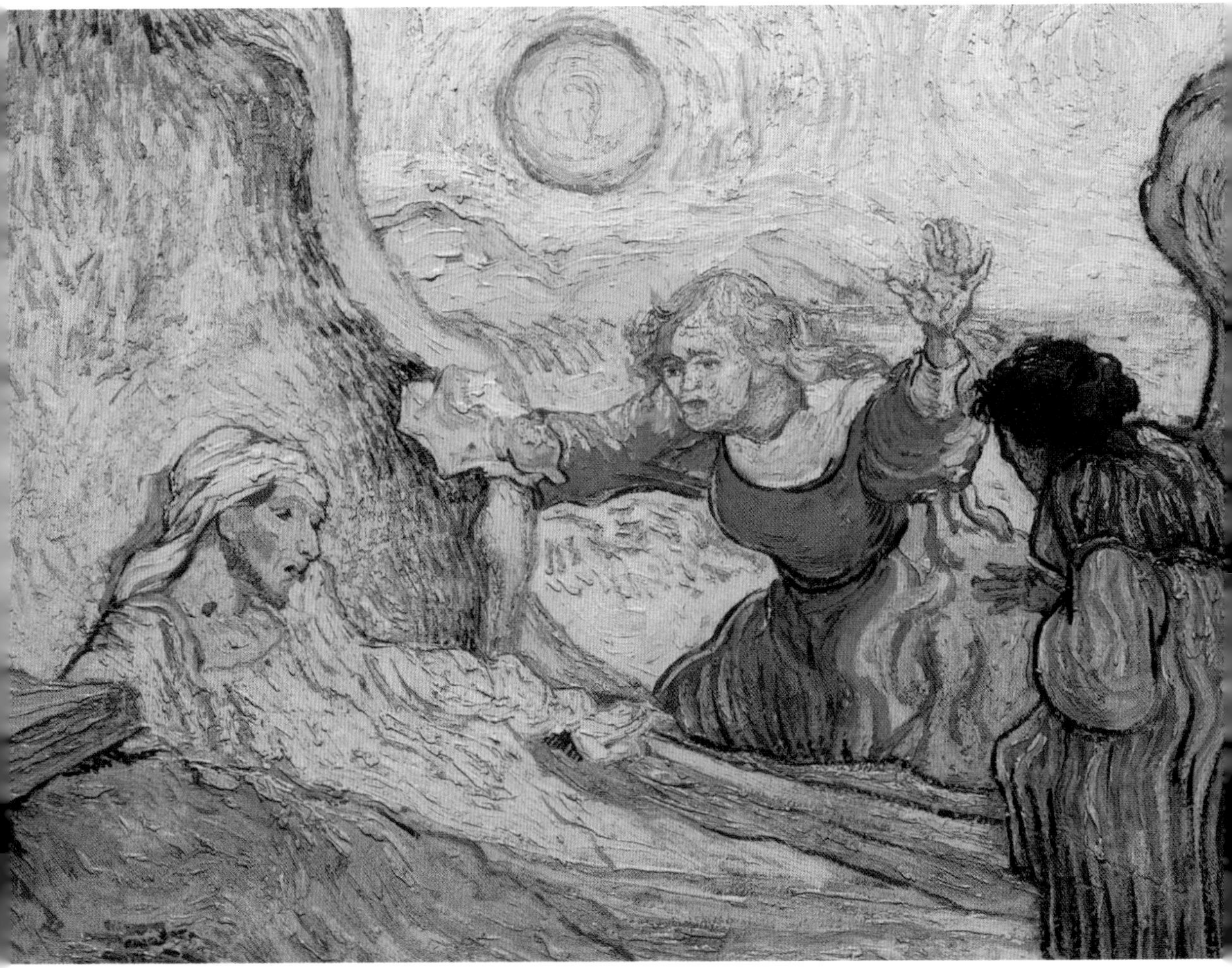

van Gogh, *The Raising of Lazarus*, 1890, Van Gogh Museum, Amsterdam

The art of loving

VINCENT VAN GOGH

(1853–1890), a Dutch painter

> *He would not even look up to heaven, but beat his breast and said, "God, have mercy on me, a sinner."*
> —LUKE 18:13B

VINCENT VAN GOGH was a troubled man. His brother Theo felt there were two people inside him: "one marvelously gifted, refined and gentle, and the other selfish and unfeeling." Failing in many ventures, including the ministry, Vincent finally settled on art. He sensed God in the great masterpieces. "I think that everything that is really good and beautiful, the inner, moral, spiritual and sublime beauty in men and their works, comes from God," he wrote to Theo. "I cannot help thinking that the best way of knowing God is to love many things."

Vincent dreamed of founding a colony in the South of France where artists could work together. Eventually Paul Gauguin joined him in Arles, but on December 23, 1888, Vincent suffered a mental collapse. He mutilated his ear and had to be hospitalized. The next day, Christmas Eve, Theo took the night train to be at his older brother's side.

Vincent was all but driven from Arles. He was released from the hospital in January, but fearing another breakdown, he had himself admitted to a psychiatric hospital in Saint-Rémy in May 1890. It was there that he painted *The Raising of Lazarus*, mirrored after Rembrandt. Vincent used his distinctive red beard to identify himself as Lazarus in the painting. Jesus is absent; Mary is kneeling in prayer. After so much grief, Martha's joy looks conspicuously similar to a bedraggled hospital patient. "I didn't have to put myself out very much," Vincent wrote to Theo, "in order to try and express sadness and extreme loneliness."

While at Saint-Rémy Vincent also created *The Good Samaritan*. Here the beard is different. It has just a hint of red, not the blazing color of Vincent's facial

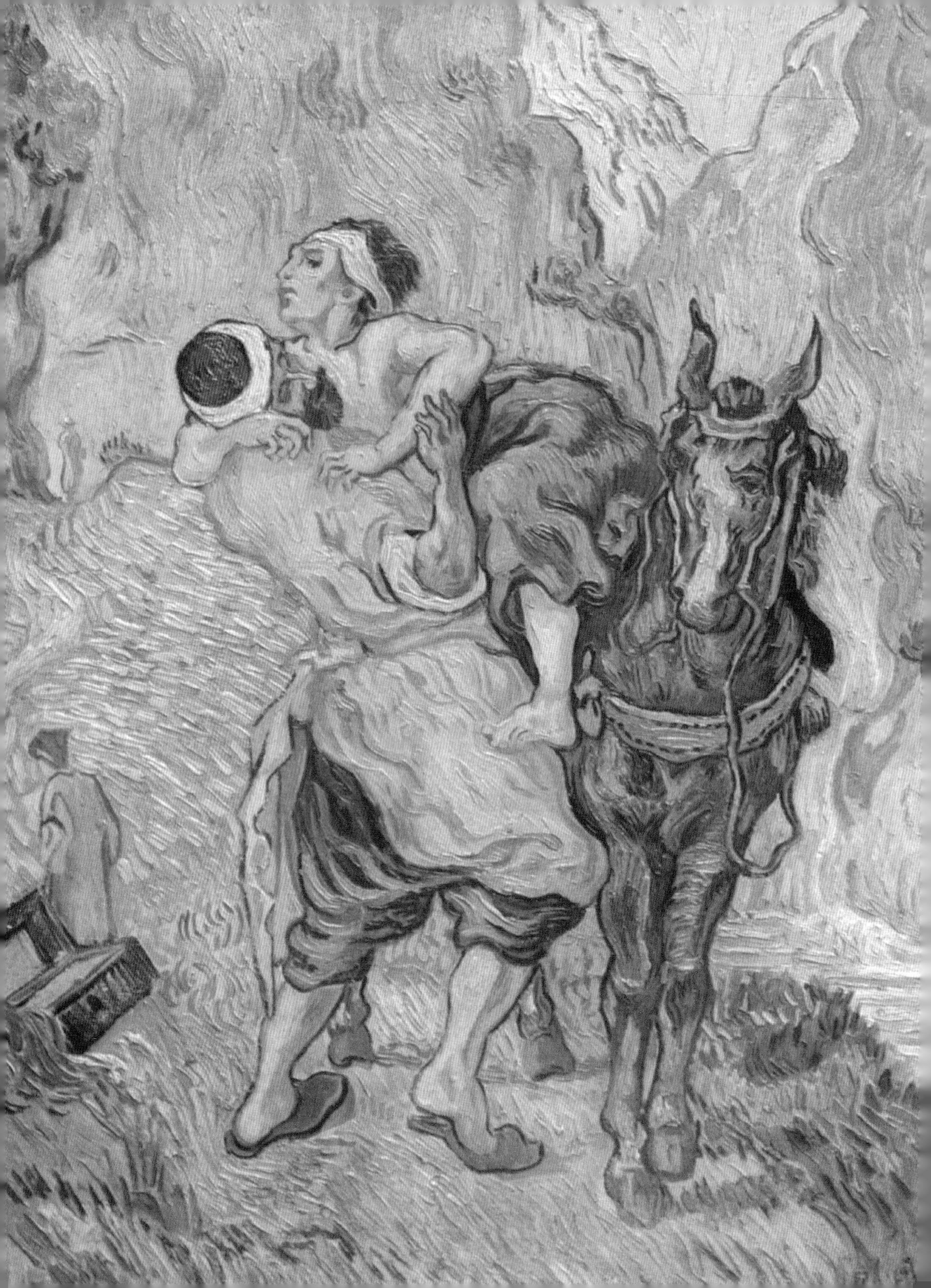

hair. It is more subdued, a fuller beard, more like Vincent's *Portrait of Theo van Gogh*. The Samaritan resembles the younger Theo, whom Vincent came to call his "wise older brother." The mix of hope and helplessness is nearly palpable in both works.

Vincent may have seen certain aspects of the parable that are often missed. The man was not simply robbed: his attackers beat him so brutally that the Samaritan had to tend to his open wounds. His savior did not offer assistance; he acted. Vincent emphasized the straining muscles of the Samaritan; he is clearly heaving the victim onto the beast. There is little question that in mirroring Eugène Delacroix's famous painting, Vincent was creating a richer, more vibrant expression of his own experience with his brother. "You really feel that for my part I am working and suffering like you," he wrote to Theo that July.

> In my pictures I want to say something consoling. I want to paint men and women with a touch of the eternal, whose symbol was once the halo, which we try to convey by the very radiance and vibrancy of our colouring.

Vincent considered portraits to be his métier. To him and other artists of the day, ideas and emotions could be expressed *in* the actual paint on the canvas as well as *through* the artist's brush. "I *should like* to paint portraits which would appear after a century to the people living then as apparitions," he wrote a month before he ended his life. "By which I mean that I do not endeavor to achieve this by a photographic resemblance, but by means of our impassioned expressions."

Vincent may have seen the artist colony of Arles as an uncaring tribe that had cast him aside in his despair and illness. Yet he was not bitter that the community he founded had turned on him. Through it all he continued to echo sentiments he admired in his brother. "I don't really have any friends except for you," Vincent told Theo. "The more I think it over, the more I feel that there is nothing more truly artistic than to love people."

Perhaps Vincent found in his wise older brother the Samaritan we all seek.

◀ van Gogh, *The Good Samaritan*, 1890, Kröller-Müller Museum, Otterlo

The Lord never tires of forgiving: never! It is we who tire of asking him for forgiveness. We need to ask for the grace not to get tired of asking for forgiveness, because he never gets tired of forgiving.

—POPE FRANCIS

Community is the fruit born through shared brokenness, and intimacy is the fruit that grows through touching one another's wounds.

—HENRI J. M. NOUWEN

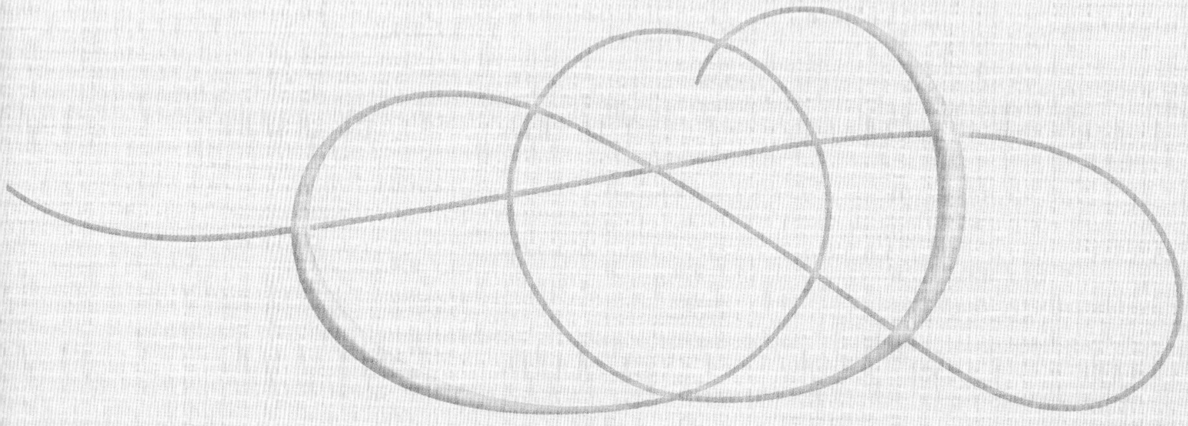

Faith is not the clinging to a shrine but the endless, tameless pilgrimage of hearts. Audacious longing, calling, calling, burning songs, daring thoughts, an impulse overwhelming the heart, usurping the mind—it is all a stalwart driving to the precious serving of Him who rings our hearts like a bell, wishing to enter our empty perishing lives.

—ABRAHAM JOSHUA HESCHEL

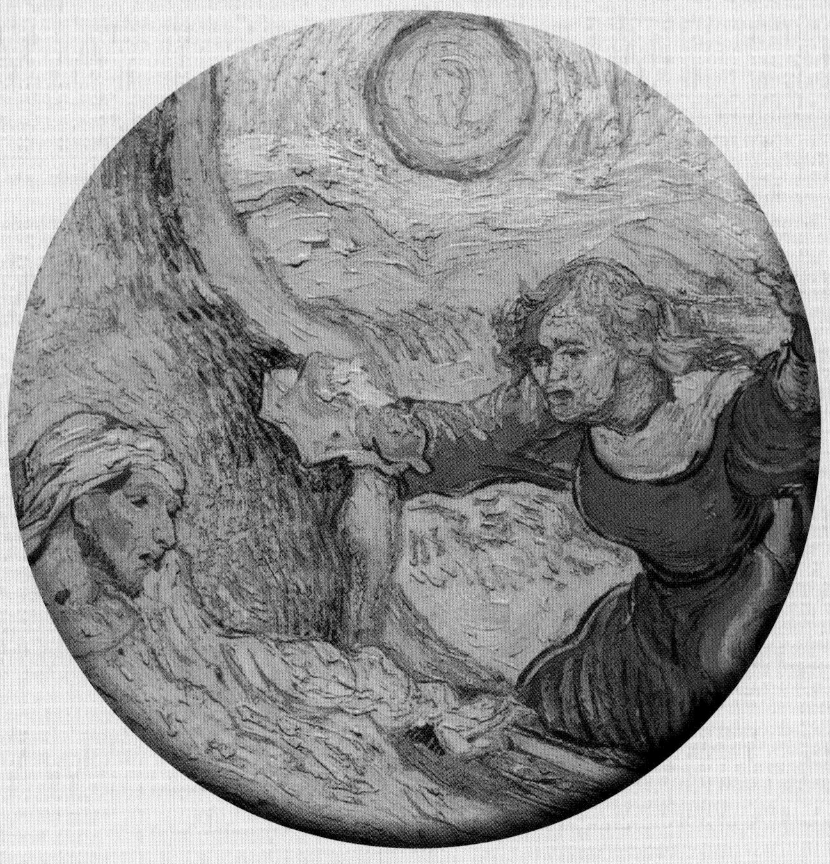

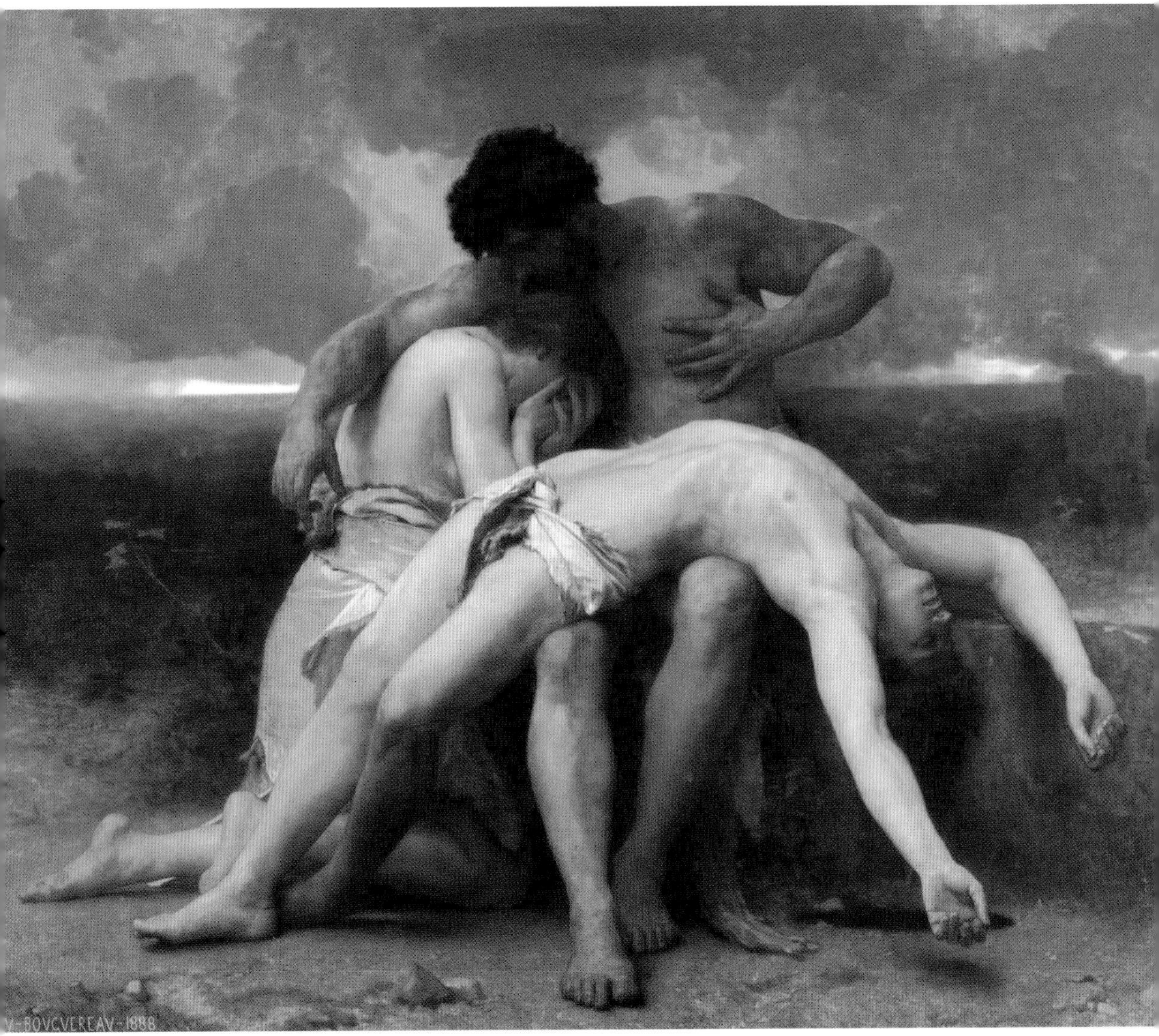

Bouguereau, *The First Mourning*, 1888, Museo Nacional de Bellas Artes, Buenos Aires

One who mourns finds joy

WILLIAM-ADOLPHE BOUGUEREAU

(1825–1905), a French painter

> *In all their distress he too was distressed, and the angel of his presence saved them. In his love and mercy he redeemed them; he lifted them up and carried them all the days of old.*
>
> —ISAIAH 63:9

THE PAINTINGS OF WILLIAM BOUGUEREAU are joyous. His portraits of children are famous for their innocence and candor. His nudes of adults are the opposite of pornography: more celebration of humanity than degradation. "In painting, I am an idealist," William said. "I see only the beautiful in art and, for me, art is the beautiful. Why reproduce what is ugly in nature? I do not see why it should be necessary." He managed to communicate his ideals in ways that few artists ever achieve. He left the world 826 paintings. "Each day I go to my studio full of joy," he wrote near the end of his life; "in the evening when obliged to stop because of darkness I can scarcely wait for the next morning to come. If I cannot give myself to my dear painting I am miserable."

All of which makes William something of a puzzle. He and his future wife, Nelly, moved in together in 1856. They had three children before they married: Henriette, Georges, and Jeanne, who was born on Christmas Day, 1861. Jeanne was four years old when she died in 1866, just eight days after her parents' wedding. Two years later William and Nelly had another child, Paul. Georges died in 1875; he was fifteen. A year later Nelly had a fifth child, Maurice. In 1877 Nelly contracted tuberculosis; she and baby Maurice died within two months of each other. In 1900, Paul died of tuberculosis as well. He was thirty-two. By this time four of William's five children were dead. Only Henriette and William's second wife, Elizabeth, survived the artist when he died in 1905.

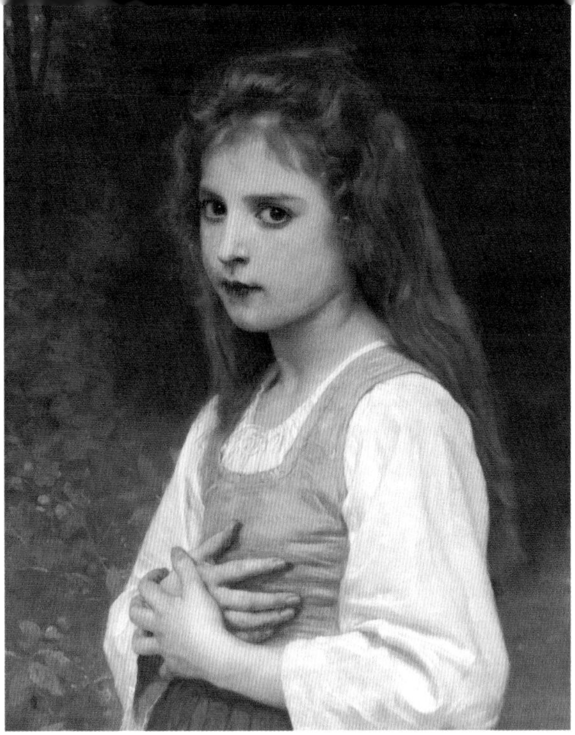

Bouguereau, *Jeanne*, 1888, private collection

This was an onslaught of grief. How to explain the apparent contradiction between such joyous work and William's personal loss? As with many artists, he seems to have found expression for his deepest sorrows in depictions from the Bible.

The First Mourning, painted in 1888, describes the precise moment Adam and Eve discovered the body of Abel, murdered by his brother, Cain. William's depiction is suggestive and heartbreaking. The first mourning, as he put it, was not the death of a spouse or even that of a brother. A bereaved father himself, William knew there is no mourning that compares to that of losing a child.

Modern research would have come as no surprise to him. One study that assessed mourning reactions concluded that bereaved parents have "significantly higher intensities of grief" than those who lost a parent or a spouse. Several other studies have drawn the same conclusion. One phrase is repeated almost universally by bereaved parents and those who know them: *they never get over it.* It is "a permanent change," as one researcher put it; "there is no going back."

William's insight deserves pause. Of all deaths, losing a child was the first in the Bible; the parallel to his own grief and the death of God's Son on the cross could not have been lost on the artist. The framing is nearly identical to the mother's posture and the position of the dead child in an earlier work, *The Virgin of Consolation*, from 1875. There are other similarities to his 1876 *Pietà*: the angels who weep; Mary, whose grief has left her incapable of expression. *The Madonna of the Roses* was painted in 1903 after four of William's children had died. In it Jesus is so completely human, we pause at his innocence; Mary is equally present; and yet we see sorrow in those peaceful eyes.

A clue to William's source of peace lies in a portrait of his daughter, *Jeanne*. William finally painted her twenty-two years after her death, in 1888. Her portrait is a masterpiece. William used all his skill: the lighting, shading, and angle are held up as examples for aspiring artists even today. His talent for capturing the ineffable is apparent in her expression. Yet that is not what speaks to us. Somehow William did more than paint a portrait of his daughter.

Many bereaved parents agree that we would choose the few years we had with our child over none at all. It was worth the wound. As Leo Tolstoy observed, "Only people capable of loving deeply can experience profound grief." One ten-year study found that nearly all bereaved parents feel they will see their children in heaven. Most believe that death is a temporary parting. This certainty is felt almost immediately in the initial shock and disbelief of grief. Later, they sense that they have an active interaction with their child. They all report a bond with their child in heaven. This has proven true even with parents who do not believe such a place exists. Another study found that bereaved parents are incapable of sustaining belief that their child is *not* continuing in an afterlife. There is little doubt that William felt a similar bond with his children; his belief in heaven was absolute. We look at Jeanne and want to weep. In it, we sense William's tears of memory, of loss, of hurt, of hope.

William *found* joy in art and *put* joy in art. The bulk of his work feels like a gift. And perhaps it was. In his tremendous output we sense that, in giving, William seemed to have found a way to deal with all that he had lost. There may be no more profound a testament to the artist's view than in a painting from 1897. With three of his children dead, William placed himself in a painting he entitled simply *Compassion!*

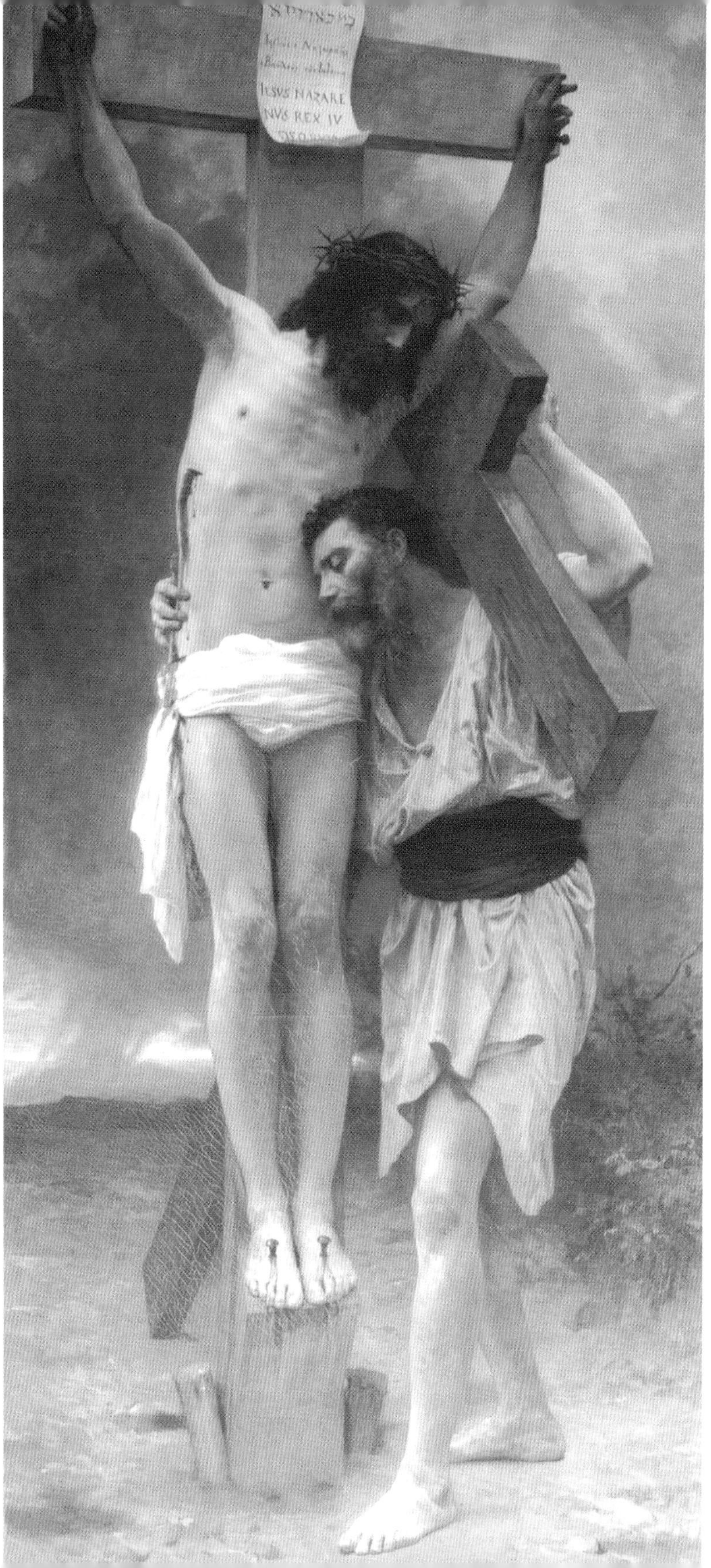
IESVS NAZARE
NVS REX IV

Paralyzed and silent in her bed, my daughter Paula taught me a lesson that is now my mantra: You only have what you give. It is in giving that I connect with others, with the world and with the divine.

—ISABEL ALLENDE

God's intervention is also seen in those sudden, unexpected experiences, at times of utter despair, when all at once the mind is filled with the absolute certainty of God's love. It is like an unexpected signpost upon an uncertain road.

—PAUL TOURNIER

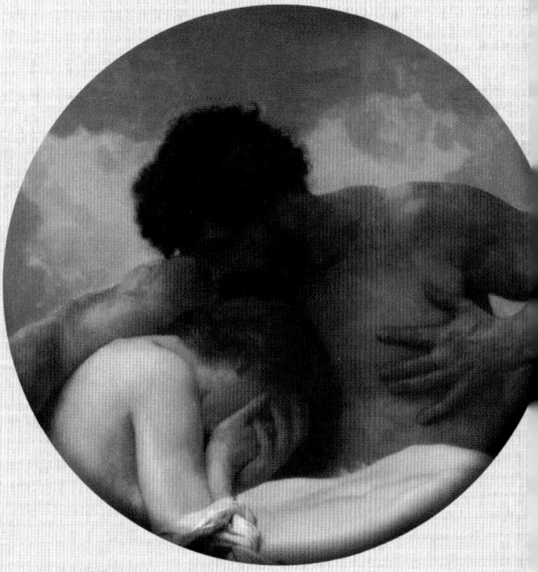

Now the sun will rise as bright,
as though no sorrow had fallen in the night.

This sorrow fell on me alone,
the sun, it shines on everyone.

Do not wrap yourself around the night,
bathe it in eternal light.

My tent is dark, the lamp is cold,
bless the light, the Joy of the World!

—FRIEDRICH RÜCKERT

◀ Bouguereau, *Compassion!*, 1897, Musée d'Orsay, Paris

ABOUT THE RÜCKERT POEMS

FRIEDRICH RÜCKERT (1788–1866) was a translator and professor of Asian languages. Hailed by *The Atlantic Monthly* as "the last of the grand old generation of German poets," many of his *lieder*, or songs, were set to music by the great composers of the day. But for three decades he hid from view his most personal work.

The day after Christmas 1833, Friedrich's youngest child, three-year-old Luise, showed symptoms of scarlet fever. She died on New Year's Eve. His son Ernst died on January 16, twelve days after the boy turned five. Friedrich's four remaining children survived. He was kind and attentive, grateful for each moment with them, yet his grief was unassuaged. "That I should drink and eat, eat and drink," he wrote, "forgetting all the while that you are lost to me!" Over the first six months of 1834 Friedrich composed hundreds of poems on loss and mourning. "Spare me these delights!" he cried. "They cannot fool my heart, adding grief to grief." He averaged two to three poems each day. Some are his finest, others less so; none was intended for publication. He kept Luise and Ernst's pastel portraits with him for the rest of his life. Six years after Friedrich's death, in 1872, his son Heinrich compiled 425 of the poems in *Kindertodtenlieder (Songs on the Death of Children)*.

Gustav Mahler (1860–1911) later set five poems from the book to music; his *Kindertotenlieder* premiered in 1905. (The absent *d* is an easy way to tell them apart.) Gustav's Rückert adaptations are moving, but his most profound work was still to come. In 1907 his four-year-old daughter, Putzi, died of diphtheria and scarlet fever. His next composition, *Das Lied von der Erde (Song of the Earth)*, speaks of life, death, parting, and redemption. It was Gustav's masterpiece.

The Rückert poems in this book are original translations by David Bannon. They have never been published in English before, save one that is part of the Mahler cycle, though that is also a new translation. These and other translations are indicated in the bibliography.

NOTES

Let the reader, where we are equally confident, stride on with me; where we are equally puzzled, pause to investigate with me; where he finds himself in error, come to my side; where he finds me erring, call me to his side. So we may keep to the path, in love, as we fare toward Him "whose face is ever to be sought."

—ST. AUGUSTINE

All author names refer to works listed in the bibliography.

EPIGRAPH

VIIn1 ***The celebration:*** Bonhoeffer, 21, 25; edited.

VIIn2 ***Every image:*** John Damascene, 92–93. See also Gregory I to Serenus, c599–600 in Schaff, ser. 2, v13, 53; Besançon, 149, 394; Howes, 7.

VIIn3 ***Art inflames:*** Frängsmyr, 35; Solzhenitsyn, Nobel Media.

INTRODUCTION

XVn1 ***funerary art:*** See Wilken, 49; Blainey, 64; Hollingsworth, 96; Stokstad, 220, 222; Morabito, 21 January 2017; Levine, "Jewish Archaeology," in Katz, 524–25.

XVn2 ***scenes of deliverance:*** See Jaś Elsner, "'Pharaoh's Army,'"in Kessler, 12, 10–44.

XVn3 ***often-illiterate:*** See Clark, 79, 81; Jensen, *Understanding*, 21–22.

XVn4 ***texts... emphasized:*** See Freeman, 218; de Borchgrave, 11–12; Wilken, 53; Grant, 189; Ferngren, 2.

XVn5 ***The healing Jesus:*** See Jefferson, 2–3; Williamson, 4, 6; Crossan, *Essential*, 18–20; Keller, 19; Panofsky, 42; Withrow, 243–45, 305–06, 324–27, 329–30.

XVIn1 ***Art speaks:*** See Malchiodi, ix; Neimeyer, *Lessons*.

XVIn2 ***part of us:*** See Peppers, 47, 50; Gorer, 192–99.

XVIn3 ***Grief is as individual:*** Doka, *Journey*, 8; emphasis in original; see also May, 261, 263; Janoff-Bulman, 6–12.

DECEMBER 1

3 ***abandoned and vulnerable:*** See Worden, *Counseling*, 123.

5n1 ***Art is a human activity:*** Tolstoy, *What Is Art?*, 50; emphasis in original; edited.

5n2 ***Life isn't much:*** Buechner, *Whistling*, 1.

5n3 ***You need something to love:*** "Etwas brauchest du zu lieben," Rückert, 391.

DECEMBER 2

7 *an apple by Cézanne:* Cited by Merton, 28 June 1959. *Search for Solitude,* 298. See also Auden, *Complete Works,* 776.

8n1 *exhausted and serene:* See Anderson, *Paradise Lost,* 240.

8n2 *Her tomb is far away:* August, 1897, Goldwater, 20–21.

8n3 *I have an enemy:* Cited in Anderson, *Paradise Lost,* 240.

8n4 *small steps:* Schiff, 129–40.

8n5 *crushing weight of grief:* See Doka, *Journey,* 6.

8n6 *completely discouraged:* Goldwater, 20–21.

9 *The questions themselves:* See Gauguin's discussion of the nature of the soul, *The Modern Spirit and Catholicism,* unpublished (1897), cited in Jacobs, 56.

10n1 *unconsciously, perhaps:* Ibid., 65.

10n2 *a signature:* Ibid., 53.

10n3 *Bereavement often opens:* Ano, 461–80.

10n4 *marked spirituality:* Park, 707–29; Calhoun, *Posttraumatic Growth,* 7–13; Calhoun, *Handbook*; Thompson, *Expressive Arts,* 39.

10n5 *quest for meaning:* Neimeyer, *Behaviour Change,* 65–79.

11n1 *creators of modern art:* Tillich, *Courage,* 147–48.

11n2 *Suffering:* Park, "Religion and Spirituality," in Neimeyer, *Grief and Bereavement,* 358, 359, see 355–63; edited. Also Tedeschi, *Helping,* 10, 11; Kushner, 133–34, 148; Rosenblatt, *Help Your Marriage,* 5.

11n3 *Holly-tree:* Rückert, 13.

DECEMBER 3

13n1 *had once condemned:* Jensen, *The Cross,* 231–32.

13n2 *My small daughter:* Carrdus, 135–51. Also Luther, *Writings,* 40; Martin to Mr. and Mrs. Matthias Knudsen, 21 October 1531, *Spiritual Counsel,* 61.

15n1 *I would gladly: On Women,* 199.

15n2 *defiant raging:* Martin to Jakob Propst, 9 October 1542, Linton, 38f.

15n3 *yet to be so sad: On Women,* 200.

15n4 *broke down in tears:* Linton, 20–29f.

15n5 **Christ on the Cross:** Noble, 138–62.

15n6 *grotesque:* Ross, vii, 6–7.

15n7 *The blood of Jesus:* 1 John 1:7.

16n1 *Those pure disciples:* Dillard, "Luke," in Corn, 37.

16n2 *I thought to teach:* "Ich wollte mir erziehn eine Spinnemädchen," Rückert, 70.

17 *If I am not:* Jeanne d'Arc, 24 February 1431. "Si je n'y suis, Dieu veuille m'y mettre; et si j'y suis, Dieu veuille m'y garder." *Histoire complète,* 94.

DECEMBER 4

19 ***The moon has risen:*** Tanner, 11774, 11775.

20n1 ***Let God Guide us:*** Introduction, Mathews, xiii–xiv.

20n2 ***work of desolation:*** See Attig, "Seeking Wisdom," in Stillion, 11, 84.

20n3 ***nature seemed:*** Tanner, 11774.

21n1 ***The artist should preach:*** Merton, *Raids,* 171; from *Lugano Review*, 43–45; see *Literary Essays,* 378.

21n2 ***My role, I think:*** "Meine Rolle, denk' ich," in Rückert, 153.

21n3 ***God is both:*** Borg, 111, 133; Edited; emphases in original.

DECEMBER 5

23n1 ***lost their fears of death:*** Knapp, 183, 202.

23n2 ***constant companion:*** See Fish, "Differences of Grief Intensity," in Rando, *Parental Loss*, 223, 417, 426.

24n1 ***loving in separation:*** Attig, 187, 188. See also McGoldrick, 19; Rosenblatt, "Grief That Does Not End," in Klass et al., *New Understandings,* 55.

24n2 ***I had no idea:*** Finkbeiner, 194; for cancer patient interviews, 191–194.

24n3 ***Lord of the universe:*** cited in Telushkin, *Wisdom*, 347. Also Boswell, 406; Schama, 450–53; Grayzel, 362–65; Telushkin, *Literacy,* 193–94.

25n1 ***needs to be broken:*** Rohr, 12.

25n2 ***Yet a little while:*** Rossetti, 193–94. See also Hurley, 95.

25n3 ***God enters into:*** Fretheim, 124, 128; edited.

DECEMBER 6

27n1 ***pulled his brother to safety:*** Koerner, 81.

27n2 ***Caspar knew death:*** Boime, 512.

27n3 ***similar . . . to losing a child:*** Rando, *Go on Living,* 157.

27n4 ***little social acknowledgment:*** Ibid., 159.

27n5 ***platitudes:*** Dyregrov, 45–48.

27n6 ***Caspar . . . felt responsible:*** Cain et al., 34 (4), 747; Stephenson, "Grief of Siblings," in Rando, *Parental Loss,* 324, 326. See also Stephenson, *Mourning,* 172.

27n7 ***inescapable:*** Knapp, 140. Also Pearlman et al., 5, 17.

27n8 ***92 percent:*** Finkbeiner, 131.

27n9 ***never quite learned to live with:*** Dahlenburg, "Major Depression," in Bogousslavsky, 112–20. Also Hogan, "Sibling Loss," in Doka, *Children and Adolescents*, 161, 162, 164, 168; Schumacher, "Helping Children Cope," in Hansen, 82–94; Pearlman et al., 5; Jeffreys, 15; Murphy et al., *Stress* 16(1), 17–25.

28n1 ***The firs stand around:*** "Immergrün, durch alle Zeiten während," See Eberlein, 206; trans. from Boime, 567.

28n2 ***Art serves as a mediator:*** "Äußerungen bei Betrachtung . . ." in Eimer, v1; trans. by Cahen-Maurel, "The Simplicity of the Sublime,"in Nassar, 191, 193.

28n3 ***true isolation:*** Packman et al., 817–41.

28n4 ***Close your bodily eye:*** Vaughn, 103.

29n1 ***Quietly in the night:*** O'Donohue, *Eternal Echoes,* 170, 178–79; edited.

29n2 ***Over all graves:*** "Über alle Gräber wächst zuletzt das Gras," Rückert, 153.

29n3 ***Prayer comes to pass:*** Heschel, *Quest,* 15, 16.

DECEMBER 7

31n1 ***Murderous, licentious:*** Berenson, 91.

31n2 ***David, another troubled artist:*** Birch et al., 243; Buechner, *Peculiar Treasures,* 27; Finkelstein, 12.

31n3 ***First and Third Commandments:*** See Tillich, *Eternal Now*, 92–100; Telushkin, *Literacy,* 56–57; Alt, 145, 156.

33n1 **Death of the Virgin:** See the Louvre, *Death of the Virgin.*

33n2 ***scandalous and impious:*** Hughes, 84–85, 89.

33n3 ***wounded and . . . killed:*** Ranuccio Tomassoni, who died from a wound to the groin. See Hughes, 95.

34n1 ***Roman stories of charity:*** Maximus, 180.

34n2 **The Seven Works of Mercy:** Graham-Dixon, 342; Ward, *Guardian of Mercy;* Mother Teresa, *A Call to Mercy.*

34n3 ***a pauper's grave:*** Seward, 193–97; Graham-Dixon, 414–24. See also Hughes, 82–95.

35n1 ***If we believe:*** Baillie, *Presence of God,* 207; edited.

35n2 ***Come, bring your sampler:*** "The Wounded Heart," Herrick, 13.

35n3 ***God creates:*** 7 July 1838, Kierkegaard, 59; emphasis in original.

DECEMBER 8

37 ***spiritual nature:*** Diderot, *Œuvres,* 158; *Diderot on Art II,* 86; Danto, 36–43.

38n1 ***failed to complete:*** See Callard-Szulgit, 32–35.

38n2 ***father's . . . guilt:*** Cain, *Survivors,* x; Jordon, xxvii, xxviii. Li et al., *Death Studies* 38(3), 165–71; Li et al., *Omega*, 75(2), 1–18.

38n3 ***bad death:*** Murphy et al., *Death Studies*, 27(1), 39–61; Doka, *Gender,* 23. Also Cleiren et al, 37–44; Farberow et al., 592–98; Farberow, 23–34; Harwood et al., 185–94.

38n4 ***more troubled by grief:*** Bailley et al., 256–71; Mitchell et al., 12–18; Murphy et al., *Stress* 16(1), 17–25.

38n5 ***children are blamed:*** Feigelman et al., *Omega*, 63(4), 291–316.

38n6 ***Their grief is rarely acknowledged:*** Doka, "Disenfranchised Grief," in Dickinson et al., 212–15; reprinted from Doka, *Hidden Sorrow*, 3–9.

40 ***One uses color:*** "On se sert des couleurs, mais on peint avec le sentiment," quoted in Keller, 148.

41n1 ***Beauty springs:*** "Est beau ce qui procède d'une nécessité intérieure de l'âme. Est beau ce qui est beau intérieurement." Kandinsky, *Du Spirituel dans l'art*; emphasis in original. Kandinsky, *Concerning*; and *On the spiritual*, 95.

41n2 ***I live:*** Byron, 1.

41n3 ***The great secret:*** Rilke to Margo Sizzo, 23 January 1924, in Macy, February 27.

DECEMBER 9

43n1 ***The idea for* The Angelus:** Trans. and Dali anecdote from Schneider, *America*, 24 March 2015.

43n2 **The Angelus:** Dali, 64. Dali later wrote an essay on the piece, *The Tragic Myth of Millet's Angelus*.

45n1 ***Important reality:*** Kugel, 190–91; emphasis in original; edited.

45n2 ***The crucial question:*** "Der entscheidende . . ." Jung, 130; Carr, 69.

45n3 ***The time draws near:*** Excerpted from *In Memoriam*, 45–46.

DECEMBER 10

47 **Christ in the Garden of Olives:** See Morgan, 234–36.

48n1 ***The effect must be for the soul:*** Delacroix, *A Small Philosophic Dictionary of the Fine Arts*, begun in 1857 and never finished; cited in Prideaux, 176.

48n2 ***This struggle is regarded:*** Trans. from Eugene-Delacroix.com, "Jacob" and "Entombment."

49n1 ***Man must be alone:*** Wiesel, *Messengers*, 125, 126; emphasis in original; edited.

49n2 ***A Dirge:*** Shelley, 123.

49n3 ***He's a mysterious:*** Kselman, 280, 291, 302; edited.

DECEMBER 11

51n1 ***unsullied purity:*** Cited by Friends of the Dublin Art Colony.

51n2 **TIME *Magazine:*** Abbott's first *Angel*, painted in 1887 with Mary as his model. *TIME* 142(27), cover.

51n3 ***For* men, *the dawn:*** Abbott to the Editor of *Bruno's Weekly*, 11 March 1916. See Anderson, *American Heritage*, 24–32.

52n1 ***the horror of dying:*** Abbott to Everton Sainsbury, 5 May 1880; cited in Anderson, *Thayer*, 17, 38.

52n2 ***the eleven-year-old child:*** See Sim et al., 1211–20; Andrews, 38–50.

52n3 ***portraits of his children changed:*** See McGoldrick, 15; Buckle, 113–27; Vess et al., 115–28.

52n4 ***the hills around them:*** Faulkner, 23, 24. See Tedeschi, *Helping,* 13; Rosenblatt, *Help Your Marriage,* 5. Also Rosenblatt, *Parent Grief,* 16, 93.

53 ***this dear mountain:*** Cited by the National Gallery of Art.

54n1 ***When we run:*** Taylor, 57.

54n2 ***Thousand minstrels:*** in Longfellow, *Places,* 67–72; excerpted and edited.

55 ***Angels often:*** Jeanne d'Arc, 12 March 1431. "Elles viennent souvent sans être appelés . . ." *Histoire complète,* 139, 141; edited from the trial manuscript. When asked if the voice was that of an angel or a saint, Jeanne replied, "It is from God." Jeanne d'Arc, 24 February 1431. "Cette voix vient de la part de Dieu." *Histoire complète,* 93. See also Spoto, 140f.

DECEMBER 12

59n1 ***The immanent God:*** May, *Addiction,* 124; edited.

59n2 ***For my particular grief:*** Shakespeare, 65.

59n3 ***We can never struggle:*** "Car il me paraissait certain . . . ," quoted in Canciani, 80.

DECEMBER 13

62n1 ***Do not 'recover':*** Martison et al., 259–67; Seigal, 10, 12.

62n2 ***measurable . . . components:*** Spratt, 299–306.

62n3 ***demonstrable differences:*** See McCoyd, 20–22.

62n4 ***appreciate life:*** Rosenblatt, *Parent Grief,* 2–4.

63 ***a sketched-in hope:*** See Klass, *Omega*, 19(1), 33; Rosof, 5–19; Roach, 68; Rubin, "Parental Response," in Stroebe et al., *Handbook,* 219–40.

64n1 ***Every great loss:*** Remen, 38.

64n2 ***Modes of aesthetic:*** Crowther, 153; edited.

65 ***What is dying:*** "Was ist sterben? was ist todt sein?" Rückert, 143.

DECEMBER 14

67n1 ***my goldsmith:*** See Hutchison, 10–11, 19, 20; Russell, 39.

67n2 ***remained Catholic:*** Hutchison, 179.

67n3 ***a very real physical affect:*** Knapp, 178–79; Klass, *Death Studies*, 17(4), 343–68.

68n1 ***Hands of an Apostle:*** See Hutchison, 105; Levey, "Dürer and the Renaissance," in Dodwell, 16.

68n2 ***Albrecht's own:*** See Russell, 10–11, 120.

68n3 ***seventeen siblings:*** Hutchison, 19; Worden, *Grief Counseling,* 118; Davies et al., 297–313.

68n4 ***twentieth anniversary:*** See Tuck, 342; also Dues, *Catholic Customs,* 157–60.

69n1 ***Suffering contains:*** Wiesel, *Gates,* 201.

69n2 ***In the midst of life:*** From a Gregorian chant that became part of the burial service in *The Book of Common Prayer.*

69n3 ***Shut out suffering:*** Robertson, 26 April 1846, in Baillie, *A Diary*, Day 119; edited.

DECEMBER 15

72 ***turn outward:*** Neimeyer, "Developmental Theory," in Neimeyer, *Techniques,* 9.

73n1 ***Let us think:*** Pope Francis, *Church*, 3–4.

73n2 ***The two disciples:*** Nouwen, *Bread,* October 2; edited.

73n3 ***Jesus answered:*** "Jesus . . . answerid by this word, and seyd: . . ." *Shewings*; modern English from *Revelation*, 54–55; edited.

DECEMBER 16

75 ***not unheard of:*** Boswell, 207, 259, 301, 341.

77n1 ***You can kiss your family:*** Buechner, *Telling,* 3.

77n2 ***We would be quite:*** "L'on seroit même surpris . . .," *Maximes,* 97, trans. Edmonson, 115. See David, *Practice,* 89; and Delaney, 108.

77n3 ***God is nearer:*** Julian, *Revelation*, 124.

DECEMBER 17

79 ***masterpieces to order:*** Varriano, 125, 155.

80 ***self-preservation:*** See Zeff; Aron; and Sand.

81n1 ***Bear in mind:*** Cain, *Quiet,* 265; edited.

81n2 ***All of us are called:*** Martin, *Becoming,* 63.

81n3 ***God still speaks today:*** de Caussade, 1, 3, 4, 15; edited.

DECEMBER 18

84 ***limber up his fingers:*** Quoted in Schneider, *Watteau,* 102.

86 ***so badly treated:*** Ibid., 103.

87n1 ***To talk of accepting death:*** Cited in Lipsitt, 216–26; edited.

87n2 ***Lift me above:*** "Hebt mir von des Himmels Ecken," Rückert, 185–86.

87n3 ***You can keep forever:*** Lewis to Phyllis Elinor Sandeman, 31 June 1947, *Letters, vII,* 668; emphasis in original.

DECEMBER 19

89n1 ***lifelong grief:*** Klass, "The Deceased Child" in Klass, et al., *New Understandings,* 214–15; Silverman, "Children's Construction," in Klass, et al., *New Understandings,* 85.

89n2 *death of an infant:* Peppers, 27.

89n3 *persists indefinitely:* Weiss, "The Attachment Bond," in Parkes et al., *Attachment,* 74, 75.

89n4 *shedding ten thousand tears:* Smedes, 123.

90n1 *I mean by a picture:* Quoted in Cartwright, 94.

90n2 *comes at a price:* Smedes, 123.

91n1 *What Christ came to do:* Forsyth, 354, 356–57; edited.

91n2 *What can I give him:* Excerpted from "A Christmas Carol," *Poetical Works,* 246–47.

91n3 *Nothing irredeemable . . . Irredeemable harm:* Willard, *Conspiracy,* 327; Willard, *Renovation,* 151; edited.

DECEMBER 20

93n1 *The medium:* See Rosenblatt, *Bitter, Bitter Tears.*

93n2 *Peace, let it be:* Details of the séance in Marshall, 144.

95n1 *reunion with loved ones:* Greeley, 813–35.

95n2 *sense the deceased:* Benore, 1–22; Klugman, 249–62; Davies, *Funerary Rites,* 229; Cleiren, 129; Hay, 83; Stroebe et al., 44(3), 143–58; David, Jesus Seminar, 3–6; cited in Crossan, *Birth,* 13–14, 709; also Tedeschi, *Helping,* 8, 9, 10, 13.

95n3 *not without precedent:* See Henri Nouwen to Mr. and Mrs. Healey, 9 Jun 1974 and 2 August 1974, in *Love, Henri,* 27; O'Donohue, *Anam Cara*, 261.

95n4 *interacted with Lewis:* Phillips, 117–18.

95n5 *tangible expression:* Buechner, "Faith and Fiction," in Zinsser, 45–46, 47; Buechner, *Secrets,* 169–70.

95n6 *Martin Luther . . . approved of:* Linton, 135.

95n7 *even among atheists:* Bernstein, 210, 212.

95n8 *They relate stories:* For interviews see Redfern, 197–214; Al-Chokhachy; Toom, 1–13.

95n9 *a vision of Jesus:* For details, Gatrall, 85–86. Tissot recorded the words that Jesus seemed to be whispering to the women: "See, I have been more miserable than you: I am the solution to all your problems; without me civilization is in ruins." See Wood, 143; Dolkart, 11.

95n10 *Bible paintings:* See Vincent van Gogh to Theo van Gogh, Cuesmes, 24 September 1880, in *Self-portrait,* 60–61.

96n1 *I feel very strongly:* Lewis to Vera Mathews on the death of her father, 27 March 51, *Letters, vIII,* 103–4; edited.

96n2 *Is it not at least:* Peale, 41–42.

97 *With a slow and noiseless:* Excerpted from "Footsteps of Angels," *Poems*, 4–5. The visitor was Longfellow's wife, Mary, who died during a miscarriage in 1835. Also Klass, *New Directions,* 54.

DECEMBER 21

99n1 ***Karl . . . less so:*** Jo found Rudolf Steiner's work appealing. Karl met Steiner only once, in November 1913. Steiner had Karl's hospital poems and letters to Jo published in 1919.

99n2 ***It is terrible:*** "Es ist schrecklich," Karl to Joanna Thylmann, 11 July 1913, Thylmann, 77.

100n1 ***the very first grenade:*** "die allererste Granate," Karl to Joanna Thylmann, Montmédy, 5 August 1916, Thylmann, 162. This was likely during the German offensive to consolidate the line between Fleury and the Thiaumont-fortification, 1–12 August 1916.

100n2 ***Awakening:*** "Aufwachen," August 1916, Thylmann, 164–5.

100n3 ***On the morning:*** "Am Morgen des 29. August, nach tagelangen Visionen," Thylmann, 165.

102n1 ***This is a road:*** Interviewed in Zapata, 105.

102n2 ***The ache of loss:*** Wolterstorff, 156, 157; edited.

103 ***I realize that suffering:*** Interviewed in Zapata, 105, 156.

DECEMBER 22

105 ***his final painting:*** See Feigelman et al., *Devastating Losses,* xv.

108 ***It*** **is** ***bad:*** Wright, 26 June 2014.

109n1 ***Nature is unsettled:*** "Unruhig ist's in der Natur," Rückert, 198.

109n2 ***A messenger comes:*** Wieseltier, 166.

DECEMBER 23

111n1 ***minor theatricals:*** See Flanders, 10–13; Miles, 105–6: Vauchez, 290–91.

111n2 ***Savvy artists:*** Mühlberger, 34.

112n1 ***Parents distanced themselves:*** Ariès, *Centuries,* 38; Ariès, *Western Attitudes.*

112n2 ***repeated as fact:*** Plumb, 7.

112n3 ***not survive anyway:*** Ibid., 7.

112n4 ***Mary mourned less:*** See van Vurst, 33.

112n5 ***If only I had died:*** 2 Samuel 18:33. See Parkes, *Bereavement,* 39; also the diary of Ralph Josselin, a 17th-century Essex clergyman, in Thorley, 51–55.

112n6 ***never consolation:*** See Wiesel, "Job," *Great Figures*; edited. Also Grout, 93–113; Freud to Ludwig Binswanger, 04 December 1929, in Berger-Zell, 183.

112n7 ***modern scholarship:*** Boswell, 38–39; Linton; Woods; Gies; Pollock, 12.

112n8 ***moved back to Correggio:*** See Pearlman et al., 7.

112n9 ***output considerably diminished:*** See Klass, *Omega*, 19(1), 33; Murphy et al., *Research* 25(6), 425–37. Also McBride, 59–73; Williams, "Effects of Grief," in Doka, *Loss in Later Life*, 191–206; and Doka, *Journey,* 27–30.

113n1 ***You will not awaken:*** Schiff, 132.

113n2 ***Never did I see:*** "Niemals anders sah ich dich erwachen," Rückert, 74. See Brunner, 11, 15–16, 91; Miles, 271–72; Flanders, 28–30.

113n3 ***The passing joys:*** Groeschel, 39–40.

CHRISTMAS EVE

115n1 ***gifted, refined and gentle:*** See the Van Gogh Museum, "Brotherly Love."

115n2 ***to love many things:*** Vincent to Theo van Gogh, Cuesmes, 22–24 June 1880, *Letters*, 88.

115n3 ***sadness and ... loneliness:*** Vincent to Theo van Gogh and Jo van Gogh-Bonger, Auvers-sur-Oise, c. 10 July 1890. See Morgan, 14; and *Letters*, 420.

117n1 ***wise older brother:*** Quoted in "Brotherly Love," Van Gogh Museum.

117n2 ***hope and helplessness:*** Vincent sought, as Henri Nouwen wrote, "to touch people by tenderly expressing his solidarity with the human condition." Cited in Nouwen, *Essential*, 15.

117n3 ***You really feel:*** Vincent to Theo van Gogh and Jo van Gogh-Bonger, Auvers-sur-Oise, c. 10 July 1890, *van Gogh Letters*, http://vangoghletters.org/vg/letters/let898/letter.html.

117n4 ***In my pictures:*** Vincent to Theo van Gogh, Arles, 3 September 1888, *Letters,* 394; edited.

117n5 **I should like *to paint:*** Vincent to Wilhelmina J. van Gogh. First half of June 1890, *Complete Letters,* 470; emphasis in original.

117n6 ***I don't really have any friends:*** Vincent to Theo van Gogh, The Hague, 22 July 1883, *van Gogh Letters*, http://vangoghletters.org/vg/letters/let364/letter.html.

117n7 ***to love people:*** Vincent to Theo van Gogh, Arles, 18 September 1888, *Self-portrait*, 329.

117n8 ***the Samaritan we all seek:*** Theo died six months after Vincent ended his life. See Feigelman et al., *Devastating Losses*, xv.

118n1 ***The Lord never tires:*** Pope Francis, 17 March 2013, in *Mercy*, 4.

118n2 ***Community is the fruit:*** Nouwen, *Bread,* January 4.

119 ***Faith is not:*** Heschel, *Grandeur,* 332.

CHRISTMAS DAY

121n1 ***In painting:*** Rehs Galleries (2018).

121n2 ***Each day:*** Bouguereau.org (2017).

122n1 ***higher intensities of grief:*** Sanders, 303–22; Hindmarch, 5, 30; Cleiren et al., 22–36; Middleton et al., 235-41; Leahy, 207–17.

122n2 ***the same conclusion:*** Knapp, 183.

122n3 **never get over it:** Gorer, 84, 85, 121–22; Buckle, 1; Tedeschi, *Helping,* 13.

122n4 ***there is no going back:*** Klass, *Parental Grief,* 120. See also Finkbeiner, 244; Leming, 497, 500; Knapp, 183; Attig, 13; Edelstein, 29; Janoff-Bulman, "Disillusionment," in Harvey, 35–47; Kauffman, 1–2.

122n5 ***first in the Bible:*** See Sandmel, 77; Kass, 149; Wiesel, "Adam and Eve," *Great Figures*; Wiesel, *Messengers,* 62.

123n1 ***Only people capable:*** Tolstoy, *Childhood,* 100. See Parkes, *Bereavement,* 28; Thompson et al., *Handbook,* 1; Shear, "Grief Is a Form of Love," in Neimeyer, *Techniques,* 15, 17, 18; Cooper, "Complicated Grief," in Stroebe et al., *Complicated Grief,* 17.

123n2 ***who do not believe:*** Klass, *Death Studies*, 17(4), 343–68.

123n3 ***incapable of sustaining belief:*** Knapp, 36.

125n1 ***Paralyzed and silent:*** Allende, *All Things Considered*, 4 April 2005; Allende, *This I Believe,* 14–15; edited.

125n2 ***God's intervention:*** Tournier, 172; edited.

125n3 ***Now the sun will rise:*** "Nun will die Sonne so hell aufgehn," Rückert, 369. Listen: Waltraud Meier, *Mahler* (RCA Legacy, 1999): track 6.

ABOUT THE RÜCKERT POEMS

127n1 ***The last of the grand:*** Taylor, *Atlantic*, 33; also Taylor, *Essays*, 92.

127n2 ***That I should drink:*** From "Daß ich trinken soll und essen," Rückert, 69.

127n3 ***Spare me these delights:*** From "Rathet mir nicht zum Vergnügen," Rückert, 142.

127n4 ***Some are his finest:*** See Revers, "*Kindertotenlieder,*" in Painter, *Mahler and His World*, 174.

127n5 ***pastel portraits:*** Friedrich had the portraits made in Autumn 1833.

127n6 ***Six years after:*** In 1881, after Heinrich's death, Marie Rückert rearranged 241 of the poems according to Friedrich's diary in a new edition, *Lied und Leid* [Song and Sorrow]. See Rückert, *Gesammelte*, 477.

127n7 ***his four-year-old daughter:*** Maria Anna, called Putzi, 3 November 1902–5 July 1907. See Gartenberg, *Mahler*, 115, 119; Lebrecht, *Why Mahler?*, 124, 145; Wildhagen, "*Das Lied von der Erde*," in Barham, *Mahler*, 135.

NOTES

128 ***Let the reader:*** *Saint Augustine*, ii.

BIBLIOGRAPHY

Papers, Journals, Periodicals, Documents, Audio/Video, and Internet Sources

Allende, Isabel, "In Giving I Connect With Others," *All Things Considered* (National Public Radio): 4 April 2005, https://www.npr.org/2005/04/04/4568464/in-giving-i-connect-with-others

Amishai-Maisels, Ziva, *Gauguin's Religious Themes*. Ph.D. diss., Hebrew University, Jerusalem, 1969 (Garland, 1985).

Anderson, Ross, "Angel in the Parlor: The Art of Abbott Thayer," *American Heritage*, 34(1) (1982).

Andrews, Catherine, and Sylvia Marotta-Waters, "Spirituality and Coping Among Grieving Children: A Preliminary Study," *Counseling and Values*, 50(1) (October, 2005): 38–50, https://doi.org/10.1002/j.2161–007X.2005.tb00039.x.

Ano, Gene, and Erin Vasconcelles, "Religious Coping and Psychological Adjustment to Stress: A Meta-analysis," *Journal of Clinical Psychology*, 61(4) (October, 2004): 461–480, https://doi.org/10.1002/jclp.20049.

Bailley, Steven, Michael Kral, Katherine Dunham, "Survivors of Suicide Do Grieve Differently: Empirical Support for a Common Sense Proposition," *Suicide and Life-Threatening Behavior*, 29(3) (Autumn, 1999), https://www.ncbi.nlm.nih.gov/pubmed/10531638.

Benore, Ethan, and Crystal Park, "Death-Specific Religious Beliefs and Bereavement: Belief in an Afterlife and Continued Attachment," *The International Journal for the Psychology of Religion,* 14(1) (2004): 1–22, https://doi.org/10.1207/s15327582ijpr1401_1.

bouguereau.org, "Biography of William-Adolphe Bouguereau" (2017): https://www.bouguereau.org/biography.html,edited.

Cain, Albert, Irene Fast, and Mary Erickson, "Children's Disturbed Reactions to the Death of a Sibling," *American Journal of Orthopsychiatry*, 34 (4) (July, 1964): 747, 741–52, http://dx.doi.org/10.1111/j.1939–0025.1964.tb02375.x.

Carrdus, Anna, "Consolation Arguments and Maternal Grief in Seventeenth-century Verse: The Example of Margarethe Susanna von Kuntsch," *German Life and Letters*, 47(2) (1994): 135–51, http://dx.doi.org/10.1111/j.1468–0483.1994.tb01526.x.

Cartwright, Julia, "The Garden of Hesperides," *The Art Journal, 1900* (H. Virtue & Co., 1900).

Cleiren, Marc, René Diekstra, Ad Kerkhof, Jan van der Wal, "Mode of Death and Kinship in Bereavement: Focusing on 'Who' rather than 'How'," *Crisis*, 15(1) (1994): 22–36, http://psycnet.apa.org/record/1994–41119–001.

——, Onja Grad, Anka Zavasnik, Rene Diekstra, "Psychosocial Impact of Bereavement after Suicide and Fatal Traffic Accident: A Comparative Two-country Study," *Acta Psychiatrica Scandinavica*, 94(1) (July, 1996): 37–44, https://doi.org/10.1111/j.1600–0447.1996.tb09822.x.

Cvinar, Jacqueline, "Do Suicide Survivors Suffer Social Stigma: A Review of the Literature," *Perspectives in Psychiatric Care*, 41(1) (January, 2005): 14–21, https://doi.org/10.1111/j.0031–5990.2005.00004.x.

David, Stacy, "Appearances of the Resurrected Jesus and the Experience of Grief," unpublished paper, Jesus Seminar, Santa Rosa, CA (1995).

Davies, Betty, John Spinetta, Ida Martinson, Sandra McClowry, Emily Kulenkamp, "Manifestations of Levels of Functioning in Grieving Families," *Journal of Family Issues*, 7(3) (September, 1986): 297–313, https://doi.org/10.1177/019251386007003005.

Eugene-Delacroix.com, "Jacob Wrestling with the Angel" (2010), http://www.eugene-delacroix.com/jacob-wrestling-with-the-angel.jsp.

——, "The Entombment" (2010), http://www.eugene-delacroix.com/the-entombment.jsp.

Farberow, Norman, Dolores Gallagher, Michael Gilewski, Larry Thompson, "An Examination of the Early Impact of Bereavement on Psychological Distress in Survivors of Suicide," *The Gerontologist*, 27(5) (October, 1987): 592–98, https://doi.org/10.1093/geront/27.5.592.

——, "The Los Angeles Survivors-After-Suicide Program: An Evaluation," *Crisis*, 13(1) (1992): 23–34, https://www.ncbi.nlm.nih.gov/pubmed/1395706.

Feigelman, William, John Jordan, Bernard Gorman, "Parental Grief after a Child's Drug Death Compared to Other Death Causes: Investigating a Greatly Neglected Bereavement Population," *Omega*, 63(4) (August, 2011), https://www.ncbi.nlm.nih.gov/pubmed/22010370.

Friends of the Dublin Art Colony, *Monadnock Art*, http://www.monadnockart.org/artists-past/abbott-handerson-thayer.

van Gogh, Vincent, Van Gogh Museum, *Vincent van Gogh: The Letters* (2018), http://vangoghletters.org/vg/.

Van Gogh Museum, "Brother Love: Vincent & Theo" (2018), https://www.vangoghmuseum.nl/en/stories/brotherly-love.

Greeley, Andrew, and Michael Hout, "Americans' Increasing Belief in Life after Death: Religious Competition and Acculturation," *American Sociological Review*, 64(6) (Dec., 1999): 813–35, http://www.jstor.org/stable/2657404.

Grout, Leslie, and Bronna Romanoff, "The Myth of the Replacement Child: Parents' Stories and Practices after Perinatal Death," *Death Studies*, 24(2) (2000): 93–113, http://dx.doi.org/10.1080/074811800200595.

Harwood, Daniel, Keith Hawton, Tony Hope, Robin Jacoby, "The Grief Experiences and Needs of Bereaved Relatives and Friends of Older People Dying through Suicide: A Descriptive and Case-Control Study," *Journal of Affective Disorders*, 72(2) (November, 2002): 185–94, https://doi.org/10.1016/S0165-0327(01)00462-1.

Hughes, Robert, "Caravaggio: Portrait of the Artist as a Bad Lot," *Horizon*, XVII(3) (Summer, 1975).

Jacobs, Jay, "Where Do We Come From? What Are We? Where Are We Going?", *Horizon*, XI(3) (Summer, 1969).

Kapoor, Anish, interviewed by Alastair Sooke, "'I Don't Know Where I'm Going,'" *The Telegraph* (26 September 2006), http://www.telegraph.co.uk/culture/art/3655568/I-dont-know-where-Im-going.html.

Klass, Dennis, "Solace and Immortality: Bereaved Parents' Continuing Bond with Their Children," *Death Studies*, 17(4) (July/August 1993): 343–68, https://www.tandfonline.com/doi/abs/10.1080/07481189308252630.

——, Samuel Marwit, "Toward a Model of Parental Grief," *Omega*, 19(1) (1988–1989): 33, http://dx.doi.org/10.2190/BVUR-67KR-F52F-VW35.

Klugman, Craig, "Dead Men Talking: Evidence of Post Death Contact and Continuing Bonds," *Omega*, 53(3) (2006): 249–62, https://doi.org/10.2190/40UP-PKC5-D4RV-E1QV.

Leahy, Julia, "A Comparison of Depression in Women Bereaved of a Spouse, Child, or a Parent," *Omega*, 26(3) (May, 1993): 207–17, https://doi.org/10.2190/YLG9-P4R7-W2VW-KAFR.

Li, Jie, Margaret Stroebe, Cecilia Chan, Amy Chow, "The Bereavement Guilt Scale: Development and Preliminary Validation," *Omega*, 75(2) (October, 2015): 1–18, https://www.researchgate.net/publication/307746082.

——, Margaret Stroebe, Cecilia Chan, Amy Chow, "Guilt in Bereavement: A Review and Conceptual Framework," *Death Studies* 38(3) (March, 2014): 165–71, https://www.researchgate.net/publication/260193605.

Lipsitt, Don, "The 'Dying Role': Its Time Had Come," *Psychiatry: Interpersonal and Biological Processes*, 79(3) (2016): 216–26, https://doi.org/10.1080/00332747.2016.1222198.

Louvre, *Death of the Virgin* (2018), https://www.louvre.fr/en/oeuvre-notices/death-virgin.

Mahler, Gustav, *Mahler: Kindertotenlieder, Rückert-Lieder* (RCA Legacy, 1999). https://archive.org/details/Kindertotenlieder1.NunWillDieSonnSoHellAufgehnmeierMaazel.

Martison, Ida, Betty Davies, Sandra McClowry, "Parental Depression Following the Death of a Child," *Death Studies,* 15(3) (1989): 259–67, http://www.tandfonline.com/doi/abs/10.1080/07481189108252429.

McBride, Joseph, and Steven Simms, "Death in the Family: Adapting a Family Systems Framework to the Grief Process," *The American Journal of Family Therapy*, 29(1) (2001): 59–73, https://doi.org/10.1080/01926180126032.

Merton, Thomas, "Answers on Art and Freedom," *Lugano Review*, 1(1) (1965).

Middleton, Warwick, Beverley Raphael, Nada Martinek, Paul Burnett, "A Longitudinal Study Comparing Bereavement Phenomena in Recently Bereaved Spouses, Adult Children and Parents," *Australian & New Zealand Journal of Psychiatry*, 32(2) (April, 1998): 235–41, http://journals.sagepub.com/doi/abs/10.3109/00048679809062734.

Mitchell, Ann, Yookyung Kim, Holly Prigerson, MaryKay Mortimer-Stephens, "Complicated Grief in Survivors of Suicide," *Crisis*, 25(1) (2004), http://dx.doi.org/10.1027/0227-5910.25.1.12.

Morabito, Adriano, interviewed by Maria Cristina Valsecchi, "Rome's Ancient Catacombs," *National Geographic* (21 January 2017): https://www.nationalgeographic.com/archaeology-and-history/archaeology/rome-catacombs/.

Morgan, Ted, "The Strange End of Vincent van Gogh," *Horizon*, XVI(4) (Autumn, 1974).

Murphy, Shirley, Clark Johnson, Lang Wu, Juan Fan, Janet Lohan, "Bereaved Parents' Outcomes 4 to 60 Months after Their Children's Deaths by Accident, Suicide, or Homicide: A Comparative Study Demonstrating Differences," *Death Studies*, 27(1) (2003): 39–61, https://doi.org/10.1080/07481180302871.

——, Ick-Joong Chung, L. Clark Johnson, "Patterns of Mental Distress Following the Violent Death of a Child and Predictors of Change over Time," *Research in Nursing & Health*, 25(6) (December, 2002): 425–37, https://doi.org/10.1002/nur.10060.

——, Clark Johnson, Ick-Joong Chung, Randal Beaton, "The Prevalence of PTSD Following the Violent Death of a Child and Predictors of Change 5 Years Later," *Journal of Traumatic Stress*, 16(1) (February, 2003), 17–25, https://doi.org/10.1023/A:1022003126168.

National Gallery of Art, "Mount Monadnock", https://www.nga.gov/Collection/art-object-page.166476.html.

Neimeyer, Robert, "Meaning Reconstruction in the Wake of Loss: Evolution of a Research Program," *Behaviour Change*, 33(2) (June, 2016): 65–79, https://doi.org/10.1017/bec.2016.4.

Packman, Wendy, Heidi Horsley, Betty Davies, Robin Kramer, "Sibling Bereavement and Continuing Bonds," *Death Studies*, 30(9) (November, 2006): 817–41, https://doi.org/10.1080/07481180600886603.

Palombo, Joseph, "Parent Loss and Childhood Bereavement: Some Theoretical Considerations," *Clinical Social Work Journal*, 9(1) (1981): 3–33, https://doi.org/10.1007/BF00757091.

Park, Crystal, "Religion as a Meaning-Making Framework in Coping with Life Stress," *Journal of Social Issues*, 61(4) (December, 2005): 707–29, doi:10.1111/j.1540-4560.2005.00428.x.

Plumb, J. H., "The Great Change in Children," *Horizon*, XIII(1) (Winter, 1971).

Rehs Galleries, "William A. Bouguereau" (2018): http://www.rehsgalleries.com/view_image.html?image_no=38.

Robertson, Frederick, "Typified by the Man of Sorrows, the Human Race," from an autograph manuscript: http://www.fwrobertson.org/sermons/ser94.htm.

Rosenblatt, Paul, Douglas Jackson, Rose Walsh, "Coping with Anger and Aggression in Mourning," *Omega*, 3(4) (January, 1973): 271–84, http://dx.doi.org/10.2190/MNMJ-G1QN-05U1-WVPA.

Sanders, Catherine, "A Comparison of Adult Bereavement in the Death of a Spouse, Child, and Parent," *Omega*, 10(4) (1980).

Schneider, Nathan, "The Angelus at Work," *America* (24 March 2015): https://www.americamagazine.org/content/all-things/angelus-work.

Shoor, Mervyn, and Mary Speed, "Delinquency as a Manifestation of the Mourning Process," *The Psychiatric Quarterly*, 37(3) (July, 1963): 540–58, http://dx.doi.org/10.1007/BF01617752.

Sim, Julius, Linda Machin, Bernadette Bartlam, "Identifying Vulnerability in Grief: Psychometric Properties of the Adult Attitude to Grief Scale," *Quality of Life Research*, 23(4) (May, 2014): 1211–20, https://www.ncbi.nlm.nih.gov/pubmed/24129670.

Solzhenitsyn, Alexandr, Nobel Media, "Alexandr Solzhenitsyn - Nobel Lecture". Nobelprize.org, AB 2014. Web 27 February 2018, http://www.nobelprize.org/nobel_prizes/literature/laureates/1970/solzhenitsyn-lecture.html.

Spratt, Mary, and Douglas Denney, "Immune Variables, Depression, and Plasma Cortisol over Time in Suddenly Bereaved Parents," *Journal of Neuropsychiatry and Clinical Neurosciences*, 3(3) (August, 1991): 299–306, https://doi.org/10.1176/jnp.3.3.299.

Stroebe, Wolfgang, Margaret Stroebe, Günther Domittner, "Individual and Situational Differences in Recovery from Bereavement: A Risk Group Identified," *Journal of Social Issues*, 44(3) (Fall, 1988): 143–58, https://doi.org/10.1111/j.1540-4560.1988.tb02082.x.

Taylor, Bayard, "Friedrich Rückert," *Atlantic Monthly*, 18, (105) (July 1866), collected in *The Atlantic Monthly*, v18 (Ticknor & Fields, 1866), https://archive.org/details/atlantic18bostuoft.

TIME Magazine, "The New Age of Angels," 142(27) (27 December 1993).

Toom, Victor, "Finding Closure, Continuing Bonds, and Codentification after the 9/11 Attacks," *Medical Anthropology: Cross-Cultural Studies in Health and Illness*, (June, 2017): 1–13, https://doi.org/10.1080/01459740.2017.1337118.

Twain, Mark, audio dictation and Notebook 40, University of California, Mark Twain Collection.

van Vurst, Jim, "Mary's Loneliness," *St. Anthony Messenger*, 123(8) (January 2016).

Vess, James, John Moreland, Andrew Schwebel, "Understanding Family Role Reallocation following a Death: A Theoretical Framework," *Omega*, 16(2) (March, 1986): 115–28, https://doi.org/10.2190/8DE3-UHG5-TUHV-QKK2.

Wiesel, Elie, *Great Figures of the Bible: Legends and Legacies of Our Biblical Heroes* (Yale Roe Films, public television air date 1999; DVD release, 2004).

Wright, N. T., transcribed from "Theology of Joy: N. T. Wright with Miroslav Volf." (Yale Center for Faith and Culture; Tübingen, Germany): 26 June 2014. Published on 24 September 2014. Italics added to indicate Wright's verbal emphases, https://www.youtube.com/watch?v=2u3PGZc8VsU [Minute 9:53-11:25].

Books

Al-Chokhachy, Elissa, *Our Children Live On: Miraculous Moments for the Bereaved* (Llewellyn, 2012).

Allende, Isabel, "In Giving I Connect with Others," *This I Believe: The Personal Philosophies of Remarkable Men and Women* (Henry Holt, 2007).

Alt, Albrecht, *Essays on Old Testament History and Religion*, trans. R. A. Wilson (Doubleday, 1968).

Anderson, Ross, *Abbott Handerson Thayer* (Everson Museum, 1982).

Anderson, Wayne Vesti, *Gauguin's Paradise Lost* (Viking ebook, 1971, 2013).

Ariès, Philippe, *Centuries of Childhood: A Social History of Family Life [L'Enfant et la vie familiale sous l'Ancien Régime]*, trans. Robert Baldick (Knopf, 1962).

——, *Western Attitudes toward Death: From the Middle Ages to the Present [Essais sur l'histoire de la mort en Occident: du Moyen Âge à nos jours]*, trans. Patricia Ranum (Johns Hopkins University Press, 1975).

Aron, Elaine, *The Highly Sensitive Person* (Birch Lane, 1996).

Attig, Thomas, *How We Grieve: Relearning the World* (Oxford University Press, 1996).

Auden, W. H., *Collected Poems*, ed. Edward Mendelson (Modern Library, 2007).

——, *The Complete Works of W.H. Auden: Prose*, vIV, 1956–1962, ed. Edward Mendelson (Princeton University Press, 2010).

Augustine, *Saint Augustine*, ed. and trans. Garry Wills (Penguin, 1999).

Bade, Patrick, *Edward Burne-Jones* (Parkstone, 2011).

Baillie, John, *A Diary of Readings* (Scribner's Sons, 1955).

——, *The Sense of the Presence of God: Gifford Lectures, 1961–1962* (Scribner's, 1962).

Barham, Jeremy, ed., *The Cambridge Companion to Mahler*, Wildhagen section trans. Barham and Trefor Smith (Cambridge University Press, 2007).

Berenson, Bernard, *Caravaggio: His Incongruity and His Fame* (Chapman & Hall, 1953).

Berger-Zell, Carmen, *Abwesend und doch präsent: Wandlungen der Trauerkultur in Deutschland* (Neukirchener Theologie, 2013).

Bernstein, Judith, *When the Bough Breaks: Forever After the Death of a Son or Daughter* (Andrews and McMeel, 1997).

Besançon, Alain, *The Forbidden Image: An Intellectual History of Iconoclasm* (University of Chicago Press, 2000).

Birch, Bruce, Walter Brueggemann, Terence Fretheim, David Peterson, *A Theological Introduction to the Old Testament* (Abgindon Press, 1999).

Blainey, Geoffrey, *A Short History of Christianity* (Rowman & Littlefield ebook, 2011).

Bogousslavsky, Julien, and François Boller, eds., *Neurological Disorders in Famous Artists,* Frontiers of Neurology and Neuroscience, 19 (Karger, 2005).

Boime, Albert, *A Social History of Modern Art, v2: Art in an Age of Bonapartism, 1800–1815* (University of Chicago Press, 1990).

Bonhoeffer, Dietrich, *Dietrich Bonhoeffer's Christmas Sermons,* ed. and trans. Edwin Robertson (Zondervan, 2005).

de Borchgrave, Helen, *A Journey into Christian Art* (Fortress Press, 1999, 2000).

Borg, Marcus, *Jesus: Uncovering the Life, Teachings, and Relevance of a Religious Revolutionary* (HarperOne, 2006).

Boswell, John, *The Kindness of Strangers: The Abandonment of Children in Western Europe from Late Antiquity to the Renaissance* (Pantheon, 1988).

Broude, Norma, ed., *Gauguin's Challenge: New Perspectives After Postmodernism* (Bloomsbury, 2018).

Brunner, Bernd, *Inventing the Christmas Tree*, trans. Benjamin Smith (Yale University Press, 2012).

Buckle, Jennifer, and Stephen Fleming, *Parenting After the Death of a Child: A Practitioner's Guide* (Routledge, 2010).

Buechner, Frederick, *Peculiar Treasures: A Biblical Who's Who* (HaperSanFrancisco, 1979).

——, *Secrets in the Dark: A Life in Sermons* (HarperSanFrancisco, 2006).

——, *Telling the Truth: The Gospel as Tragedy, Comedy, and Fairy Tale* (HarperCollins, 1977).

——, *Whistling in the Dark: An ABC Theologized* (Harper & Row, 1988).

Byron, George Gordon, *Manfred: A Dramatic Poem*, 1, i, 7–11 (John Murray, 1817), https://archive.org/details/manfreddramaticp02byro.

Cain, Albert, ed., *Survivors of Suicide* (Thomas, 1972).

Cain, Susan, *Quiet: The Power of Introverts in a World That Can't Stop Talking* (Crown, 2012).

Calhoun, Lawrence, and Richard Tedeschi, *Posttraumatic Growth in Clinical Practice* (Routledge ebook, 2013).

——, Richard Tedeschi, eds., *Handbook of Posttraumatic Growth: Research and Practice* (Routledge, 2014).

Callard-Szulgit, Rosemary, *Perfectionism and Gifted Children*, 2nd ed. (Rowman & Littlefield, 2012).

Canciani, Domenico, *L'intelligence et l'amour: Réflexion religieuse et expérience mystique chez Simone Weil,* trans. D. Bannon (Beauchesne, 2000).

Carr, Edward Hallett, *What Is History?* (Vintage Books, 1961).

de Caussade, Jean-Pierre, *The Sacrament of the Present Moment*, trans. Kitty Muggeridge (HarperOne, 1989).

Clark, Gillian, *Christianity and Roman Society* (Cambridge University Press, 2004).

Cleiren, Marc, *Adaptation After Bereavement: A Comparative Study of the Aftermath of Death from Suicide, Traffic Accident, and Illness for Next of Kin* (Leiden University Press, 1991).

Corn, Alfred, *Incarnation: Contemporary Writers on the New Testament* (Viking, 1990).

Corr, Charles, and David Balk, ed., *Children's Encounters with Death, Bereavement, and Coping* (Springer, 2010).

——, and Donna Corr, ed., *Handbook of Childhood Death and Bereavement* (Springer, 1996).

Crossan, John Dominic, *The Birth of Christianity: Discovering What Happened in the Years Immediately After the Execution of Jesus* (HarperCollins ebooks, 1998).

——, *The Essential Jesus: What Jesus Really Taught* (HarperSanFrancisco, 1994).

Crowther, Paul, *How Pictures Complete Us: The Beautiful, the Sublime, and the Divine* (Stanford University Press ebook, 2016).

Dali, Salvador, *The Secret Life of Salvador Dali*, trans. Haakon M. Chevalier (Dial Press, 1942), https://archive.org/details/in.ernet.dli.2015.76092.

Danto, Arthur, *Unnatural Wonders: Essays from the Gap between Art & Life* (Columbia University Press, 2005).

Davies, Douglas, *Death, Ritual and Belief: The Rhetoric of Funerary Rites*, 3rd ed. (Bloomsbury Academic, 2017).

Dickinson, George, Michael Leming, Alan Mermann, *Dying, Death, and Bereavement 98/99* 4th ed. (McGraw-Hill, 1998).

Diderot, Denis, *Diderot on Art II: The Salon of 1767*, trans. John Goodman (Yale University Press, 1995).

——, *Œuvres de Denis Diderot: Salons*, Tome II (J.L.J. Brière, 1821).

Dodwell, C. R., ed., *Essays on Dürer* (Manchester University Press/University of Toronto Press, 1973).

Doka, Kenneth, ed., *Disenfranchised Grief: New Directions, Challenges, and Strategies for Practice* (Research Press, 2002).

——, ed., *Disenfranchised Grief: Recognizing Hidden Sorrow* (Lexington, 1989).
——, *Grief Is a Journey: Finding Your Path Through Loss* (Atria, 2016).
——, and Terry Martin, *Grieving Beyond Gender: Understanding the Ways Men and Women Mourn*, rev. ed. (Routledge ebook, 2010).
——, ed., *Living with Grief: Children, Adolescents, and Loss* (Routledge, 2000).
——, and Amy Tucci, eds., *Living with Grief: Children and Adolescents* (Hospice Foundation of America, 2008).
——, ed., *Living with Grief: Loss in Later Life* (Hospice Foundation of America, 2002).
Dolkart, Judith, *James Tissot: The Life of Christ* (Merrill, 2009).
Dues, Greg, *Catholic Customs & Traditions: A Popular Guide* (Twenty-Third Publications, 1989).
Dyregrov, Kari, and Atle Dyregrov, *Effective Grief and Bereavement Support: The Role of Family, Friends, Colleagues, Schools and Support Professionals* (Kingsley, 2008).
Eberlein, Kurt, ed., *Caspar David Friedrich: Bekenntnisse* (Klinkhardt & Biermann, 1924).
Edelstein, Linda, *Maternal Bereavement: Coping with the Unexpected Death of a Child* (Praeger, 1984).
Eimer, Gerhard, with Günther Rath, eds., *Kritische Edition der Schriften des Künstlers und seiner Zeitzeugen*, v1 (Kunstgeschichtliches Institut der Johann Wolfgang Goethe-Universität, 1999).
Faulkner, Barry, *Sketches from an Artist's Life* (Bauhan, 1973).
Feigelman, William, John Jordan, John McIntosh, Beverly Feigelman, *Devastating Losses: How Parents Cope with the Death of a Child to Suicide or Drugs* (Springer, 2012).
Ferngren, Gary, *Medicine and Health Care in Early Christianity* (Johns Hopkins University Press, 2009).
Finkelstein, Israel, and Neil Asher Silberman, *David and Solomon: In Search of the Bible's Sacred Kings and the Roots of the Western Tradition* (Free Press ebook, 2006).
Finkbeiner, Ann, *After the Death of a Child: Living with Loss through the Years* (Johns Hopkins University Press, 1996).
Flanders, Judith, *Christmas: A Biography* (Thomas Dunne, 2017).
Forsyth, P.T., *The Person and Place of Jesus Christ* (Hodder & Stoughton, 1909).
Freeman, Charles, *A New History of Early Christianity* (Yale University Press ebook, 2009).
Pope Francis, *The Church of Mercy: A Vision for the Church* (Loyola Press, 2014).
——, *The Name of God Is Mercy*, trans. Oonagh Stransky (Penguin Random House ebook, 2016).
Frängsmyr, Tore, and Sture Allén, *Nobel Lectures, Literature 1968–1980* (World Scientific Publishing Co., 1993).
Fretheim, Terence, *The Suffering of God: An Old Testament Perspective* (Fortress, 1984).
Gartenberg, Egon, *Mahler: The Man and His Music* (Schirmer, 1978).

Gatrall, Jefferson, *The Real and the Sacred: Picturing Jesus in Nineteenth-Century Fiction* (University of Michigan Press, 2014).

Gies, Francis, and Joseph Gies, *Marriage and the Family in the Middle Ages* (Harper Perennial, 1988).

van Gogh, Vincent, *The Complete Letters of Vincent van Gogh, v3* (Little, Brown and Co., 1958), https://archive.org/details/completeletterso03gogh.

——, *The Letters of Vincent van Gogh*, ed. Ronald de Leeuw, trans. Arnold Pomeran (Penguin ebook, 1996).

——, *Van Gogh: A Self-Portrait—Letters Revealing His Life as a Painter*, ed. and trans. W. H. Auden (New York Graphic Society, 1961), https://archive.org/details/vangoghselfportr00gogh.

Goldwater, Robert, *Paul Gauguin* (Harry N. Abrams, 1983).

Goodall, Jane, *Reason for Hope: A Spiritual Journey*, with Phillip Berman (Warner, 1999).

Gorer, Geoffrey, *Death, Grief, and Mourning* (Doubleday, 1965).

Graham-Dixon, Andrew, *Caravaggio: A Life Sacred and Profane* (WW Norton, 2010).

Grant, Michael, *Jesus: An Historian's Review of the Gospels* (Scribner's Sons, 1977).

Grayzel, Solomon, *A History of the Jews: From the Babylonian Exile to the Present, 5728–1968*, new rev. ed. (Meridian, 1947, 1968).

Groeschel, Benedict, *Behold, He Comes: Meditations on the Incarnation* (St. Anthony Messenger Press, 2001).

Hansen, James, and Thomas Frantz, *Death and Grief in the Family*, The Family Therapy Collections, v8 (Aspen Systems Corporation, 1984).

Harvey, John, ed., *Perspectives on Loss: A Sourcebook* (Psychology Press, 1998).

Haugk, Kenneth, *Experiencing Grief: Journeying through Grief, Book Two* (Stephen Ministries, 2004).

Hay, David, *Religious Experience Today: Studying the Facts* (Mowbray, 1990).

Herrick, Robert, *Hesperides or Works Both Human and Divine of Robert Herrick*, 2nd ed. (Routledge, 1885), https://archive.org/details/hesperidesorwork00herr.

Heschel, Abraham, *Man's Quest for God: Studies in Prayer and Symbolism* (Scribner's, 1954).

——, *Moral Grandeur and Spiritual Audacity*: *Essays,* ed. Susannah Heschel (Farrar, Straus and Giroux, 1997).

Hindmarch, Celia, *On the Death of a Child*, 3rd ed. (Radcliffe, 2009).

Hollingsworth, Mary, *Art in World History,* trans. Julia Weiss (Routledge ebook, 2004).

Howes, Graham, *The Art of the Sacred: An Introduction to the Aesthetics of Art and Belief* (I. B. Tauris, 2007).

Hurley, Michael, *Faith in Poetry: Verse Style as a Mode of Religious Belief* (Bloomsbury, 2018).

Hutchison, Jane Campbell, *Albrecht Dürer: A Biography* (Princeton University Press, 1990).

Janoff-Bulman, Ronnie, *Shattered Assumptions: Towards a New Psychology of Trauma* (Free Press, 2002).

Jeanne d'Arc, *Histoire complète de Jeanne d'Arc: du procès qui l'a condamnée et de sa réhabilitation*, v3, ed. Philippe-Hector Dunand, trans. D. Bannon (Édouard Privat, 1899), https://archive.org/details/HistoireCompleteDeJeanneDArc3

Jefferson, Lee, *Christ the Miracle Worker in Early Christian Art* (Fortress Press, 2014).

Jeffreys, J. Shep, *Helping Grieving People - When Tears Are Not Enough: A Handbook for Care Providers*, 2nd ed. (Routledge, 2011).

Jensen, Robin, *The Cross: History, Art, and Controversy* (Harvard University Press, 2017).

——, *Understanding Early Christian Art* (Routledge, 2000, ebook 2011).

Joan of Arc, see *Jeanne d'Arc.*

John Damascene, *On Holy Images,* trans. Mary H. Allies (Thomas Baker, 1898), https://archive.org/details/stjohndamasceneo00alliuoft.

Jordon, John, and John McIntosh, eds., *Grief After Suicide: Understanding the Consequences and Caring for the Survivors* (Routledge, 2015).

Julian of Norwich, *Revelation of Love,* ed. and trans. John Skinner (Image/Doubleday, 1997).

——, *The Shewings of Julian of Norwich*, ed. Georgia Ronan Crampton (Medieval Institute Publications, 1994), http://d.lib.rochester.edu/teams/text/the-shewings-of-julian-of-norwich-part-1#936.

Jung, Carl, *Erinnerungen, Träume, Gedanken von C.G. Jung*, aufgezeichnet und herausgegeben von Aniela Jaffé, translated by D. Bannon (Rascher, 1962), https://archive.org/details/erinnerungentr00jung.

Kandinsky, Wassily, *Concerning the Spiritual in Art*, trans. Michael Sadler, https://archive.org/details/TheSpiritualInArtByWassilyKandinsky.

——, *Du Spirituel dans l'art et dans la peinture en particulier*, trans. D. Bannon (Gallimard, 1988).

——, *On the Spiritual in Art*, trans. and ed. Hilla Rebay (Solomon Guggenheim Foundation, 1946), https://archive.org/details/onspiritualinart00kand.

Kass, Leon, *The Beginning of Wisdom: Reading Genesis* (Free Press, 2003).

Katz, Steven, ed., *The Cambridge History of Judaism, v4: The Late Roman-Rabbinic Period* (Cambridge University Press, 2006).

Kauffman, Jeffrey, ed., *Loss of the Assumptive World: A Theory of Traumatic Loss* (Brunner-Routledge, 2002).

Keller, Hiltgart, and Bodo Cichy, *20 Centuries of Great European Painting: A Collection of Masterpieces* (Sterling, 1957).

Kessler, Herbert, and David Nirenberg, eds., *Judaism and Christian Art: Aesthetic Anxieties from the Catacombs to Colonialism* (University of Pennsylvania Press, 2013).

Kierkegaard, Søren, *The Soul of Kierkegaard: Selections from His Journals,* ed. and trans. Alexander Dru (Dover, 2003).

King, Barbara, *How Animals Grieve* (University of Chicago Press ebook, 2013).

Klass, Dennis, Phyllis Silverman, Steven Nickman, eds., *Continuing Bonds: New Understandings of Grief* (Taylor & Francis, 1996).

—— and Edith Steffen, eds., *Continuing Bonds in Bereavement: New Directions for Research and Practice* (Routledge ebook, 2017).

——, *Parental Grief: Solace and Resolution* (Springer, 1988).

Knapp, Ronald, *Beyond Endurance: When a Child Dies* (Schocken Books, 1986).

Koerner, Joseph Leo, *Caspar David Friedrich and the Subject of Landscape*, 2nd ed. (Reaktion Books, 1990; 2nd revised digital ed., 2009).

Kselman, John, interviewed by Bill Moyers, *Genesis: A Living Conversation* (Doubleday, 1996).

Kugel, James, *The God of Old: Inside the Lost World of the Bible* (Free Press, 2003).

Kushner, Harold, *When Bad Things Happen to Good People* (Avon, 1981).

La Grange, Henry-Louis de, *Mahler, v2: The Years of Challenge, 1897–1904* (Oxford University Press, 1995).

Brother Lawrence, Laurent de la Résurrection (Frère Laurent), *Maximes spirituelles fort utiles aux âmes pieuses, pour acquérir la présence de Dieu* (Edme Couterot, 1692).

——, *Practicing the Presence of God*, trans. Robert Edmonson (Paraclete, 2007).

——, *The Practice of the Presence of God,* trans. Mary David (Newman, 1945; Paulist, 1978).

——, *The Practice of the Presence of God*, trans. John Delaney (Image, 1977).

Lebrecht, Norman, *Why Mahler? How One Man and Ten Symphonies Changed Our World* (Pantheon, 2010).

Leming, Michael, and George Dickinson, *Understanding Dying, Death, & Bereavement,* 5th ed. (Harcourt, 2002).

Lewis, C. S., *The Collected Letters of C.S. Lewis, vII: Books, Broadcasts, and the War, 1931–1949,* ed. Walter Hooper (HarperCollins ebooks, 2004, 2009).

——, *The Collected Letters of C.S. Lewis vIII: Narnia, Cambridge, and Joy 1950–1963,* ed. Walter Hooper (HarperCollins, 2007).

Liberman, Alexander, *The Artist in His Studio* (Random House, 1988).

Linton, Anna, *Poetry and Parental Bereavement in Early Modern Lutheran Germany* (Oxford University Press, 2008).

Loh, Maria, *Still Lives: Death, Desire, and the Portrait of the Old Master* (Princeton University Press, 2015).

Longfellow, Henry Wadsworth, ed., *Poems of Places: America, New England, vII* (Houghton, Mifflin & Co, 1881), https://archive.org/details/poemsofplaces26long.

——, *Poems of Henry Wadsworth Longfellow* (Crowell, 1901), https://archive.org/details/poemsofhenrywads00long.

Luther, Martin, *Luther: Letters of Spiritual Counsel*, ed. and trans. Theodore Tappert (Regent College, 2003).

——, *Luther on Women: A Sourcebook*, trans. Susan Karant-Nunn Merry Wiesner-Hanks (Cambridge University Press, 2003).

——, *Martin Luther: Selections from His Writings*, ed. John Dillenberger (Anchor Books, 1961).

Macy, Joanna, and Anita Barrows, trans. and eds., *A Year with Rilke: Daily Readings from the Best of Rainer Maria Rilke* (HarperOne, 2009). See also https://onbeing.org/programs/joanna-macy-wild-love-world/.

Malchiodi, Cathy, *The Art Therapy Sourcebook*, 2nd ed. (McGraw-Hill, 2006).

Marshall, Nancy Rose, and Malcolm Warner, *James Tissot: Victorian Life/Modern Love* (Yale University Press, 1999).

Martin, James, *Becoming Who You Are: Insights on the True Self from Thomas Merton and Other Saints* (Paulist Press, 2006).

Mathews, Marcia, *Henry Ossawa Tanner: American Artist* (University of Chicago Press, 1969).

Maximus, Valerius, *Memorable Deeds and Sayings: One Thousand Tales from Ancient Rome*, trans. Henry John Walker (Hackett, 2004).

May, Gerald, *Addiction & Grace: Love and Spirituality in the Healing of Addictions* (HarperOne, 1988).

May, Rollo, *The Cry of Myth* (Delta, 1991).

McCoyd, Judith, and Carolyn Ambler Walter, *Grief and Loss Across the Lifespan: A Biopsychosocial Perspective*, 2nd ed. (Springer, 2016).

McGoldrick, Monica, and Froma Walsh, *Living Beyond Loss: Death in the Family*, 2nd ed. (W.W. Norton, 2004).

McNiel, Andy, and Pamela Gabbay, *Understanding and Supporting Bereaved Children: A Practical Guide for Professionals* (Springer, 2017).

Merton, Thomas, *From the Monastery to the World: The Letters of Thomas Merton and Ernesto Cardenal,* trans. Jessie Sandoval (Counterpoint ebook, 2017).

——, *The Literary Essays of Thomas Merton,* ed. Patrick Hart (New Directions, 1981).

——, *New Seeds of Contemplation* (New Directions, 1962).

——, *Raids on the Unspeakable* (New Directions, 1966).

——, *A Search for Solitude: The Journals of Thomas Merton*, v3, 1952–1960, ed. Lawrence Cunningham (HarperSanFrancisco, 1996).

Miles, Clement, *Christmas in Ritual and Tradition, Christian and Pagan* (Unwin, 1912), https://archive.org/details/christmasinritua00mile_0.

Morgan, David, *The Forge of Vision: A Visual History of Modern Christianity* (University of California Press, 2015).

Mühlberger, Richard, *The Christmas Story: Told through Paintings* (The Metropolitan Museum of Art/Gulliver Books, 1990).

Murray, Alexandar, *Suicide in the Middle Ages* (Oxford University Press, 1998).

Nassar, Dalia, ed., *The Relevance of Romanticism: Essays on German Romantic Philosophy* (Oxford University Press, 2014).

Neimeyer, Robert, Darcy Harris, Howard Winokuer, Gordon Thornton, eds., *Grief and Bereavement in Contemporary Society: Bridging Research and Practice* (Routledge, 2011).

——, *Lessons of Loss: A Guide to Coping* (Center for the Study of Loss and Transition, 2006).

——, ed., *Techniques of Grief Therapy: Assessment and Intervention*, (Routledge, 2015).

Noble, Bonnie, *Lucas Cranach the Elder: Art and Devotion of the German Reformation* (University Press of America, 2009).

Nouwen, Henri J.M., *Bread for the Journey: A Daybook of Wisdom and Faith* (HarperOne, 1997).

——, *The Essential Henri Nouwen*, ed. and introduction by Robert Jonas (Shambhala ebook, 2011).

——, *Love, Henri: Letters of the Spiritual Life*, ed. Gabrielle Earnshaw (Convergent Penguin ebook, 2016).

Nussbaum, Martha, *Upheavals of Thought: The Intelligence of Emotions* (Cambridge University Press, 2001).

O'Donohue, John, *Anam Cara* (HarperCollins, 1997; epub ed., 2008).

——, *Eternal Echoes: Exploring Our Yearning to Belong* (HarperCollins, 1999).

Otto, Rudolph, *The Idea of the Holy,* trans. John Harvey (Oxford University Press, 1923, 1979).

Ozment, Stephen, *The Serpent and the Lamb: Cranach, Luther, and the Making of the Reformation* (Yale University Press, 2011).

Painter, Karen, ed., *Mahler and His World,* Revers section trans. Irene Zedlacher (Princeton University Press, 2002).

Panofsky, Erwin, *Tomb Sculpture: Four Lectures on Its Changing Aspects from Ancient Egypt to Bernini*, ed. H.W. Janson (Abrams, 1964).

Parkes, Colin, and Holly Prigerson, *Bereavement: Studies of Grief in Adult Life*, 4th ed. (Routledge ebook, 2010).

——, Joan Stevenson-Hinde, Peter Marris, eds., *Attachment across the Life Cycle*, (Routledge, 1991).

Peale, Norman Vincent, *The Healing of Sorrow* (Inspiration Book Service/Doubleday, 1966).

Pearlman, Laurie Ann, Camille Wortman, Catherine Feuer, Christine Farber, Theresa Rando, *Treating Traumatic Bereavement: A Practitioner's Guide* (Guilford Press, 2014).

Peppers, Larry, and Ronald Knapp, *Motherhood & Mourning: Perinatal Death* (Praeger, 1980).

Phillips, John Bertram, *Ring of Truth: A Translator's Testimony* (Hodder & Stoughton, 1967).

Pollock, Linda, *Forgotten Children: Parent-Child Relations from 1500 to 1900* (Cambridge University Press, 1984).

Prideaux, Tom, *The World of Delacroix: 1798–1863*, rev. ed. (Time-Life Books, 1972).

Rando, Therese, *How to Go on Living When Someone You Love Dies* (Bantam, 1988).

——, ed., *Parental Loss of a Child* (Research Press, 1986).

Redfern, Suzanne, and Susan Gilbert, *The Grieving Garden: Living with the Death of a Child* (Hampton Roads, 2008).

Remen, Rachel Naomi, *My Grandfather's Blessings: Stories of Strength, Refuge, and Belonging* (Riverhead, 2000).

Ricci, Corrado, *Antonio Allegri da Correggio: His Life, His Friends, and His Time,* translated from the Italian by Florence Simmonds (Heinemann, 1896), https://archive.org/details/antonioallegrida00riccuoft.

Roach, Sally, and Beatriz Nieto, *Healing and The Grief Process* (Delmar, 1997).

Rohr, Richard, *Breathing Under Water: Spirituality and the Twelve Steps* (St. Anthony Messenger Press, 2011).

Rosenblatt, Paul, *Bitter, Bitter Tears: Nineteenth-Century Diarists and Twentieth Century Grief Theories* (University of Minnesota Press, 1983).

——, *Help Your Marriage Survive the Death of a Child* (Temple University Press, 2000).

——, *Parent Grief: Narratives of Loss and Relationship* (Routledge, 2000).

Ross, Ellen, *The Grief of God: Images of the Suffering Jesus in Late Medieval England* (Oxford University Press, 1997).

Rossetti, Christina, *The Poetical Works of Christina Georgina Rossetti*, with memoir and notes &c by William Rossetti (MacMillan, 1904), https://archive.org/details/poeticalworksofc00ross.

Rosof, Barbara, *The Worst Loss: How Families Heal from the Death of a Child* (Henry Holt, 1994).

Rückert, Friedrich, *Kindertodtenlieder* [Songs on the Death of Children], ed. Heinrich Rückert, trans. D. Bannon (Sauerländer, 1872), https://archive.org/details/bub_gb_d8I4AQAAMAAJ.

——, *Gesammelte Poetische Werke*, v12, ed. Conrad Beyer (Sauerländer, 1882), https://archive.org/details/gesammeltepoetis12rc.

Russell, Francis, *The World of Dürer: 1471–1528* (Time-Life Books, 1967).

Russell, Peter, *Light in Battle with Darkness: Mahler's Kindertotenlieder* (Lang,1991).

Sand, Ilse, *Highly Sensitive People in an Insensitive World: How to Create a Happy Life*, trans. Elisabeth Svanholmer (Jessica Kingsley, 2016).

Sandmel, Samuel, *The Enjoyment of Scripture: The Law, the Prophets and the Writings* (Oxford University Press, 1972).

Schaff, Philip, and Henry Wace, eds., Gregory the Great, *Ad Serenum Massiliensem episcopum*, Migne's patrology, v77, cols. 1128–30, *A Select Library of Nicene and Post Nicene Fathers of the Christian Church*, ser. 2, v13, ed., trans. James Barmby (Christian Literature Company, 1898), https://archive.org/details/selectlibraryofn13schaff.

Schama, Simon, *The Story of the Jews, v1: Finding the Words, 1000BC–1492AD* (HarperCollins EPub Ed., 2014).

Schiff, Harriet Sarnoff, *The Bereaved Parent* (Penguin, 1977).

Schneider, Pierre, *The World of Watteau: 1684–1721*, rev. ed. (Time-Life Books, 1977).

Seigal, Catherine, *Bereaved Parents and Their Continuing Bonds: Love after Death* (Kingsley, 2017).

Seward, Desmond, *Caravaggio: A Passionate Life* (Thistle, 2013).

Shakespeare, William, *Othello, the Moor of Venice*, I, iii (Ginn and Co., 1881), https://archive.org/details/shakespearesothe02shak.

Shelley, Percy Bysshe, *The Poetical Works of Percy Bysshe Shelley*, edited by H. Buxton Forman, v5 (Bell & Sons, 1892), https://archive.org/details/poeticalworkspe02goog.

Smedes, Lewis, *My God and I: A Spiritual Memoir* (Eerdmans, 2003).

Spoto, Donald, *Joan: The Mysterious Life of the Heretic Who Became a Saint* (HarperSanFrancisco, 2007).

Staudacher, Carol, *Beyond Grief: A Guide to Recovering from the Death of a Loved One* (New Harbinger, 1987).

Stephenson, John, *Death, Grief, and Mourning: Individual and Social Realities* (Free Press, 1985).

Stillion, Judith, and Thomas Attig, eds., *Death, Dying, and Bereavement: Contemporary Perspectives, Institutions, and Practices*, (Springer, 2014).

Stokstad, Marilyn, and Michael Cothren, *Art History*, v1, 5th ed. (Pearson, 2014).

Stroebe, Margaret, Henk Schut, Jan van den Bout, eds., *Complicated Grief: Scientific Foundations for Health Care Professionals* (Routledge, 2012).

——, Robert Hansson, Wolfgang Stroebe, Henk Schut, eds., *Handbook of Bereavement Research: Consequences, Coping, and Care* (American Psychological Association, 2001). Rubin and Malkinson citation: http://dx.doi.org/10.1037/10436-009.

Tanner, Henry Ossawa, "The Story of an Artist's Life II: Recognition," in *The World's Work: A History of Our Time*, vXVIII, May to October 1909 (Doubleday, 1909): 11769–75.

Tatlock, Lynne, ed., *Enduring Loss in Early Modern Germany: Cross Disciplinary Perspectives* (Brill, 2010).

Taylor, Barbara Brown, *Learning to Walk in the Dark* (HarperOne, 2014).

Taylor, Bayard, *Critical Essays and Literary Notes* (Putnam's Sons, 1880), https://archive.org/details/criticalessaysli00tayluoft.

Tedeschi, Richard, and Lawrence Calhoun, *Helping Bereaved Parents: A Clinician's Guide* (Routledge, 2003).

Telushkin, Joseph, *Jewish Literacy: The Most Important Things to Know About the Jewish Religion, Its People, and Its History* (William Morrow, 1991).

——, *Jewish Wisdom* (HarperCollins ebook, 1994).

Tennyson, Alfred, *In Memoriam*, 4th ed. (Moxon, 1851), https://archive.org/details/inmemoriambyate00barogoog.

Mother Teresa, *A Call to Mercy: Hearts to Love, Hands to Serve* (Image, 2016).

Thompson, Barbara, and Robert Neimeyer, eds., *Grief and the Expressive Arts: Practices for Creating Meaning* (Routledge ebook, 2014).

Thompson, Neil, Gerry Cox, Robert Stevenson, eds., *Handbook of Traumatic Loss: A Guide to Theory and Practice* (Routledge, 2017).

Thorley, David, *Writing Illness and Identity in Seventeenth-Century Britain* (Palgrave MacMillan, 2016).

Thylmann, Karl, *Karl Thylmann, Briefe* [*Karl Thylmann, Letters (to Joanna Thylmann)*], ed. Joanna Thylmann, trans. D. Bannon (Privately published, Hohmann, c. 1919), https://babel.hathitrust.org/cgi/pt?id=uc1.b4902665.

Tillich, Paul, *The Courage to Be* (Yale University Press, 1952).

——, *The Eternal Now* (Scribners, 1963).

Tolstoy, Leo, *Childhood, Boyhood, Youth*, trans. Rosemary Edmonds (Penguin, 1964), https://archive.org/details/childhoodboyhood00leot.

——, *What Is Art?*, trans. Aylmer Maude (Crowell, 1899): 50, https://archive.org/details/whatisart00tols.

Tournier, Paul, *The Person Reborn,* trans. Edwin Hudson (Heinemann, 1966).

Tuck, Steven, *A History of Roman Art* (Wiley & Sons, 2015).

Twain, Mark, *Autobiography of Mark Twain*, v1, ed. Harriet Elinor Smith (University of California Press, 2010).

Varriano, John, *Italian Baroque and Rococo Architecture* (Oxford University Press, 1986).

Vauchez, André, *Francis of Assisi: The Life and Afterlife of a Medieval Saint,* trans. Michael Cusato (Yale University Press English ed. ebook, 2012).

Vaughn, William, *Caspar David Friedrich: 1774–1840*, exhibition catalogue (Tate Gallery, 1972).

Ward, Terence, *The Guardian of Mercy: How an Extraordinary Painting by Caravaggio Changed an Ordinary Life Today* (Arcade, 2016).

Werner, Emmy, and Ruth Smith, *Vulnerable but Invincible: A Study of Resilient Children and Youth* (McGraw-Hill, 1982).

Wiesel, Elie, *The Gates of the Forest*, trans. Frances Frenaye (Schocken, 1966).

——, *Messengers of God: Biblical Portraits and Legends*, trans. Marion Wiesel (Simon & Schuster, 1976).

Wieseltier, Leon, *Kaddish* (Vintage, 1998).

Wilken, Robert Louis, *The First Thousand Years: A Global History of Christianity* (Yale University Press, 2012).

Willard, Dallas, *The Divine Conspiracy: Rediscovering Our Hidden Life in God* (HarperCollins ebooks, 1997, epub ed., 2009)

——, *Renovation of the Heart: Putting on the Character of Christ* (NavPress, 2002).

Williamson, Beth, *Christian Art: A Very Short Introduction* (Oxford University Press, 2004).

Withrow, William Henry, *The Catacombs of Rome, and Their Testimony Relative to Primitive Christianity* (Hodder and Stoughton, 1888), https://archive.org/details/catacombsofromet00withuoft.

Wohlleben, Peter, *The Inner Life of Animals: Love, Grief, and Compassion*, trans. Jane Billinghurst (Greystone, 2017).

Wolterstorff, Nicholas, "The Grace That Shaped My Life," *Finding God at Harvard: Spiritual Journeys of Christian Thinkers*, ed. Kelly Monroe (Zondervan, 1996). Adapted from *Philosophers Who Believe*, ed. Kelly James Clark (InterVarsity Press, 1993). See also Wolterstorff's *Lament for a Son* (Wm. B. Eerdmans, 1987).

Wood, Christopher, *The Life and Work of Jacques Joseph Tisson, 1836–1902* (Weidenfeld and Nicolson, 1986).

Woods, Robert, *Children Remembered: Responses to Untimely Death in the Past* (Liverpool University Press, 2007).

Worden, J. William, *Children and Grief: When a Parent Dies* (Guilford, 2001).

——, *Grief Counseling & Grief Therapy: A Handbook for Mental Health Practitioners*, 2nd ed. (Springer, 1991).

Zapata, Celia Correas, *Isabel Allende: Life and Spirits*, trans. Margaret Sayers Peden (Arte Público Press, 2002).

Zeff, Ted, *The Highly Sensitive Person's Survival Guide* (New Harbinger, 2004).

Zinsser, William, ed., *Going on Faith: Writing as a Spiritual Quest* (Marlowe and Company, 1999).

ACKNOWLEDGMENTS AND ILLUSTRATION CREDITS

Lonnie, Judy, Philip, Janet, and Elaine for kindness and support; the staff of the Chester County Library and the Lewisville Community Library; the staff of Paraclete Press. Thank you all.

The images in this book are exact, faithful photographic reproductions of two-dimensional, public-domain works of art. The works of art themselves are in the public domain. Every attempt has been made "to reproduce the underlying works with absolute fidelity" in accordance with the United States District Court for the Southern District of New York ruling that "exact photographic copies of public domain works of art would not be copyrightable under United States law because they are not original." The images in this book are "'slavish copies' of public domain works of art" as defined by the court's ruling; as such, "Copyright is not available in these circumstances." [Bridgeman Art Library, Ltd., Plaintiff v. Corel Corporation, 36 F. Supp. 2d 191 (S.D.N.Y. 1999); https://www.law.cornell.edu/copyright/cases/36_FSupp2d_191.htm. See also Bridgeman Art Library v. Corel Corp., 25 F.Supp.2d 421 (S.D.N.Y. 1998)] "There is no copyright in photographic reproductions of two-dimensional works of art in the public domain." Grischka Petri, "The Public Domain vs. the Museum: The Limits of Copyright and Reproductions of Two-dimensional Works of Art," *Journal of Conservation and Museum Studies*. 12(1) (2014) p. Art. 8. https://www.jcms-journal.com/articles/10.5334/jcms.1021217/. "Bridgeman Art Library, Ltd. v. Corel Corp. set a precedent establishing reproductive images of two-dimensional artworks as not copyrightable. . . . The Southern District of New York has twice ruled that reproductive photography is most likely the only case in which a photograph is *not* copyrightable. . . . The copyright itself was found to be invalid." Katherine L. Kelley, "The Complications of 'Bridgeman' and Copyright (Mis)use," *Art Documentation: Journal of the Art Libraries Society of North America*, 30(2) (Fall 2011): 38–42. Emphasis in original. https://www.jstor.org/stable/41244063. "It's not a gray area. If they make an unadorned photo of the public domain image, that photo can't be copyrighted—period!" Christopher Sprigman, instructor of intellectual property law at the University of Virginia Law School, interviewed by Bernard Starr, "Must You Pay to Use Photos of Public Domain Artworks? No, Says a Legal Expert," *Huffington Post* (12 November 2012): https://www.huffingtonpost.com/bernard-starr/museum-paintings-copyright_b_1867076.html.

ABOUT PARACLETE PRESS

Who We Are

As the publishing arm of the Community of Jesus, Paraclete Press presents a full expression of Christian belief and practice—from Catholic to Evangelical, from Protestant to Orthodox, reflecting the ecumenical charism of the Community and its dedication to sacred music, the fine arts, and the written word. We publish books, recordings, sheet music, and video/DVDs that nourish the vibrant life of the church and its people.

What We Are Doing

BOOKS Paraclete Press Books show the richness and depth of what it means to be Christian. While Benedictine spirituality is at the heart of who we are and all that we do, our books reflect the Christian experience across many cultures, time periods, and houses of worship.

We have many series, including *Paraclete Essentials*; *Paraclete Fiction*; *Paraclete Poetry*; *Paraclete Giants*; and for children and adults, *All God's Creatures*, books about animals and faith; and *San Damiano Books*, focusing on Franciscan spirituality. Others include Voices from the Monastery (men and women monastics writing about living a spiritual life today), *Active Prayer*, and new for young readers: *The Pope's Cat*. We also specialize in gift books for children on the occasions of Baptism and First Communion, as well as other important times in a child's life, and books that bring creativity and liveliness to any adult spiritual life.

The Mount Tabor Books series focuses on the arts and literature as well as liturgical worship and spirituality; it was created in conjunction with the Mount Tabor Ecumenical Centre for Art and Spirituality in Barga, Italy.

MUSIC The Paraclete Recordings label represents the internationally acclaimed choir *Gloriæ Dei Cantores*, the *Gloriæ Dei Cantores Schola*, and the other instrumental artists of the *Arts Empowering Life Foundation.*

Paraclete Press is the exclusive North American distributor for the Gregorian chant recordings from St. Peter's Abbey in Solesmes, France. Paraclete also carries all of the Solesmes chant publications for Mass and the Divine Office, as well as their academic research publications.

In addition, Paraclete Press Sheet Music publishes the work of today's finest composers of sacred choral music, annually reviewing over 1,000 works and releasing between 40 and 60 works for both choir and organ.

VIDEO Our video/DVDs offer spiritual help, healing, and biblical guidance for a broad range of life issues including grief and loss, marriage, forgiveness, facing death, understanding suicide, bullying, addictions, Alzheimer's, and Christian formation.

Learn more about us at our website:
www.paracletepress.com or
phone us toll-free at 1.800.451.5006

SCAN
TO
READ
MORE